GOD DOES PLAY DICE

GOD DOES PLAY DICE

The Autobiography of a Holocaust Survivor

by
Klara Samuels

BainBridgeBooks
Philadelphia

Published June 1999
by
BainBridgeBooks
an imprint of
Trans-Atlantic Publications Inc.
Philadelphia PA

Website address: www.transatlanticpub.com

PRINTED IN THE UNITED STATES OF AMERICA

ISBN: 1-891696-07-6

Library of Congress Cataloging-in-Publication Data

Samuels, Klara, 1927-
        God does play dice : the autobiography of a Holocaust survivor/
by Klara Samuels.
                p.   cm
                ISBN 1-891696-07-6
Samuels, Klara, 1927- . 2. Jews—Poland—Warsaw—Biography.
        3. Holocaust, Jewish (1939-1945)—Poland—Warsaw—Personal narratives.
Warsaw (Poland)—Biography. 5. Holocaust survivors—United States
—Biography. I. Title
DS135.P63.S26   1999
940.53'18'092—dc 21
[B]   98-54705
                                                                        CIP

To my husband Bert,

my Sons Mark and Sam,

my granddaughter Miranda

my grandson Jackson

and other grandchildren yet unborn

for whom this book was written

"Quantum mechanics is certainly imposing
But an inner voice tells me that it is not yet the real thing.
The theory says a lot, but does not really bring us
any closer to the secret of the 'old one.'
I, at any rate, am convinced that He is not playing at dice."

—Albert Einstein, December 4, 1926
in a letter to physicist Max Born.

Einstein could not believe that chance
or fortuitous events play such
an important role in the universe.

PREFACE

For years I have been urged by my friends to write down how I survived the war. I was reluctant to commit to such a vast project, and unsure I was up to it. One day, in the fall of 1996, my husband brought home a flyer about a memoir group meeting at our local Barnes and Noble, and suggested we both go. The group leader, Zella Geltman, my husband and other participants in the group encouraged me to persevere and praised my efforts.

Writing about my childhood was fun, but the war years were extraordinarily difficult. For the stories to sound convincing, I had to force myself not only to remember the past, but literally to relive it, complete with the feelings I had at the time. I usually wrote in the morning, and the mood would linger with me for hours, as if my body were in the present and my mind in the past. Now that it is over, I believe that the catharsis of going back has helped me to understand myself and those around me more deeply. It is never too late to learn and to grow!

This book is appended with a brief history of Poland. I believe this background will be helpful. I have tried to write my story objectively and truthfully, and to show how the horrors of the war years alternated with much better periods in my life. Above all, the love and devotion of my parents helped me to survive the war sanely and with faith in humanity.

Klara Samuels
West Orange, New Jersey
January 1999

CONTENTS

Photographic inserts are found following page 160.

My father's family.
Read from right to left

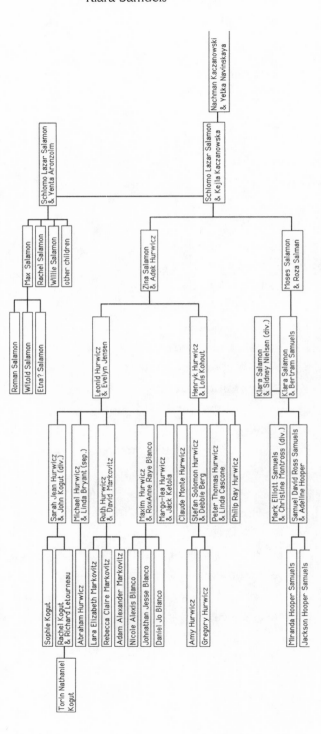

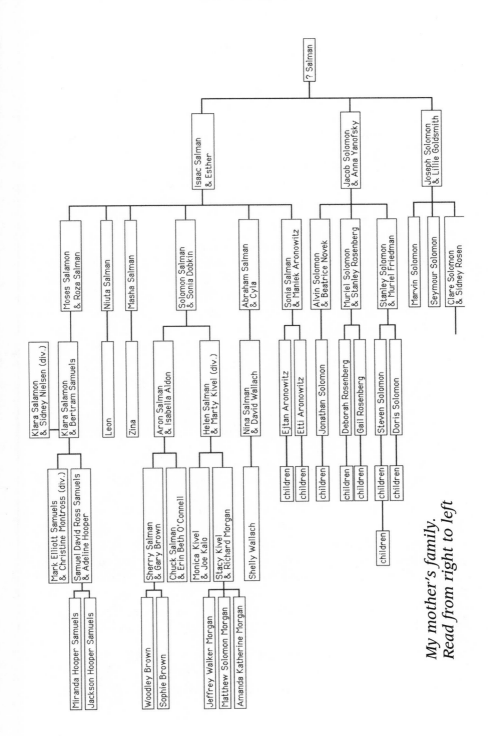

My mother's family.
Read from right to left

INTRODUCTION

The Holocaust was a cataclysmic tragedy of an unprecedented magnitude and nature. Vast numbers of people have perished, and continue to, because of war, disease and natural catastrophes. But never before had such hatred been unleashed with such an organized, officially sanctioned malevolence by one people against another.

Enslaving Africans was a prolonged process motivated by greed and indifference to human life, as was the near eradication of American Indians. Agricultural collectivization in the Soviet Union, the Cultural Revolution in China and the de-urbanization of Cambodia are all examples of class warfare – internal developments each resulting in the death of millions of a country's own people. The Biafran famine, the Hutu and Tutsi killings in Rwanda and the Somalian famine are examples of tribal warfare caused, at least in part, by artificial borders imposed on Africa years ago by its colonizers. Similarly, the hatreds giving rise to the ethnic cleansing in Yugoslavia date from that country's past involving the Ottoman Empire and the Austro-Hungarian Empire. All of these and other atrocities bear some similarities to the Holocaust, but differ from it drastically in either intent, scope or degree of outrage. The massacre of Armenians by the Turks early in this century probably comes closest, and as a result many Jews and Armenians feel a kinship arising from their similar histories.

The consequences of the Holocaust for the world's Jewry cannot be underestimated. Fully half of the world's Jewish population perished, not cleanly but after unimaginable suffering. We will never know how the small Jewish town culture (*shtetl*) would have evolved, what contributions the six million dead would have made to Jewish, Polish and world culture. We can assume that it would have been a considerable one, since the Jews had already produced such great individuals as Karl Marx, Sigmund Freud, Albert Einstein, Felix Mendelssohn and Marc Chagall.

The Holocaust provided a focus of unity for the remaining world Jewry, and since we Jews are an articulate people, we brought it forcefully to the world's attention. The world responded with a momentary fit of guilt –

surely an aberration – which provided an impetus for the creation of the State of Israel. Clearly, the story of Israel would have been quite different without the Holocaust. The sympathy engendered towards the Jews in general in the aftermath of the catastrophe contributed, in my opinion, to the weakening of anti-Semitism in many places, chiefly in the United States. Thus the Jewish survivors, both in Israel and outside of it, have unintentionally benefited from the tragedy of their brethren.

As I write this, 53 years have passed since the end of the war. The world has moved on. As memories of the Holocaust fade, it becomes a distant echo for the Jews; just another story to be relegated to history books for others. Is this natural? Of course! Should it be allowed to happen? To this I say emphatically: No!

The Holocaust is a cautionary tale for all of humanity, not just Jews. In peeling away its specificity, the why's of its happening to Jews, of its per-petrators being German, and of the time it happened, a basic flaw of human nature is revealed. Yes, we are capable of unreasoning prejudice and hatred of those we perceive as "outsiders." We know how to delude ourselves into believing these "outsiders" are so inferior, so vicious, so ter-rible as to be subhuman, thus allowing us to treat them as such. Under normal circumstances we are unaware of such potential in ourselves, and righteously view ourselves as civilized people incapable of such atrocities.

The facts of the Holocaust argue otherwise. When a people is cornered and suffering, perhaps because of severe economic dislocations and resulting adversities, they want to blame someone and find a scapegoat. It is at such times that we are most vulnerable and can easily succumb to the call of a sick but charismatic leader who articulates our malaise and focuses it conveniently on some people alien to us.

Viewing the Holocaust in this light and retelling its history to all the chil-dren of the world may help us to guard against other catastrophes such as the outrage in Bosnia. I wish the Holocaust could have been written and canonized as part of the Bible, for surely it is as much a part of our human experience as the Exodus from Egypt.

What of the survivors of the tragedy? We are few in number and dying off rapidly. As a group we have succeeded brilliantly, at least materially. This should not be surprising. Only the quick-witted and enterprising, and the strong of body and spirit had any chance to survive. Those who did and continued to display these attributes used them to rebuild their lives. The Jews are traditionally known as capable merchants and entrepreneurs on the one hand, and thinkers and intellectuals on the other. This dual aptitude can be found among the survivors as well: some have succeeded in business and some in the professions, arts and sciences.

The cost to our psyches is harder to measure. The hatred, the horrors, the losses we suffered, the very duration of our hopelessness have marked us for life. There are no precedents to help us deal with such massive injuries. No one knew how to help us and, in the real sense, no one did. Each of us had to face the demons as best we could and each of us, consciously or unconsciously, selected a path to follow.

I could have stayed in New York City rather than move to Buffalo, joined survivor organizations, and continued to dwell on or in my past. I did not do so. For me the healing led away from the tragedy until the passage of sufficient time and the normality of my life made me strong enough to face it. I did not do it alone. My husband Bert was greatly instrumental in leading me back to the mainstream, with his sympathy and by providing the atmosphere of normality around me that allowed me to follow a path away from the darkness and towards life.

Why should I be compelled to live by the standards of the Holocaust for the rest of my life? Wouldn't it be in a sense a defeat for me, and an ultimate victory for Hitler, if my whole life were to stay referenced by those years?

Yes, I feel an obligation to speak up, and I do so, particularly by addressing the young whenever I am asked to. But I do not feel self-righteous about it. No blame should be attached to those survivors who choose not to speak out. To live a normal life, prosper and bring up a family is in itself a triumph for each survivor, a victory over the evil and death that Hitler brought to the world. Stories of individual survivors range from those devoting their entire lives to keeping the memory of the Holocaust alive before the world, to those who licked their wounds in the anonymity of withdrawal. Most of us, including myself, fall somewhere in the middle of this range.

Once I decided to write this book, I deliberately refrained from reading other survivors' accounts. I wanted my memories and my reflections on them to be truly mine. At times, it can be quite easy to appropriate ideas you hear or read about, and forget they are not your own.

I hope this book will stand as my contribution to the story.

CHAPTER 1

ROOTS

My father was born in 1891 in the hamlet of Stawiski, near the town of Lomza, where the family lived. Lomza was originally part of Poland, but during the 19th and first part of the 20th centuries it belonged to Russia. It was a small town—a population of around 50,000—more or less a county seat. A large part of the population was Jewish. Enough Jews from the area emigrated to the United States in the last hundred years to form and sustain a "Lomza Society," an organization which purchased a tract of cemetery plots in the Forest Hills area of Queens. By sheer coincidence, my American-born husband's entire family is buried there. This made me immediately acceptable to his mother. There is no record of prior contact between our two families, but it is very likely that some of our ancestors knew each other. I can imagine them sitting somewhere in heaven saying to themselves, "Moishe, Shlomo-Lazer's daughter Klara and Bert, the son of Shmuel, not bad. The circle is closed."

The Lomza Jewish population disdained last names as a newfangled invention of the *goyim* (gentiles). Sometime during the 1920s, my father visited Lomza looking for his birth certificate. When he introduced himself as Moses Salamon to the local worthies at the town hall where the births of Jewish children were registered, they failed to recognize his name. Finally, after some prompting, an old man's eyes lit up. "Ah!" he said, "Moishe, Shlomo-Lazer, Keila, Srulki, Rivke! So that's who you are!"

He had just recited two generations of my father's ancestors; only then did he ask for news of the family.

One of my great-grandfathers on my father's side was a Talmudic scholar. He was not an official rabbi, but a *rebbe*, a wise man. His wife ran a store and made a living, in addition to cooking, cleaning, shopping and bringing up the children while he spent his days studying the Bible and Talmud. In any other society, my great-grandfather would be considered a layabout, but among Jews he was not only highly respected, but considered a matrimonial catch. For hundreds of years, such love of learning bestowed stature on these life-long students, but no material rewards. It was not until my generation that the tangible payoff came, when the value of learning and education became more generally recognized so that those who achieve it are rewarded with money as well as esteem.

At one point my great-grandfather fell ill. A gentile doctor was called in and prescribed red meat cooked in butter. Utter consternation! A visit to the rabbi produced this solution: if the doctor says it is a matter of life and death, you must do it. According to Jewish law, life has priority over all other laws and regulations, such as *kashruth* (the collected rules for staying kosher). The doctor, when appealed to, insisted on the treatment. Maybe to him it was a joke on the Jews. Maybe he was diagnosing anemia and truly believed in the efficacy of his prescription. At any rate, a pan was sacrificed for the purpose—never to be used again—and the hamburgers were fried in butter on an open fire outside so as not to contaminate the house. My great-grandfather consumed this delicacy with tears running down his face, for he was forced to sin against God. Here was a man who knew where he stood.

My father remembered this grandfather fondly. As an old man, he had quizzed my father on his learning at the *cheder* (a Hebrew religious elementary school), praised him and showed his affection for the little boy. Of his own father, my father spoke little. He had been a minor supplier to the Russian army and was already ill when my father was a small child. He had been married once before and produced nine living children with his first wife. After his first wife died, he married Keila, my father's mother, who was younger than three of my grandfather's children with his first wife.

I only knew one of my father's half brothers, Max. Uncle Max was a *felcher* (a sort of paramedic or nurse practitioner), who had a big practice in Warsaw. He and his wife were a childless, prosperous couple. Periodic dinners at their house were a command performance. Uncle Max had only one leg; the other had been lost during World War I and, disdaining a prosthesis, he propelled himself on crutches.

Their apartment on Leszno Street, just a couple of blocks from ours, was large, somber and full of heavy, massive furniture and dark red velvet drapes. Knick-knacks and faded pictures of funny-looking people in old-fashioned clothes filled every available flat surface—a truly Victorian place. Dinners were formal, with many indigestible courses following each other—an agony for a little girl who was a rotten eater. A child was expected to sit quietly and be invisible. Today they would call my aunt and uncle family-oriented, but not child-oriented.

Max died in the late 1930s. In my young life, he was the first person known to me to die, and I could not imagine where he had gone. I was judged too young to go to the funeral, but was included in the *shiva* (literally "sitting"—a Jewish custom of visiting the bereaved for one week after the funeral). The apartment seemed even darker than usual, hushed—my uncle's booming voice gone forever. We never went back. It seems that my aunt was not fond of her husband's family; she only tolerated us while he was alive.

In spite of the relative poverty of his family, my father had a happy childhood. He was a good student and progressed from the *cheder* to the Russian *gymnasium* (high school) where he learned Russian. He already spoke fluent Yiddish, Hebrew and Polish. The gymnasium, like his home, was authoritarian and strict. At one point my father requested to attend a performance of *Hamlet* which was playing in town, but was denied on the grounds he had already seen it.

In a separate incident, a state inspector came to observe a physics class one day. A student asked a question and the teacher's answer was deemed inadequate; the teacher was fired on the spot. My father admired this way of maintaining standards. He must have not liked this particular teacher since he felt no pity for the poor man.

My father did not resent such regimentation. On the contrary, he felt all this was appropriate and in his own best interest. It kept him focused and self-disciplined. I must admit, however, that with my father, theory and practice were sometimes quite distant and that my own childhood did not embody too many of my father's antiquated ideas.

By the first decade of the 20th Century, modern culture had begun to reach Lomza. First came the tomato. Though a plant, it was suspected of being *trayf* (not kosher) because of its red color. Accordingly, a deputation of housewives went to the rabbi to solicit his opinion. The rabbi decided that since apples were also red, tomatoes were kosher. Even so, they never became a staple of the Jewish diet like the cucumber, the latter mostly in its pickled form.

Then the movies arrived, at that time consisting mostly of short features. One such feature showed an accident between a cart and a train. My father told of a man who went to see it night after night, hoping one night the accident would be averted.

After high school my father went to college in Königsberg (now called Kalinin) in what was then Germany. This city had been home to the philosopher Immanuel Kant. My father supported himself by tutoring and escorting wealthy Russian tourists around town. He was quite poor and came to frequent a restaurant where he could get cheap food and in large quantity. He remained a patron even after discovering horse meat was used to make the hamburger there.

My father was about five feet tall and already balding, not terribly social, and yet he never felt he was inferior to anyone. He had a solid belief in the superiority of intellect and education, both matters of pride for him and the Jews. Sometime around 1910 he transferred to the University of Kharkov in present-day Ukraine, where he graduated as a medical doctor in 1912. He dreamed of being a surgeon but during his internship fell in love with bacteriology, which he ended up specializing in.

The years immediately after were happy. The bacteriological research he enjoyed so much in turn sparked his lifelong romance with chemical research. My father was always trying to make something out of something else. During the war he succeeded in making—and selling—vodka from milk. In Palestine, after the war, he made saccharine in his lab and sold it to both Jewish and Arab bakeries.

My father spent World War I practicing medicine in Russia while at the same time avoiding groups and individuals hostile to Jews, which were practically everybody. In his professional capacity, he served both sides, and was rarely paid by either.

At one point during the Russian Revolution, a Bolshevik soldier held a gun to my father's head, an event which contributed to his vehement hatred of communism and caused the appearance of two white patches of hair on the back of his head. On another occasion, my father was awakened one night by loud noises in the apartment. He heard glass and furniture breaking, loud shouting and crying. In the dark, he hastily remade his bed and slid under it. There he remained while the thugs ransacked his meager belongings, luckily never looking carefully into the dark recesses under the bed. He never found out which political party, if any, they belonged to.

In 1921, my father escaped from the continuing chaos in Russia and arrived in Warsaw with his mother, Keila, and enough money for eight trips on the tram. His father had died sometime during World War I. Fortunately, his younger sister Zina and her husband, Adek Hurwicz, were by that time settled in an apartment and supported by Adek's law practice. Zina was my father's only full sister and much loved by him. Zina eventually became my favorite aunt, and both she and Adek would prove to be instrumental at many points in my life.

While living with Zina and Adek, my father began to establish himself as a bacteriologist in Warsaw. This required both an investment in a laboratory and acquaintances with numerous physicians in order to get the necessary referrals. He began working in various Jewish clinics and became friendly with a number of Jewish doctors who referred patients to him. By 1923 he had his own laboratory in the large apartment he now shared with his mother. He was on his way.

My parents' meeting is shrouded in a bit of mystery. In 1924, my mother, Roza Salman, came to Warsaw to visit her oldest sister Masha, who was already married and had lived in the city for some time. Masha already knew my father through common friends. The first meeting between my parents took place at a get-together at Masha's house. The mystery is whether the meeting was accidental or planned. People like to believe in love at first sight and don't like to admit they met loved ones through a matchmaker. Since my mother never wanted to talk about this, I assume she was introduced to my father with some hope in mind.

My mother was completely different from my father. While he came from a small, poor Jewish town in Poland, she came from a wealthy, even aristocratic, Jewish family from Minsk, the capital of present-day Belarus. While my father lived dangerously during World War I and the Russian Revolution, she was sheltered and protected by her family even during those difficult days. He was a self-made man while she was a dependent woman.

My maternal grandfather, Isaac, originally owned three tanneries in and around Minsk. He owned his own house and the entire street it was on, renting the other houses to his relatives who paid him whatever rent they could afford whenever they could. The family was decidedly assimilated. Only Russian was spoken in the house. My mother spoke no Yiddish. Isaac, of course, lost his real estate holdings during the Russian Revolution, but he was able to escape with a substantial amount of money, first to Germany and then to Poland. When I knew him, he was again a rich man in Vilnius, the present-day Lithuanian capital which was then part of Poland and known as Wilno. There he bought another tannery as well as a wool factory. He also owned property in Warsaw, where my mother and her brother, Abrasha, were established.

Among her siblings, my mother was the only one with artistic talent. She played the piano and had a concert-hall-size, but very true coloratura, soprano voice. Amazingly for the time, her talent was appreciated and developed by her father, who allowed her to study voice and piano in Frankfurt for five years. But she never sang or played professionally, as in my grandfather's eyes a professional performer ranked close to being a prostitute. She was pretty and petite like her mother, Esther, and her sister Masha.

My mother had several brothers and sisters who would be major figures at various points in my life. Her oldest brother, Solomon, fled Europe during World War II and established himself in New York City. Solomon succeeded Isaac as the family patriarch and became quite well off in his own right. In America, he and his wife "Big Sonia" owned property in North Carolina as well as New York, and they moved back and forth between the two. Out of harm's way during the war, Solomon and Sonia would act as the family's financial safe house and later as my sponsors when I came to America.

Masha was my mother's favorite sister. She married young and produced one daughter, Zina (not to be confused with Moses' sister of the same name). Masha died of breast cancer while still in her twenties. Her husband never remarried and he and Zina remained very much part of the family.

Abrasha, my mother's younger brother, was sweet, merry and handsome, but never displayed much of a business acumen. He had to be continually supported by Isaac and later Solomon. I believe he studied to be an engineer. After World War I, he settled in Warsaw with his wife, Cyla. Their daughter, Nina, was 18 months younger than I and one of my dearest friends. By the end of World War II, Abrasha and his family had settled in Tel Aviv. There I lived with them for a year immediately after the war.

My mother's sister Aniuta, called Niuta for short, was the black sheep of the family, very cosmopolitan and well-connected. She smoked, drank socially, gambled and was considered a bad influence on her nieces and nephews. However, she proved her loyalty by staying with Isaac after he was denied permission to leave Europe by the Soviets even though she had secured for herself the necessary papers to flee. Niuta and her son Leo, and Masha's daughter Zina died along with my grandfather Isaac in the Holocaust, although Niuta's husband managed to escape to Australia.

"Little Sonia" was my mother's youngest sister. Like Abrasha, she moved to Palestine and was financially supported from time to time by her father and oldest brother. She married her high school sweetheart, Maniek, an active Zionist who moved to Palestine to work on a kibbutz immediately after high school. On the pretense of wishing to go to college in Jerusalem, Sonia soon followed, despite the fact that Isaac never approved of the relationship.

Writing about my aunts and uncles brings their faces and personalities vividly before my eyes. But I must say that to a child or even a young woman, they seemed an ordinary group. Now, when I think of them all together, they seem a colorful bunch with very different personalities, lives and destinies.

After a short courtship, my father went to Vilnius to ask Isaac for his daughter's hand. Although business was bad for Isaac that year and he did not feel he could "afford" a dowry suitable for a doctor, he agreed to the marriage. He thought his sheltered and somewhat spoiled daughter would have a good life with this man, who in four short years had made a good life for himself and his widowed mother.

The engagement was announced. In Vilnius, my father was introduced to my mother's family and friends, who judged him reasonably worthy. In turn, my mother met my father's friends in Warsaw. She got along very well with his sister Zina, and Adek; in time the two couples would become inseparable. She was also looking forward to being near Masha, but Masha soon moved back to Vilnius before her untimely death.

Shortly before the wedding, misfortune struck. My father's mother died in the street of a heart attack. The nuptials had to be postponed and the festivities scaled down. My father was still in mourning when the wedding took place in February 1926.

The dowry would prove to be a contentious point between my father and my mother's family. It included a sum of money, a pitiful one according to my father, and the accoutrements needed to start married life. My father had recently moved with his mother to the large apartment on Nowolipie Street in Warsaw where he had his laboratory, and the furnishings were as yet very sparse. The dowry included furniture, china, linen and a piano to be bought by Isaac. Because of the dislocations during World War I, my mother did not have a hope chest.

However, the furniture didn't live up to expectations and the piano, which had neither a good tone nor appearance, was eventually exchanged for a Bluchner, a very good brand. To make matters worse, the money was grudgingly handed over in dribs and drabs. Perhaps it really was a bad year for Isaac, but the way he went about this did a lot of damage. My father was not a forgiving man. He cherished his grudges. Whenever he talked about my mother's family, there was a note of contempt in his words and tone. He never went to Vilnius with my mother and me to visit his in-laws. When Isaac came to Warsaw, my father was polite but never cordial. Even a young child like myself could detect this ambivalence. Luckily, Vilnius was far away and contact was kept to a minimum.

My parents had 13 very good years together before the Nazi invasion. My father grew more and more successful and respected as a doctor. Soon after I was born, we moved to an apartment on Leszno Street, in a prestigious Jewish area of Warsaw. Now we belonged to Warsaw, and Warsaw belonged to us.

CHAPTER 2

BEFORE THE WAR

I was born on October 26, 1927, following 24 hours of difficult labor. In the end, I had to be pulled out with a pair of
forceps, leaving a long, curved scar on my right cheek. My
mother cried when she first saw me. No doubt she visualized a permanently disfigured, unmarriageable spinster. The scar, which was quite
prominent when I was a child, gradually faded as I grew up. I can still see
its traces when I am particularly tired or sick.

I weighed about 10 pounds at birth. No doubt my size contributed to the
long, agonizing labor. My poor mother! No wonder I was an only child. As
an adult I yearned for a large, extended family but, as a child, I did not
miss the absence of siblings and took all the attention lavished on me as
my due.

Years later, when I was a teenager during the war, I met the wife of my
mother's obstetrician. "You were followed by several abortions," she told
me bluntly. Apparently, at that time in Poland the opinion of two doctors
was all that was needed to perform a legal abortion – amazing in this
most Catholic of countries.

Having only one child was in fashion at that time for members of the middle class. Most of my classmates were only children, as were some of my
cousins. It was the first time women had access to any, albeit imperfect,

21

birth control measures and they were taking full advantage of it. In part, it must have been a reaction to the large families they all came from. Even in the United States, my American mother-in-law felt she, as the oldest girl in a family of eight, had never had any childhood. She was always diapering, cleaning, feeding and, in general, mothering her younger siblings, who trailed after her and denied her any privacy at all.

My mother died during the war and I was separated from my father for many years during my adult life. Most of my friends and relatives perished in the Holocaust, and those few who survived washed up on various distant shores. Thus, for most of my adult life I had few opportunities to reminisce about my childhood and practically no mementos at all to help me recall it.

Retracing my childhood is thus difficult. It may not be this way for everyone, but then many people have more landmarks to help them navigate among their memories and fix the correct times and places. I have no family albums depicting me at various ages, at various vacation sites, or commemorating important family events. Photos immortalize scenes connecting you with your family or friends, weaving in an orderly manner the progress of your life.

Only two pictures of me as a child survived the war. They had been sent to my Aunt Sonia in Palestine, who gave them to me after the war. One of them was taken in Druskienniki, a summer resort. It is a small black-and-white snapshot, taken when I was five or six. I am standing on a tree stump and leaning against the trunk of the adjacent tree wearing a striped, short-sleeved sweater and a pleated mini skirt. My legs are bare. I wear anklets and Mary Jane shoes. My face is round and sweet, but the pointed chin hints at strength and determination. My eyes are round, my nose small and straight and my mouth stretched in a gentle half-smile.

My childhood memories are not organized chronologically, but rather as a vast swampy mass, out of which specific memories stick out like twigs. My earliest memory is a fragment, but gives a glimpse of my family. My mother, my nanny and I were spending the summer at a resort near Warsaw. I was under three and very scared of the dark. My mother, who was very soft-hearted, allowed me a small night-light. It was a miniature lamp with a small pink shade enclosing the small area around me in a comforting, rosy glow. One night, I was awakened by an angry roar from my father. He had just come to spend the weekend with us and discovered that I was being "coddled beyond all reason." He would have no wimp for a daughter, he yelled. In the dark, he loomed like a giant to a small frightened child, although he was only about five feet tall. Most children have nocturnal fears, fears of the dark, of monsters and the like. Mine were aggravated by my father. Needless to say, from then on I slept in the dark.

Of all the adults in my life, my father was by far the most important. I have a photograph of him taken in Israel soon after the war. Of course, he is several years and one terrible war older than he was in my childhood memories, but it best represents how I remember him. In the photograph he is wearing his white lab coat and sitting at the lab bench looking into the microscope. There are deep bags under his eyes and a fringe of fine, black hair surrounding his bald pate. I can just see one of the two distinct white patches of hair, each the size of a walnut, on the back of his head, reminders of his harrowing experience during the Russian Revolution. His glasses lie nearby on the bench.

In my mind I see him lifting his tired eyes from the microscope, rubbing them wearily and replacing the glasses before letting his little daughter look through the eyepiece, while he explains what I am seeing. He had very poor vision, suffering from both severe myopia and astigmatism. His choice of bacteriology as a career, which requires long hours of intense peering through the microscope, was very poor from the standpoint of this disability.

I was a very healthy child, although I was told that when I was three months old I contracted the dreaded diphtheria. A pediatrician was called in, but misdiagnosed my illness. "Only your father's correct diagnosis and heroic measures saved your life," my mother told me worshipfully, raising my father's standing in my eyes to even greater heights.

No matter how busy he was, my father always had time for me. I was free to enter the lab rooms. If my problem was serious enough, I could interrupt almost any activity. Sometimes I would be even called in to reassure some terrified child whose blood was to be taken. At such times my father would solemnly rub my finger with a cotton ball dipped in ether. This made my finger cold and insensitive. Then he would pretend to pierce it with a needle at the end of a pressure rod. Occasionally, if this did not suffice, he would actually prick me with the needle, producing a tiny bead of blood. I was very proud of being used as such a model and would gravely assure the little patient that the procedure was painless.

The white mice, guinea pigs and the occasional rabbit which inhabited the lab were all fascinating for a small child. I knew their functions. The rabbit, for example, was used for a pregnancy test. My father injected the urine of a pregnant woman into one large ear and after several days sacrificed the rabbit. The rabbit was then examined. When finished my father would send the carcass to the building superintendent as a free meal for his family. My father spoke to me matter-of-factly about such procedures. He was eager to instruct me and hoped I would come to love his work.

My father was intimately involved in my education, my readings and my interests. I became used to telling him details about my classes and the books I was reading. When I claimed religion and history were dull, he produced exciting, dramatic books about both, took me on museum trips, talked about Zionism and Palestine, and made me see both subjects as stories about the past with a vital impact on the present. He understood the importance of motivation in learning.

I loved my mother, but early on recognized her as a sort of fellow child, though bigger and with more clout. I felt free to criticize her, indulge her, even argue with her. I inherited little of her innate sweetness and natural goodness. As a child, I probably considered those traits weaknesses to be exploited to my advantage. I certainly did not appreciate her enough, but I am sure she was unaware of it. She was one of the world's innocents. All her friends loved her and my father adored her. His personality changed a great deal after her death and he never formed a romantic attachment after losing her.

My father was successful as a doctor and his reputation kept growing. Soon we moved from the apartment on Nowolipie to one on Leszno Street. Both streets were inhabited primarily by Jews – but what a difference! On Nowolipie Street, modern-looking Jews mingled with black-robed, fur-hatted men with *peyes* (sideburns) and boys looking like miniature replicas of the men. Many of the Orthodox men carried religious texts and often continued reading while walking in the street. Orthodox women were also totally covered though not veiled, wearing long, somber dresses, their worn faces peering from the babushkas (scarves worn over heads and shoulders). Hawkers sold herring, incomparable bagels, clothing and other goods directly from their carts, advertising them in loud sing-song voices. One heard more Yiddish than Polish in the street. In short, it was a scene not unlike the Lower East Side in New York at the same time, which, of course, was populated by these kinds of people.

Leszno, by contrast, was a wide, tree-lined street. Trams ran in both directions; in addition, open, horse-driven carriages transported the more affluent citizens. Ours was a typical Warsaw apartment house built sometime around the turn of the century. Leszno apartments were expensive and for the most part occupied by assimilated Jews. Comprising about six floors, the building represented a microcosm of urban life. Our apartment had three rooms facing the street and four facing the courtyard, and even boasted a balcony, from which one could watch life in the street and the occasional parade.

My father was shaved every other day by the local barber who came to the house; since he had a tough, black beard, he usually looked like he needed a shave. The tailor also came for fabric selection—my mother's domain—and for the several fittings needed, for which my father would grumblingly emerge out of his lab. When clad in the semi-finished garment, my father, who loved his comfort, would spread his arms and lift them up and then invariably complain that the jacket was too tight; to which the tailor would always answer, "Dr. Salamon, what is this, are you planning to do gymnastics in this suit?"

We had four people to help in our house. Two of them, Panna (Miss) Renia and Panna Fela worked in the lab. They performed the routine analyses and did all the cleaning up. Both had come as untrained and semi-educated young girls; my father liked to train his help himself and to his specifications. On the domestic side there was a live-in maid, or rather a succession of them, and a cook who was married and came to work every morning. The maids, by contrast to Renia and Fela, were never Jewish; they always came straight from the country. At least once a month, my parents hosted a dinner for about 30 people, all doctors and their wives. Usually a second maid was borrowed for the evening from my Aunt Zina. For these affairs my mother did some of the cooking. No cook could better her in making gefilte fish or marinated cold salmon for an appetizer. After everything was prepared, my father would come in to inspect it. He never felt the food was sufficient in quantity and variety, so off he would go to the deli downstairs, and up would come additional mounds of nuts and sweets, herring in various sauces, chopped liver, smoked flounder and eel. I can still see the long table, extended to full capacity, the gleaming silverware on the white satin tablecloth, the centerpieces of great fishes (including heads) decorated with parsley and carrots, the crystal chandeliers twinkling above.

My mother liked little girls to have long hair worn in two braids and adorned with colorful bows at the tips. I hated my braids, not for any aesthetic reasons, but because the process of brushing and plaiting was so painful. Even though my hair was always straight and fine, somehow it would snarl into knots, and my governess was none too gentle with it. I could not see why I should suffer so needlessly, and decided short hair would eliminate the problem.

My mother's hairdresser lived and had a shop in the second courtyard of the building, and of course she knew me, so she had no reason to suspect anything was amiss when I showed up one morning claiming my mother had sent me for a haircut. Proudly, though somewhat apprehensively, I strolled back home.

My mother wept over my lost tresses as though I had just lost my virginity. How could I be so naughty, so willful, and hurt her so much! I was afraid of punishment, but totally unmoved by her tears. After all, it was my hair, wasn't it? My father, when apprised of my misdeed, dutifully scolded me, but I could see his heart wasn't in it. Probably he thought the whole thing trivial; he may even had been proud of my action.

When school was out, mother and I vacationed away from the city. Summers were spent in the country, "to breathe the fresh air," as my mother used to say. We usually did not go alone. One time we vacationed with Aunt Cyla and Cousin Nina. Nina was eighteen months younger than I, so that particularly in the early years she followed my lead, tagging along and falling in with my suggestions.

It so happened that Nina's ex-nanny lived in the country near the rooms we rented from a wealthy peasant. One morning I decided to go visit her. The nanny was old, fat, jolly and, most importantly, made excellent cookies. I was quite small then and Nina just a toddler, so I knew we would not be allowed to go there alone. No problem. We just wouldn't tell anyone we were going! Nina, who was an obedient child, protested gently but I insisted. Besides, who could resist the temptation of escaping the confines of our yard and strolling the country lanes without being rushed along? Then we could observe every garden, step into every puddle, back-track in case we missed something, and – in the end – have a visit with an uncritical, friendly adult who did not inspect our fingernails before giving us a cookie.

My mother and my aunt felt that by going to the country, feeding us and handing down a set of rules ensuring our safety, they had fulfilled their maternal obligations. They devoted their time to the housekeeping, of which there wasn't much, since the peasants provided cleaning and some of our food, and other adult activities, such as gossiping, leaving us to our own devices. Even when we went visiting, the adults would occupy themselves with their affairs, while we children were told to "go and play." Forbidden to roam at will, with no swimming pool, no sports, and no other playmates, we would get bored from time to time.

Back home, our mothers, having noticed our absence, were tearing their hair out with anxiety. Our host's entire family combed the neighborhood with visions of gypsies camping nearby, intent on kidnapping us. Also, the open well in the middle of the yard must have loomed in their thoughts. Our mothers were in hysterics, unable to think clearly and come up with the pretty obvious solution. Finally, we were spotted walking nonchalantly back home. We were both scolded but only I was punished, since it was rightly surmised that I had conceived our excursion.

When I was five, we spent the summer at the sea shore, on the Baltic sea, in a little fishing village called Karvia. That summer is forever tied in my memory with my cousin Henry. Henry is five years older than I, and ten-year-old boys are not known to spend a lot of time with their much younger female cousins. In addition, Henry had a friend his own age, who stayed nearby. Nevertheless, that summer I became Henry's project. He decided it was time for me to learn to read and write, as well as to swim. An ambitious plan, which proved to be totally successful. Henry showed me the letters and I copied them and learned to form words from them. I doubt that the pedagogy was particularly sophisticated, but two factors worked in Henry's favor. First of all I idolized him and was willing to go through fire and water to please him, let alone just learn to read and write. I was eager to do whatever he suggested in whatever time he was willing to spend with me. Secondly, I was pretty smart. Anyway, by the end of the summer, to the amazement of our parents, I could read books and write whole stories.

Teaching me to swim proved more difficult. We started by my wiggling on the sand, trying to coordinate arm and leg movements looking like a little frog (I was learning the breast stroke), after which the same activity was transferred to the water with Henry supporting me under my belly. I was fairly well-coordinated, but, although not especially afraid of water, I was, in general, a physical coward, so that it took a long time before Henry could remove his hand without causing a panic accompanied by wild flailing of arms and legs, as all instructions were forgotten. I must give him credit for his patience and good humor while we persevered. At last I could navigate by myself, but now a new problem arose. The water was shallow near the shore, then the bottom dropped off precipitously, and then, as I continued to swim out, there was a stretch of shallow water again, a sort of shelf out in the sea. Well, I was afraid to swim by myself across the deep stretch, so that, unless Henry was by my side, I was confined to the despised shallow part where "little children" ran shrieking in and out of the water and "old ladies" stood about gossiping and splashing water up to their armpits and into their ample bosoms. Finally, Henry, exasperated with my timidity, resorted to a subterfuge. He took me out onto the shelf and abandoned me there. After much soul-searching, I threw myself into the sea and made my way back. After that I was an independent swimmer and went out and back with a minimum of trepidation.

Nina and I were good friends all through childhood, although we were very different. Though younger, Nina soon grew taller, since both of her parents were tall, while both of mine were diminutive. When I was little I resented it, and harbored a secret – and absurd – fear that since she was the taller of us two, she would also become the older one.

Another one of my earliest memories is connected with the radio. In my mind's eye I see a tall, rectangular box, taller than I, made of rich brown mahogany (no wood composite then), with a rounded top shaped like a fat rainbow. In the front there are some knobs and a big, round area covered in brown fabric, like a huge blind eye. Inside, I thought at that time, there is a little man, dressed in a neat black suit, with a white shirt and tie, working frantically to produce the voices and music issuing from the box.

When I was home by myself, I often played with dolls. However, the simple quiet domesticity of cooking, feeding, dressing and undressing my doll was not enough for me. I would perform all those chores, but always within a displaced framework. My "child" and I might be castaways on a desert island. We might be princesses exiled through some dim political event. (Being a princess was a big thing with me; my husband claims it still is.) We might be great patriots banished to Siberia, bundled up to survive the fierce winter. We might be in hiding, and I would rock my baby in her carriage to prevent her crying and giving us away – little did I know that such scenes would soon be played out in my real life.

Anything I read or heard would become grist for the mill of my imagination to be enacted in the next game. I had all the paraphernalia of doll-playing: the crib, the carriage, the little stove with its set of miniature pots and pans, a child-sized table and chair set where I and the dolls could sit and sip lemonade from the tiny cups and eat little pieces of cake off the tiny plates while conversing unilaterally in French.

Despite being identified as Jews, my family was not very religious. Except on holidays, there was little mention of religion in my home. We were not kosher and we did not light candles or pronounce blessings on Friday nights. Although we belonged to the Great Synagogue of Warsaw, we rarely attended services. When I was older I attended several services there on High Holy Days. I found them excruciatingly boring and soon escaped with my friends to play in the halls away from the sanctuary.

Our maid for a time, Teresa, felt this relative secularism was a great void in my life. She often took me to the Catholic church less than a block away, which had a chapel devoted to Saint Teresa. I learned the common Catholic prayers and practices and was introduced to the priest as the "little Jewish girl who wanted to convert." Although I loved Teresa dearly and went along with what was clearly her great desire, privately I remained skeptical. Of course, I could not help but be impressed by the rich and colorful appointments in the church and the pageantry of the services or the processions we watched from our balcony. They compared favorably with the services in our synagogue, but services in a foreign tongue, be it Latin or Hebrew, sounded like a lot of mumbo-jumbo to a child not brought up in a religious tradition.

My situation should sound very familiar to many American Jews. Our home was more or less secular, with no regular rituals performed. I learned later that this was not my father's choice. He would have preferred a kosher home with some semblance, at least, to the Orthodox home he had been brought up in. This was an instance of his giving in to his wife. My mother had been brought up in a relatively assimilated home. She spent some years in Germany and wanted to move even further from Judaism. The most she was willing to do was go to the synagogue twice a year, and only then for a couple of hours at a time—a pattern which I am repeating now. Hanukkah was considered a children's holiday, and I would get the traditional *gelt* (money), some real and some made of chocolate.

We also had a Christmas tree, gaily decorated with colored glass balls, tinsel and long strands of cotton batten, little Santas and elves, but without any Christian symbols such as angels. At the top we had a big Star of David. My parents knew that the Christmas tree had pagan origins and couldn't see why it was any less appropriate in a Jewish home than in a Christian one. Of course I loved the glitter and the pine smell. The tree was always put up early because my mother and I would leave for a winter vacation before Christmas.

As far as I was concerned, Passover was the most important Jewish holiday. The two seders were celebrated at home. The first and more important one was always in our house. I had mixed feelings about it. It was a party in which children were included. It was the one time that rules for bedtime were relaxed. On the other hand, the *davening* (praying) went on too long, although at least at our seder most of it was in Polish, my first language. As many as 30 people might sit down to the seder. Since wine and mead (honey wine) flowed liberally, while the children received grape juice, everyone was merry, singing the *Dayeynu* at the top of our voices. Once, my Aunt Zina drank too much mead, and the heavy wine went to her feet instead of her head. She sounded perfectly rational, if overly loud and rambunctious, but was unable to stand up. Everyone found her situation hilarious, she most of all. My eyes must have had a look of amazement. Such goings on were totally unexpected from the usually serious adults.

While growing up, political events were of little interest to me. There were always newspapers in the house, and I overheard my parents and their friends discussing public events from time to time, but I paid little attention. Sometime in the late 1930s, my friend Zula's parents took in a refugee Jewish family from Germany. I am sorry to say that rather than feeling compassion towards this exiled family, who spoke no Polish, they seemed to me like lesser human beings, and I made no effort to imagine their bewilderment and terror. It is ironic considering the fate that would befall us soon enough.

My parents read a Jewish newspaper, written in Polish, which had a separate section for children once a week. I awaited this section eagerly. One of the features consisted of book reviews written by children, and I became a contributor. Several of my book reviews were published, as well as one letter to the editor on a subject now forgotten. As I write this chronicle, the feeling of pride in seeing my name in print comes back to me. Were it not for the disruption of war, I might have pursued this writing interest professionally.

Uncle Adek was another important adult in my life. I loved his wife Zina, my father's sister, who was also my mother's closest friend. Zina was soft, plump and cuddly. I was not plump, being always a finicky eater, but otherwise I looked like a miniature version of her. She and my father also resembled each other, but capricious genes made me look just like my aunt and not at all like my mother.

Adek was a difficult man, loved but also feared in his home. He was a successful lawyer, a marvelous raconteur—an art almost lost today—who, when so inclined, could also cut you down with just a few sarcastic words if you did anything to displease him. He was an absolute tyrant in his home and office. The latter was located in the apartment, so I had an opportunity to see how he treated his subordinates when he was angry.

Adek's opinions, voiced clearly and with great self-assurance, were widely accepted and respected by his contemporaries. He was a true intellectual. He had been a Hebrew teacher before becoming a lawyer, but was not religious at all. When his older son Leo married a Swedish girl in the United States during World War II, she converted to Judaism and went to a *mikvah* (an Orthodox Jewish ritual bath). She did this to please her in-laws who were then in Russia, but after Zina and Adek came to America they all had a good laugh about this. Incidentally, Adek could not practice law in the United States. In his late sixties, he earned a master's degree in English and became a professor of Russian language and literature at the University of Chicago.

It may seem puzzling that such an august personage would bother with his little niece, but he did. My mother and I visited Zina and Adek frequently, prompting Adek to come out of his office to take a break. Apparently my company was preferable to the "women's chatter" as he put it. "Come," he would say to me, "let us go for a promenade." We would walk the length of the living room and the long, dark hall (which had held such fears for me when I was little) and back and forth for half an hour or more. "Walking is the best exercise," he would say, "as it helps the digestion."

Adek was by far the best-informed man I knew, perhaps because everything interested him. "Tell me something interesting you heard in school today," he would order. It might be a historical event, a geographical fact, a poem, or the fact that the zero had been invented 1,000 years ago—how did they manage without it before, I wondered? I would be treated to such things as the inadequacies of the Roman numeral system, particularly in account-keeping and construction, and the marvels the Romans accomplished in spite of it, or to a recitation of a verse from the "Pan

Tadeusz" (an epic poem by Poland's greatest poet, Adam Mickiewicz), or to the legislative mess during the French Revolution. His lessons were given extemporaneously and supported by solid facts. He provided another lesson which I was to use later in my teaching: grab every opportunity to widen your students' horizons, even if the topic does not lie within your sanctioned sphere of competence.

Then came school. For five years I attended the Teachers' Union (TU). It was a private, Jewish girls' school located on Rymarska Street, about a ten-minute walk from my house. The school occupied two buildings, one for grammar school and one for high school. Shortly after I started there, the short distance between the two buildings was bridged by a connecting corridor on the second floor, eliminating the necessity of bundling up in the winter each time we needed to go to the high school.

The student body came from comfortable or affluent, assimilated Jewish families, and all the teachers were also from the Jewish middle class. Instruction, however, took place in Polish. Polish flags hung in each classroom. The Polish government was spoken of reverently, and the spirit of patriotism prevailed.

My parents sent me to TU to shield me from the anti-Semitism which I would have surely encountered in public schools. But also, truth be told, they sought to protect me from "undesirable elements," that is to say, any contact with children from blue-collar and poor families. Since most of my classmates were there for similar reasons, we all tended to be somewhat spoiled and snobbish. The few scholarship students among us, while not shunned, were somewhat excluded from our various circles of friends—really a polite term for cliques.

School lasted roughly from 8:30 a.m. to 1:30 p.m., Monday through Friday, and a shorter day on Saturday. As we progressed from grade to grade and the number of subjects grew, it became impossible to study every subject every day, so most subjects were taught two or three times a week, making a more varied and interesting schedule. The exceptions were classes in language skills and math, which met every day.

Each day included a period of physical activity, gymnastics alternating with rhythmics. I was not particularly enamored with gym; I didn't like the changing in the crowded locker room, particularly changing back into our school uniforms. Since there were no showers, our sweaty bodies had to be stuffed back into the white blouses and navy pleated short skirts which constituted the required dress in school.

The gym was large and airy and very noisy, with 26 young voices reverberating from the walls. This was accompanied by the shrill voice of our teacher calling the commands, counting or getting our attention with her piercing whistle. We did group calisthenics and worked on vertical ladders mounted on the walls and on the mats. Once I fell from the fifth or sixth rung of the ladder and landed so hard that I lost my voice for about 15 minutes. No one noticed my predicament, and I went through 15 minutes of terror, fearing that the loss would be permanent. But my voice returned with no ill effects. On the floor mats we did the usual somersaults and later cartwheels, a feat I never truly mastered.

Gym teachers usually pick athletes as their favorites and no one could accuse me of being one, but somewhere along the line, our gym teacher Panna Janka and I grew to like each other. On rainy days when I didn't go to the park after school, I would sometimes go to see her in her room and chat about the books I read, the movies I had seen, or problems with my parents and friends. In turn, she would share with me tidbits of her life that were appropriate for her young friend. It was an odd friendship, but a genuine one. I think that I tended to be more intellectually mature than some of my friends, and this drew me to adults who were willing to take me seriously. Panna Janka was one of them. Years later, our paths would cross again under the most bizarre circumstances.

School occupied only the morning hours, leaving me time for many other activities. When I was in the lower grades, if weather permitted, school was always followed by a play period in the nearby park. In those days I was not yet allowed to walk anywhere by myself, so the maid picked me up after school and took me to Ogrod Saski (Saxon Garden), a short stroll down Senatorska and Zelazna Brama Streets. Other friends would come as well. So while the maids congregated and gossiped, we played "tag," "it" or "hide and seek," releasing the pent-up energy accumulated during the morning, when we were mostly sedentary.

I have a very clear memory of an incident in the Saxon Gardens. I was very little, it was winter and snow was on the ground. For whatever reason, the maid was unavailable and my mother took me to the park to play, a very rare occurrence. I was dressed in a black seal coat and matching bonnet. I had warm, knit leggings and high, black rubber boots. Red mittens, secured by a red string around my neck, matched my glowing red cheeks. I spotted Krysia, later called Chris, in the distance. Chris's mother, Marysia, was a bacteriologist, and her father a pediatrician, so our parents must have at least heard of, if not actually known, each other.

She too wore a seal coat and, by an odd happenstance, she too was there with her mother, an event as rare in her life as in mine. As if prompted by an invisible signal, we hurled ourselves into each others' arms, hugging and kissing gleefully. We must have looked like two little black, fluffy balls colliding in midair!

From that day on our friendship was acknowledged and we visited each other often to play. My two best friends were Chris and Zula, the latter of whom I knew from school. We formed an inseparable trio at school, but when we visited each other at home, usually only one friend was invited. Indeed, it was hard for three girls to settle down to play quietly—always an important objective for adults.

Chris's home on Orla Street was always a very interesting place to visit. She lived with her parents and grandparents, Mr. and Mrs. Alabaster. I knew that alabaster was a type of marble and, in my mind, the slow-moving grandparents themselves resembled marble statues: tall, staid and elegant. They were very religious, probably bordering on Orthodox, and the house was kosher, with great packs of round matzos appearing around Passover. Their lifestyle seemed so divergent from ours as well as from that of Chris' parents.

Chris' mother traveled extensively, and from time to time she would bring back interesting things from her excursions. She brought a roulette wheel, a mah-jongg set, a troll from Scandinavia and little flags of different countries. We were allowed to play with all those things. In fact, when asked, Mrs. Marysia would explain them and tell us about the countries she had visited—far better than any geography lesson! We would play roulette, using the chips that came with the wheel, but neither of us ever caught the gambling bug in later life.

Marysia was my role model. She was certainly different from my mother and her cronies. She differed first in appearance. Where they were all plump, she was slim. Instead of wearing rich, ornate dresses, she favored simple, elegant yet expensive suits. Once she told me, "I am too poor to afford cheap clothes. I buy good, ageless classics, and they last me forever." She did not bleach or color her hair and did not have an elaborate coiffure or put nail polish on her short, blunt nails. She was not beautiful in a classic sense. But her animated face, her good physique and her energetic movements made her appear years younger than my mother and her friends.

She was the only truly educated woman I knew, holding a degree in bacteriology from the University of Warsaw. Not only was she the only professional woman in my life, she was also the only working woman my family knew socially. I saw her reading professional literature and non-fiction on a variety of subjects, so unlike the other women I knew who idled their lives away and confined their reading to fiction and their conversation to gossip.

Sometimes Marysia, Chris and I would converse in French. Like them, I spoke fluent, unaccented French because of having had a governess and of my continuing French lessons. Chris had relatives in France, and Marysia spoke French almost as fluently as Polish. My parents both spoke fluent German and Russian, and my father also spoke Yiddish and some Hebrew. But I am afraid, being the little snob that I was, I considered French much more chic.

When Chris and I got older, we sometimes ventured further from home to Marszalkowska Street or even Novy Swiat, both elegant non-Jewish areas with plenty of shopping. Chris was more familiar than I with this world because of her parents' lifestyle. Since we were both show-offs, we would pretend to be French and converse loudly in French, criticizing and mocking everything we saw around us. At such times, I would call Chris "Cri-Cri" and she would call me Claire. We would stop in a café and order a lemonade or a dish of ice cream, watching the waiters confer until they found somebody on the premises who could understand French. Recalling the successful deception back home, we would dissolve into giggles.

I understand now Marysia did not have an easy life. For instance, I was never sure why she and her family lived with her parents. At some point her husband disappeared from the apartment. I heard they were separated and later divorced. In the Jewish community at that time, divorce was considered a disgrace and a scandal, and a woman was usually blamed for not "managing things better." In that generation women were not equal partners in marriage. Men handled financial and other important decisions. Women got around this by being manipulative and convincing the men that they were the originators of various ideas. Most of the time the women acted in good faith and for the good of the family. This was an ancient pattern; feminism had never been heard of in my parents' circle.

Marysia was also an active athlete. She skied in the winter, even doing short jumps while my mother rode around in horse-driven sleds. She skated beautifully, and often took Chris and me with her. In the early summer when it was hot, but before we went away for the summer, she would take us to the Lazienki Park where there was a portion of a lake cordoned off for swimming. There I would practice my breast stroke, while she ate up the distance using the freestyle stroke. She was always open and honest with both of us, treating me as a young friend. She was truly a woman for me to admire and emulate.

My friend Zula's mother, Ruta, was also my friend. She and her sister-in-law Freda were more worldly than my mother. I think my mother met Ruta through some activity in my school; soon she became close friends with Freda and Ruta. Sometimes when I visited Zula, Ruta would take me aside and exhort me to encourage Zula to read. Ruta was an intelligent woman and despaired of her daughter. Zula disliked school and any intellectual activity such as reading. She didn't like any sports, but loved to eat. When we were together she frequently finished my meals. In spite of our different interests, Zula and I played together well and remained good friends. Apparently I was able to accommodate myself to her based on those interests we did share. Possibly Zula was doing the same. At that time, when we were 10 and 11 respectively, she was already interested in boys and I was not.

Freda had a son, Robus, a little older than Zula and I. Although he occasionally condescended to spend some time with us, essentially he moved in a different sphere, so I had no reason to visit Freda's house. Freda's husband was also a doctor, and since she was my mother's friend the two couples socialized. Freda came to our apartment from time to time. She and Robus went with us to the winter resort, Krynica, just about every winter for two or three weeks. Whenever we had a chance, Freda and I would go for a walk and talk to each other about ourselves. On other occasions we would spin long, fantastic tales.

In Krynica, we once created a fairy tale about a Christmas tree, told in the voice of the tree itself. We told about how it felt to grow up among one's relatives and be rudely snatched up by an axe man, wounded and bewildered, only to be transported to a cheerful, bustling home. We imagined how the wound was bandaged with soothing wet cloths and how the tree was stood upright, decorated, proud to be loved and admired. Of course after Christmas, the tree was stripped of all ornaments and discarded, left to die alone feeling sad and betrayed.

Yes, we were kindred souls, Freda and I. When I was with her, I didn't feel I was with an adult who might judge me, or praise or criticize according to some mysterious standards, but with an older sister accepting me for what I was. I told her things I told no one else and, I think to some extent, she did the same with me. Perhaps she dreamed of having a daughter, or maybe she needed an outlet for sharing her creativity, romanticism, and dreams, feeling reluctant to expose that side of her to her peers. We shared the poems we wrote. She hoped to publish hers and I supported her in this although, truth be told, I did not always fully understand their meaning.

These rare interludes with Freda, like my times with Marysia, gave me a window on adult life. I learned that an adult could feel lonely among her friends who did not share her sensibilities. Freda deplored the down-to-earth blandness of her peers, "the absence of poetry in their souls." I felt privileged to be the recipient of such confidences and saw her as a some-what tragic figure.

In the summer of 1939, I went on vacation to Brok-Nad-Bugiem with five school friends and a teacher's aide. It was my first vacation without my mother. All through the summer, the parents sent only occasional delega-tions to check on us , but late in August, when the political situation took an ominous turn, things changed.

Hitler demanded the "Corridor." In response a general mobilization was announced in Poland. It was time for us to go home. But how was it to be done? We walked over to the station and found utter chaos. Trains were no longer running on time, and, when they did pass through, they were full of soldiers travelling to reach their units. Civilians mobbed every passing train. It was every man for himself. Six little girls with one adult young woman, burdened with a mountain of luggage including bicycles, had no chance at all. Telephone calls began flying between Warsaw and Brok. In the end, Chris' father, who owned a car, came to transport Chris, Zula and me, while the rest of the group went home in a taxi.

The trip gave me a taste of wartime travel. Roads were jammed with mil-itary trucks and civilian carts, all overloaded, causing frequent break-downs of men and equipment. Every crossroad threatened gridlock, as the long snakes of vehicles moved east or west, and the peasants tried to harvest their fields in a hurry. We moved slowly along the hot, dusty road, tempers short, and panic just contained. The 100-mile trip lasted long into the night.

Finally I was back in the bosom of my family. My parents hugged me, kissed me, and listened to my excited retelling of the harrowing trip. But their minds weren't really on it, and soon I was put to bed.

The next morning I discovered that things at home were the same and yet they were totally different. Instead of shopping for clothes and school supplies for the fall, my parents were shopping for food. Hoarding food became a passion in Warsaw, despite all the official placards pleading with the population to refrain from depleting the city's food stocks.

Since gas masks were unobtainable, surgical masks were distributed along with a solution to permeate them, in case of a gas attack. People always prepare for the last war, instead of the next one. Walking about in the city, I saw trenches being dug in parks. I couldn't understand what they were supposed to accomplish, but had faith that somebody knew. Everyone walked fast, while the streets were filled with soldiers strutting along confidently, one might say even arrogantly, the only ones around without fear in their eyes.

My father had already been considering emigration, and had recently sold the apartment house he owned for cash. Thus, most of our possessions were in what is mistakenly called liquid form. In fact we owned $24,000 in $5 or $10 gold pieces (some were in 5 or 10 gold ruble pieces). All this wealth was packed in a small suitcase which I could barely lift. Hundred dollar bills were painstakingly wound around the whalebones of my mother's corset, or sewn into my father's vacation cap. My mother's diamond lavaliere, which, as the oldest daughter, she had inherited from her mother and grandmother, was hidden in a specially hollowed heel of my father's shoe. All through the war, he wore those shoes during dangerous times, saving them from excessive wear at other times. After the war, when we removed it, the lavaliere, fashioned in delicate filigree, was broken in half, but salvageable. We made it into a ring, a brooch, and a small pendant, all of which I still have. All around us people were doing the same things. One very rich friend of my grandparents, Mrs. Rowinska, had a set of diamonds concealed as cloth-covered sweater buttons.

I was as frightened as everyone else, but underneath it, I felt a glimmer of excitement. The possibility that there might be no school, that life was going to change, routines were being abandoned, seemed interesting and unusual, so that half of me hoped it would all blow over, and the other half secretly, guiltily, hoped it wouldn't.

CHAPTER 3

SEPTEMBER 1939

The first bombs fell at dawn on September 1, 1939. I was awakened by the noise and ran into my parents' bedroom. At first we hoped that this was yet another air raid test, but soon we realized that it wasn't. World War II had begun, and I was nearly 12 years old.

During the first few days, Warsaw was busy organizing for a prolonged siege. Blackout was ordered at night and those of us who had not prepared before were rushing around to get black cloth or construction paper to cover the windows. Sirens announced the beginning of an air raid. The all clear sounded an hour or so later when the planes had finished discharging their deadly loads. There were several air raids a day, as waves of planes came over Warsaw at one- or two-hour intervals, creating the feeling of a continuous attack. During the air raids, civilians were supposed to go to bomb shelters, also known as cellars. There, we cowered in the near dark, inhaling the coal dust mixed with the smell of root vegetables put away for the winter, cringing at the sounds of the bombs.

Those who chose to stay in the apartments risked direct hits, uncontrollable fires from the incendiary bombs, and injury from flying glass or other objects thrown around by the force of nearby explosions. Those who came down to the cellars heard the muffled sounds of bomb bursts but were in danger of being buried alive as buildings above them collapsed. A Hobson's choice indeed.

Knowing myself better now, I recognize that I function better when I am in control or have an illusion of control. That is why I am uncomfortable flying. Up in the air, I am at the mercy of the elements, the machinery of the plane, and the unknown pilot. When I fly, I do like to watch the wing in case the engine catches fire. During the air raids, I think I would have preferred to stay in the apartment where at least I would have known what was happening, but I was not given the choice.

My father became a fire warden and spent hours on the roof during the air attacks. His absence added to my fears. I always felt marginally safer when he was around. For my sake he put on a front of confidence, a show of doing something to prevent disaster. When he was with us in the cellar, particularly if the bombs were falling far away, he engaged me in conversation, told me stories or encouraged me to read in the feeble light of a candle. But when the bombs were falling close to us, not even he could disguise the choking fear we all felt. "Will I be next?" each of us wondered. Since night bombardment had not been attempted yet, we were able to spend nights in our apartment, assess the damage, sweep up the glass, restore order, have a substantial supper and spend the evening listening to the radio.

Within days, England and France entered the war. All Poland rejoiced at the news; at least now we were not alone. But it was to be a long time before those two countries would get involved in practice rather than on paper, so we had to be prepared to stand alone for a while, cheered on by the encouraging British voices on the short wave radio. Then there was the vaunted Polish army. Surely it could stop Hitler's armies, or at least delay them until help came from the West. Alas, the Polish army wasn't even prepared to fight World War I, having a military force more suited to the 19th Century.

The backbones of the Polish army were the infantry (foot soldiers) and cavalry. The soldiers were armed with rifles and swords. Old-fashioned tactics and training matched the antiquated equipment. In contrast, Germany fought a new kind of war. It was called *Blitzkrieg* (lightning war), and depended on speed, communications and tanks, all meticulously synchronized for maximum effect. German fighter planes pounded airports and supply lines, destroying the meager Polish air force within days, if not hours.

While this went on, terrorizing a country accustomed only to the swish of sabers and pounding of hoofs, a massive Panzer tank invasion began, supported by armored divisions carrying the infantry to the ever-shifting front, all moving at the same, unimaginable speed. Decisions were made on the spot, and the front commanders authorized to make them were in constant radio communication with their superiors. The new communication technology was far superior to the hand signals and messengers still employed by the Polish army.

Where did this endless supply of planes, tanks and trucks come from? We now know that Hitler could not have successfully invaded Poland without taking possession of the Skoda works in Czechoslovakia, which he had acquired in his two-stage takeover of that country. Skoda manufactured cars, but it was best known for having the biggest and most modern armament factories in Europe. Czech armaments now supplemented the tanks, planes and guns Germany had been producing feverishly since Hitler had come to power six years earlier.

The timing of the attack was quite traditional: in time to grab the harvest just collected, just right to miss the worst heat of the summer, but before the rains transformed the Polish dirt roads into impassable ribbons of mud. Hitler planned to complete the action before the change in the weather, and certainly before the winter set in. He succeeded beyond his wildest dreams. Within days Poland was helpless, and the belief in German invincibility was born.

The Polish army melted before this onslaught, and the streets of Warsaw became clogged with retreating soldiers fleeing east. Many civilians decided to follow the army, braving the crowded roads, recurring air attacks and the low-flying planes strafing all moving objects. Uncle Abrasha and his family were among those who decided to go. He ran over one evening to tell us and urged us to join them, but we were not yet ready to abandon the possessions accumulated over the years. It was an instance where it proved wiser to be rash and impetuous rather than prudent and careful. Abrasha, Cyla and Nina made it to Vilnius, and from there managed to escape to Palestine.

In those first days, it was still possible to go outside in the intervals between the air raids. We would dispense water and food to the soldiers making their weary way along our street. My father gave some first aid, cleaning the wounds of the walking casualties, and bandaging them with sheets torn into strips. Even I learned to bandage arms and legs and helped all I could, hearing the exhausted "Thank you, little miss" over and over.

Stores were closed, and no patients arrived at my father's lab. One of my father's lab assistants, Miss Fela, came over one day. She and her family were in a bad way. Poor and relying on her modest earnings, they had not put up any food supplies, and were unable to pay the inflated prices for such food as was available on the instantly created black market. The Polish government had previously forbidden such gouging. My mother packed her a big bag of staples and told her to come back when this ran out. But conditions worsened rapidly and we did not see Miss Fela again until two years later.

Soon the blackout preparations and the expensive radio we had purchased were rendered useless. The Warsaw power plants were knocked out early on, making electricity service first unreliable, then sporadic and finally non-existent. Gas lines were also destroyed within a few days. This was not catastrophic because we had plenty of candles and coal and wood for the stove we used for cooking. Since the gas burners we had used for minor cooking were no longer available, we made hot tea at night and kept it in thermoses, several of which my mother had prudently laid in stock for use throughout the next day's bombardment.

However, the loss of electricity also meant loss of communications. Unlike in the United States, telephones in Warsaw had no generator back-up. When power failed, the phones didn't work. Not being able to talk to Aunt Zina and Uncle Adek or any friends added to our feeling of helplessness and isolation. Had they survived the day? Were they bombed out and in a shelter somewhere? All our relatives and friends lived within easy walking distance, but in this city under siege they might as well have been living on the moon.

Even more serious than the loss of power was the loss of running water which soon followed. I am convinced that for urban dwellers running water, more than any other convenience, makes a difference between civilized and primitive life. Every pot, bowl, pail, and any other watertight container, including the bathtub, had been kept full to anticipate this hazard. But when the faucets were empty, we were immediately reduced to hoarding this precious commodity. Water from shaving, minimal washing and cooking was saved and used to flush the toilet once a day. Within days, we were all grubby. The men were unshaven, many letting their beards grow. The odor of unwashed clothes mixed with the smell of sweat and fear. These conditions added to our loss of human dignity. The Nazis could not have asked for a better psychological preparation for what was to come.

That year Rosh Hashanah came early, on September 14. The Germans celebrated it by concentrating their bombs on the Jewish area of Warsaw on that day. It was a day out of hell. The bombing was relentless and continuous. By this time the sirens had fallen silent, as if putting us on notice that the city was abandoned. The meager anti-aircraft guns had been silenced as well, so that the enemy could rage at us at will. German artillery was now close enough to the city to supplement the air attacks with the ones on land. Poland was prostrate and virtually beaten. Only isolated areas, the largest of them being the open city of Warsaw, were still defending themselves from the invaders. German armies surrounded the city, and their long-range guns, operating day and night, contributed to the chaotic nightmare engulfing us. On Rosh Hashanah our building was hit twice, once causing a small fire which the men were able to put out. On September 23, Yom Kippur, the Germans gave a repeat performance, again concentrating their fire power on Jewish areas.

By this time everyone was an expert at distinguishing between the artillery shells (which came whistling low, paused, then hit, spraying shrapnel in all directions) from the bombs falling from above. We were also good at estimating how far and in what direction the bombs were falling, so that people would say, "They are hitting Praga today"—a suburb of Warsaw, across the Vistula River—or, "That was pretty close, sounds like Saxon Gardens or Marszalkowska Street." When the bombs were distant, we breathed a sigh of relief. This time we were safe. This time someone else was cringing, hands over ears. We stopped thinking that this someone else might be a friend, a relative, or another suffering victim. Our world was reduced to the narrowest here and now. To survive the day, to have something to put in our mouths, to have a place to put our weary heads—this was what concerned us. Sufficient unto the day, Lord, sufficient unto the day.

On September 17 we heard truly catastrophic news. The Soviet Union had entered Poland from the East and, without a single shot being fired, had occupied the area up to the Bug River. This news, brought into Warsaw from outside, sounded at first like one of the many rumors which spread like wildfire in a city deprived of legitimate news sources. But this one proved to be true. All the armchair generals were dumbfounded. Where were England and France? We did not understand that it takes a while to gear up for modern war. France would never manage this feat at all, and England was to be subjected to prolonged bombardment before it could retaliate, and only then with massive American help. We knew that Germany and the Soviet Union had signed a non-aggression pact in the spring of 1939, but we thought the Russians might exert some pacifying influence on the Germans, not wanting the Nazis on their doorstep. We didn't know that the treaty had a secret clause providing for just such a dismemberment of Poland as was taking place.

The next day our house took a direct hit and an uncontrollable fire broke out. "Evacuate the building!" came the order. It was now time to panic—every man for himself. We ran out of the cellar with no plan of where to go. The sun shone brightly somewhere above, but down below there was a haze of dust from the disintegrating buildings mixed with the smoke from the fire. The air was filled with the sounds of shells flying all around us, moans of the wounded, unanswered cries for help, and shouts of the survivors looking for their families. The ground was strewn with debris, broken furniture, bricks, boards with nails protruding from them, and the glitter of broken glass. We ran through the courtyard, the entrance portal and into the street. As we were running across the street, instinct told us to seek some shelter under a wall. Jumping across bodies and debris, my mother tripped and fell on top of a corpse. Somehow, in the midst of the fiery chaos and the mindless terror, this was to me the most terrifying of all. "No! No!" I screamed, as if her falling meant she too was dead and lost to me. With strength beyond my years, I pulled her up and we ran to my father.

We huddled in the entrance of the nearest building, breathless, thirsty, hot and bewildered. Where to now? We had many friends living nearby, and chose one of their houses as our destination, but when we got there, we found the building was a shell—a mountain of bricks with some walls still standing and some rooms exposed to our eyes and to the sky. Beds were unmade and dishes were on the table as if the inhabitants had just left for a minute and would soon run back up the now non-existent stairs. We continued running, climbing over the rubble and keeping to the walls as if, by hiding furtively, we could escape the death-planes flying over us.

When we reached our next destination, the building was still standing more or less intact and we ran up one flight of stairs to our friends' apartment, who received us tearfully, glad we were alive. The apartment had a wide, central corridor with several doors on both sides leading to various rooms. Several people were already camped in this hall. With no windows, it was protected from flying glass. More mattresses and pillows were brought out for us, and here we spent the last nine days of the siege.

In my mind these nine days are stretched almost to infinity. Terror made the adrenaline flow, so that we lived in a state of continuous emotional fever pitch. I must have eaten and slept intermittently when exhaustion and a lull in the bombing permitted me to doze off, only to be startled into awareness by a particularly close hit. I do remember that with so many people we suffered a severe shortage of water. Two or three young men in the apartment made the hazardous trip to the river to bring several buckets of water for the group. The bombardment and artillery action were now relentless. There was hardly any conversation as each one of us huddled in an almost fetal position, instinctively trying to present the smallest possible target to the unspeakable danger.

I don't know what was going through other people's minds, but I spent the time repeating over and over, "Please God, save me. Don't let me die." This became my magic mantra; surely God would not strike me down while I prayed to him. I dared not stop praying lest God punish me. I had never before, nor have I since experienced such a fervent sensation of religious faith. Voltaire's remark comes to mind, "Even if there was no God, men would have had to invent Him." Now, in my extreme situation, with everyone around me equally terrified, belief in God was the only thing I had to hang on to. Thus, slowly, very slowly the days passed. With each passing day I felt more enervated and helpless. One cannot get used to such acute danger and attain any sense of equanimity, composure, or peace.

On September 27, Warsaw formally surrendered and the guns fell silent. After the prolonged assault on our ears, our nerves and our souls, the silence felt truly deafening. We looked at each other, sharing the same thoughts. Dare we hope it was the end of at least this phase of the war? What would the advent of German occupation mean for us? On a more prosaic note, how soon would it become possible to flush the toilet and take a bath?

The next day the German army triumphantly entered Warsaw, marching through the main thoroughfares. We ventured out timidly, gulping great breaths of the outside air which was still acrid from the lingering fires. A picture of destruction greeted our eyes. I know now that about 10 percent of Warsaw was totally destroyed, though many more buildings were partially damaged. On that day, prior to any clean-up or repairs, the streets were strewn with glass, rubble and bodies. Broken windows gaped blindly from the houses around us. The city looked mortally wounded, uninhabitable. But, in fact, the damage was less than it seemed.

When we returned to our apartment it was not burned out, though the odor of smoke still hung heavy over it. At first glance it looked as if all our possessions had been smashed. The windows had to be boarded up, as glass was unobtainable at any price. In addition, the cleaning process loomed immense without the help of the servants we had been accustomed to. The cook and maid vanished right at the start of the war—that was definitely a time to be with one's family. We re-established contact with Aunt Zina. Uncle Adek and Cousin Henry had left Warsaw at the start of the bombardment with the goal of enlisting in the Polish army. They were bombed on the train going east. Unable to proceed, they weathered the month of September in a small resort near Warsaw, possibly Srodborow or Otwock. Their building had not been hit; it even retained some of its window panes. Both Adek and Henry returned to their Warsaw apartment in late September.

In times of danger and uncertainty families try to stay together. Accordingly, the decision was made for us to move in with Zina, Adek and their family, the only close relatives we still had in Warsaw.

CHAPTER 4

ATTEMPTS TO ESCAPE

Aunt Zina and Uncle Adek Hurwicz had a large apartment on Graniczna Street near the Saxon Garden, away from the heavy concentration of Jews in the city. There was plenty of room for us, since Adek's law business, which occupied part of the apartment, soon became completely dormant, if not dead. In addition, the couple's oldest son, Leo, was away.

Leo was the genius of the family. Although only 22 in 1939, he had already received an undergraduate degree in law, which is similar to a bachelor's degree in political science in the United States, and minored in physics, all the while continuing his piano studies at the Warsaw Conservatory of Music. He was living in London at the time studying for a graduate degree in economics, and was spending the summer traveling in western Europe in a scaled-down version of a nineteenth-century Grand Tour for young men of good families. He was cut off from Poland by the recent hostilities, and his parents, while anxious about his fate, were hoping that he would be able to avoid involvement in the war. Not until they were deep in Russia did they find out that this was the case. Leo managed to duck into Switzerland and continue his studies, eventually culminating in a Ph.D. in economics and a distinguished academic career in America after the war.

Within several days we were settled in at our new lodgings. Having abandoned our apartment, we hired a horse and wagon to move our clothes, food, some books and other valuables to the new quarters. Oddly enough, nothing had been looted. Perhaps thieves and hooligans had been stunned into a momentary honesty by the violent events. But how to dispose of the furniture and lab equipment, for which we had no use at the moment? Zina's maid, Cesia, came to our rescue.

It seems that this homely, meek older woman had a rather enterprising boyfriend. He picked up our effects and promised to return them on demand. The deal, however, stipulated that the two of them could use any of our belongings, as a sort of payment. Cesia continued to come and help in the apartment, and through her boyfriend, became one of our purveyors of foodstuffs.

Our lives now revolved around two goals: how to keep ourselves fed, and how to escape from the Nazis.

We brought over our hoarded food, coal and wood, and added them to the supplies stockpiled by the Hurwiczes. Since there was no way to know how long they would have to last and what the future would bring, it was important to have ample supplies on hand, as well as to keep replenishing the perishables, such as milk and bread. The black market flourished. Right in our building lived a prostitute, at least that was her profession according to my cousin Henry. She had branched out into illicit trading. Once we bought from her a whole ham, and on several occasions big pieces of pork fat, with no objections from my father, who was a sensible man despite these most *trayf* (un-kosher) purchases.

Henry and I got the job of cutting up the fat into small pieces, a task we performed competitively, vying to produce the most uniform cubes. The cut-up fat was rendered for several hours over a low flame, with some chopped onions added at the end of the process The onions and the shriveled, un-melted pieces of fat were then skimmed off the melted fat. After cooling, the resulting lard could be kept almost indefinitely without refrigeration and was used both for cooking and as a bread spread— probably the tastiest and most high-cholesterol spread there is. The onions and pieces of fat, crisp and dripping, were a delicacy.

This detailed memory indicates the extent to which food dominated our thoughts and our lives. In no time, I had gone from a capricious, finicky eater to an omnivorous devourer of any food at all. It didn't even take an actual shortage of food—just the threat of one produced this change.

For me, a great positive aspect of our present situation was Henry's proximity. As he became a teenager, involved with school, friends and sports, he lost interest in his little cousin, but my admiration for him did not diminish. Now we were living together, and since going out was perilous and not to be undertaken lightly, we spent a lot of time together. I was basking in Henry's attention. Since there was no school, I was given some academic assignments by my father, and in the nature of things Henry became my supervisor, a fact which added to my desire to excel.

In those first weeks, German occupation was making itself felt mainly in the streets. Since the city was full of rubble, with many streets impassable to large vehicles, the first order of business was to clear them. Naturally, this was to be accomplished by the local population. Accordingly, German soldiers began grabbing people rash enough to be in the street and forcing them to work until after dark. A man identified as a Jew by his appearance could provide additional amusement to the occupiers as they laughingly beat him up, pulled his beard, or generally made him grovel in the muck. Women were also forced to do this work and, if identified as being Jewish, tormented in a like manner which included beatings, foul language and exposure. Intercourse with Jews, social or otherwise, was forbidden to Germans for fear that miscegenation would dilute the noble German blood, so we did not hear of rapes.

This situation got so bad that everyone went out as little as possible, thus intensifying the siege mentality and precluding the establishment of any kind of normality. Finally, in an effort to regularize the chaotic situation, the Jewish Council proposed organizing Jewish work brigades of able-bodied Jewish men for the clean-up details.

We knew that the current situation, bad as it was, was only the beginning. Already there were rumors that all Jews would be required to wear some clearly identifying signs, which turned out to be white armbands emblazoned with the Star of David, carry identification cards, and even be herded into a ghetto. It would take the Germans some time to get organized, but we knew these and/or other means to torment us were coming. Our little group began to plan an escape.

When the Soviet Union occupied the eastern part of Poland in September 1939, it gave part of its conquest to Lithuania. Back when Lithuania and Poland were one country, a large territory between them was inhabited by a mixture of Poles and Lithuanians. In 1918, President Wilson awarded this territory, including Vilnius, to Poland. In a feat of magnanimity not

fully understood, the Soviets corrected this "error." I am sure it was perceived as such by the Lithuanians living there. The result was that Vilnius
(where my grandfather and Uncle Solomon lived) and the surrounding
area became part of a non-Communist, neutral country, from which it
might be possible to travel to Palestine or to America.

It was our plan to make our way to Vilnius and beyond. However, since
there was no border between German-occupied Poland and Lithuania, it
was necessary to cross into Russian-occupied Poland, and from there to
Lithuania—two illegal frontiers to negotiate. This early, as is usually the
case after an upheaval, the borders were still quite porous, but were
bound to solidify in time, so it was necessary to move fast. It was now
that the $24,000 in gold—the proceeds from our recently sold apartment
building—became a stone around our collective neck.

My father had carried a little suitcase containing this treasure all through
the bombardment, in and out of the cellar, and out of our burning apartment house. But now it was too dangerous to carry so much money with
us. If our guide realized what we owned, he might kill us all for it. It was
therefore decided that we would establish a beachhead in the Soviet-
occupied territory, and delay the final move to Lithuania until all the
money was smuggled to Vilnius. My father was to stay temporarily in
Warsaw to supervise that end of the operation while the rest of us started on the journey.

While Adek and my father were making arrangements for the upcoming
trip, the women were deciding what to pack and what to wear. We knew
that we might have to carry our belongings for considerable distances, so
one small suitcase per person was all that we allowed ourselves, not much
considering that winter was coming. We compensated by planning to wear
several layers of clothing on the journey. This was to become standard procedure whenever we were making a move under dangerous conditions, so
that we always presented, at such times, an abnormally obese, even comi-
cal appearance in sharp contrast to the anguish we were experiencing.

The first time we did this, I thought back to a skit I had done in
Wolokumpia, a resort near Vilnius where I had spent several vacations
before the war, when a woman patient was disrobing in a doctor's office,
removing many layers of clothing, only for the audience to hear that the
complaint concerned her eye. How my life had already changed! It
seemed a different world, and I a different person. Then the skit was a
joke; now our behavior was deadly serious.

On the surface, I had recovered from the bombardment with no ill effects and bounced back to my normal, upbeat personality. But reflecting on it now, I realize that something had been broken. It was some spring, some assurance that nothing bad would ever happen to me, giving me boundless self-confidence and the right to act as I pleased without fear of consequences, to act on a whim. Now, my imagination was reined in, and I became a more careful, calculated and even cynical person. I would be battered much more in this war and it would take a long time afterwards to regain my sense of self-worth.

One might say these changes represent the normal process of growth and maturation, and to some extent they do. But in ordinary circumstances the process is gradual, whereas the stresses I was experiencing were exposing me suddenly and shockingly to evil, danger and deprivation, causing me to grow up suddenly and robbing me of my adolescence. My personality was inexorably shaped by the war years, which were also my teenage years, so formative in any person's life.

The journey began one evening late in October 1939. A truck pulled up in front of the house, and Adek, Henry, Zina, and my mother and I got in, each carrying a little suitcase. Last tearful kisses were exchanged with my father, as well as admonitions to be careful, all in a hurried manner since we were breaking the curfew. Then we were off.

The truck lumbered through the uneventful night, covering the 100 miles or so to the village of Sarnaki near the Bug River, which constituted the boundary between German- and Russian-occupied Poland. We disembarked in front of a large hut belonging to a wealthy peasant where we were to lay low through the daylight hours. By now, this was a well-established route, involving drivers, trucks, guides, rowboats and peasants on both sides of the border. We were fed by the farmer's wife, a stout, kindly woman who commiserated with our need to escape, perhaps sincerely, perhaps because she considered it part of the deal. We lay down and tried to doze, starting at every innocent noise. The Germans, fully aware of the ongoing exodus, were making surprise visits to the farms, in addition to patrolling the border.

Suddenly disaster struck. There was a loud knock on the door followed by a harsh voice ordering the owner to open up. Several soldiers, helmets on their heads and rifles at the ready entered and took the situation in at a glance. We did not look like peasants, so what else could we be but Jews trying to escape the Nazis? We were stunned into immobility. What would happen to us? We might be summarily shot, arrested, beaten, or, at best, turned back. It all might depend on the orders of the day, or perhaps even on the caprice of our captors. We were ordered out and taken to a nearby school which had been hastily converted into a military command center.

We were left waiting for a while, trembling with fear. But when our captors from the *Wehrmacht* (German army) returned, they engaged Adek— who spoke fluent German—in a conversation. The catastrophe turned out to have been a farce. It seemed the soldiers were only looking for soap. The war had only lasted for a couple of months, but already they were crawling with lice. We gave them our supply, and they were so grateful, they gave us some gratis advice. "If you are caught on the Soviet side, tell them you want to get to Germany. Trying to thwart you, they will make you stay," they said. They took us back to the hut to wait out the rest of daylight, and promised to come back at night and let us know when the time was right to start.

Evidently, patrolling on the Soviet side followed a routine, closely observed by the local peasantry and familiar to our new, surprise guides. Accordingly, even after night fell we had to wait until just the right moment, carefully calculated to miss the patrol. The *Wehrmacht* came back and gave us the sign. Our guides carried our suitcases, and silently as shadows we filed out of the hut to negotiate the mile or so distance to the river. In spite of the soldiers' assurances, we were afraid of other patrols. No one could be trusted; even our helpers might have just been toying with us. We were walking across the stubble of a harvested field. The ground was still soft and uneven, causing much stumbling and falling, all taking place in total silence, while the nervous guards urged us to hurry out of this no-man's zone, which provided no cover. The guards' anxiety intensified our own. We walked with our hearts and adrenaline pumping, sweating from the combination of fear and physical effort in spite of the chill in the night air.

After what seemed like an interminable trek, we reached the river where the boats were waiting. We boarded silently, while the guards righted the boats, making nothing but little splashes mingling with the tiny wavelets hitting the bank of the river. The oars were wrapped in rags to prevent noise. We were told to sit low, for this was the most dangerous part of the trip. Here, if we were spotted, we would not hear the German "*Halt!*" or the Russian "*Stoi!*"—only the rattle of guns. Luckily for us the night was cloudy, so much so that the other boat was barely visible. The boats were heavily laden, but the guides were strong young men. Soon we landed on the Russian side.

Now we had to walk again, making for the hut that was visible on the horizon. Here too we passed safely, and we entered this haven, exhausted from the physical exertion coupled with a prolonged bout of enervating anxiety and fear. We were just relaxing over a hastily prepared meal of bread and soup, when a Soviet patrol entered the hut for a routine search. It all happened so fast we had no chance to hide. The soldiers fanned out to search the rest of the hut and barn, leaving only one young man to guard us. Clearly they did not fear us, disdaining even to search us. The young soldier took a look at us and asked quietly, "*Amhu?*" (of the people?) Both Uncle Adek and my mother spoke fluent Russian, but in this conspiratorial moment the young soldier did not know it, and whispered to my uncle in broken Yiddish, "Tell them you want to go to the German side." He was confirming the advice given us earlier by our German helpers. Thank God for this young Jew's sympathy and sense of obligation to his people!

We did just that when questioned by the returning patrol leader. We had been caught in Bialystok, we claimed, visiting friends. Now we wished to return to our home in Warsaw. This was the exact reverse of our actual desired route. The peasants and our guides were also in the room, but luckily we were questioned first and they, of course, confirmed what we said. I don't know how they were punished, if at all, but our group was marched under guard to the nearby train station, our guardian angel giving us a secret sign that all was well. Here, our guards waited with us until the train arrived and put us on, with no tickets, ordering the conductor not to let us out of his sight until the train arrived in Bialystok lest we attempt to get off and make our way back to the river. Thus, in comparative comfort and under the watchful eye of the conductor, we traveled for free to Bialystok, which was about 200 miles southwest of Vilnius, the city of our destination.

Bialystok (White Stream) was a somewhat large industrial city named for the small river running through it. We went directly to the apartment of a distant relative of my father's and Zina's where, for a small sum, we were all assigned to one large room. Our hosts the Einhorns, a mother and daughter, were rather poor. Our presence was a financial boon for them. All the same, they did not treat us as boarders but as family, trying to be as helpful and hospitable as they could. In fact the daughter, though older than I, became a good friend.

Here, we settled down to a busy life. Adek and my mother tried to make contact with guides who would smuggle our money to Lithuania as fast as my father was sending it from Warsaw. To minimize the risk, the money arrived in small installations of about $1,000 each, making the transfer process a complex undertaking. Letters from my father stated how much money was being sent and alluded to the worsening conditions in Warsaw. Letters to Warsaw confirmed the receipt of the money and reported on its further journey, as well as giving news of ourselves and the Vilnius branch. Uncle Abrasha and Uncle Solomon were arranging to get their families out of Europe, Aunt Niuta had just remarried, but the Lithuanian government, already heavily dependent on the Soviet Union, was balking on issuing a visa to my grandfather. He was quite wealthy, though not as rich as the officials believed. They demanded that he reveal the location of his secret treasure and hand it over before they would let him go. Most of his liquid assets had already been transferred to America. Thus the cache didn't exist, and things were at an impasse.

Back in Bialystok our life was very hard. In all of Europe the winter of 1939-40 became one of the coldest on record. Fuel was expensive and hard to get, and our room proved impossible to heat. Flannel pajamas, heavy robes, and a down comforter ensured that my mother and I were warm in the bed we shared, but I had to steel myself to get into the icy linen at night, and again to jump out of my warm nest into the freezing room every morning. Zina, Adek, and Henry were all sleeping in one bed, and since Zina was on the outside, her problem was not to fall off. During the day I was bundled up in heavy sweaters and woolen pants, and learned that the trick was to keep moving.

This led to an amusing incident. One day, a distant cousin came to visit us. He was an ultra-Orthodox rabbi, a middle-aged man with a beard, *peyes* (long, curly side-burns), and dressed in a Hasidic outfit. He shook hands with Adek, Henry and me and sat down to talk, refusing any refreshments. He was strictly kosher and did not trust the dishes, eschewing even a glass of tea. In the course of the conversation, it was revealed that I was a girl. With my short-cropped hair and pants he had not realized it. "Why didn't you warn me?" he shouted. "I committed a mortal sin, touching a female who is not my wife!" Upset and red-faced from anger, he left soon after. I was 12 at the time but looked no older than 9 or 10 and found this incident totally absurd, as did my mother, aunt and uncle.

Henry and I were given the task of standing in lines. Bialystok had been known for its breads and rolls; the roll known in America as the bialy (a chewy onion roll) originated there. The city was surrounded by fertile countryside, yet there were shortages of all necessities of life. Henry and

I stood in interminable lines for milk, bread, flour and sugar. Eggs, butter and meat were available only on the black market. We stood stamping our feet, waving our arms, hugging ourselves, and hitting each other on the back to keep the circulation going, telling each other stories to pass the time, advancing ever so slowly to the head of the line. I got into the habit which, incidentally, remains with me to this day, of looking behind me and cheering myself up when the line behind me became longer than that in front of me. Finally, triumphant with our success or dejected in failure if the stores ran out of goods before our turn came, but invariably cold, we came back home. In spite of warm socks, gloves and boots, my hands and feet always felt frozen on my return and had to be warmed up slowly and painfully by soaking in cold water. Frostbite became a common occurrence. Some people lost toes or other extremities that winter.

My education was not neglected during these months. This was not surprising, given my parents' obsession with learning. I was sent to a public school where instruction was in Russian. Before the war, compulsory education in Polish elementary schools ended at sixth grade. High school was voluntary; even state high schools charged tuition, though some students were granted scholarships. Thus, the education of poor children usually ended in sixth grade. By contrast, in the Soviet Union education was free at all levels. In view of this, and given the high degree of unemployment in Bialystok, many people as old as 20 decided to return to school.

The class I was assigned to was just such a mixture. Twelve- or 13-year-olds coming directly from sixth grade mingled with what were essentially adults who had been out of school for five or six years, and had likely not been stellar students even then. Thus there was a mixture of ages, abilities, preparation and attitudes.

The teachers were an equally motley group. Most licensed Polish teachers were unable to lecture in Russian and thus were out of a job in this new political situation. Other than being able to speak Russian reasonably fluently, the qualifications of most of our teachers were suspect indeed. The math teacher stumbled through the problems. The Russian teacher was a sweet country girl who spoke with an atrocious accent and showed up in class one time in a nightgown in the mistaken belief she was wearing a dress.

In addition, we had to learn Belorussian. By law, inhabitants of each Soviet republic had to study the official language of that republic. Although a Polish city, Bialystok was incorporated into Belarus after the

Soviet invasion. Belorussian, I argued with our teacher, was not really a language but a dialect, because it had no literature. Only one book had been written in Belorussian. I was wrong; the existence of literature, or even of a written language, is not a proper criterion for defining a language. Many primitive languages don't have either. A better criterion for my argument would have been the fact that urban population, educated or not, did not use it. It persisted only in the countryside. Furthermore, Belorussian is clearly a cross between Russian and Polish, created by a population sandwiched between the two.

I eventually gave up on Belorussian and tuned that teacher out. The revisionist Soviet history also was not worth my while. I listened skeptically to the math teacher and checked things out at home with more reliable sources. I really concentrated all my efforts on the Russian language. An important and beautiful language, it was certainly worth knowing. I was conditioned early on, or perhaps it is my nature, to participate to the fullest extent in whatever I am involved in even if it is not very good. Thus, in most subjects I did the homework, was prepared in class and asked and answered questions.

This infuriated some of the class. These near-adults and adults might have succeeded if their motivation was stronger and the instruction better. But they were there for lack of something better to do and gave up almost immediately, often acting in class like the hooligans they were. My youth and my clear ability and progress showed them up.

My lack of tact did not help either. They retaliated by teasing me mercilessly and even mistreating me physically. Nothing serious, just slapping, pinching or tripping me with their big feet as I was approaching the teacher's desk to hand in some work. School became a misery. My family tried to console me and advised me to pay no attention. In the midst of their truly serious concerns they could spare little sympathy for my predicament. Gradually I became afraid of these big lugs and their equally coarse, foul-mouthed girlfriends.

I was thinking of playing hooky, but what was I to do all day in the cold, snowy weather? Luckily fate intervened. One day as I was leaving the building, one of the biggest goons approached me furtively. "Don't be afraid, I just want to talk to you in private," he said. We ducked into an empty room and he explained his problem to me. He was in love and wanted to write a love letter to the object of his affection, but as she was more lettered than he, he was ashamed of his spelling, grammar and overall inability to express himself. If he told me the essence of his feelings, would I write the letter for him? "For a consideration, of course," he added. This was a godsend! I would do it gladly, I replied, but only if he protected me in class and paid me 50 *kopeks* per letter (roughly 50 cents).

So the deal was struck. He certainly fulfilled his part of the bargain. I don't know how he did it, but all the verbal and physical abuse stopped abruptly. For my part, I enjoyed letting my imagination flow in the most florid and romantic language I could manage. Thus I became a youthful Cyrano de Bergerac of sorts, having all the fun and none of the heartbreak of that tragic hero. In fact, I went one step further. My client must have confided the arrangement to a couple of his best friends, because I soon acquired two additional clients and my financial situation improved rapidly.

By the end of the winter, mostly all of our family's money had been laboriously moved to Vilnius, and then sent on to America to my uncle Solomon in New York City. Through smugglers' cuts, it shrank from $24,000 to $8,000. This, then, was our stake in the future. Meanwhile, my father crossed the border at the Bug River. It took three tries as, predictably, the frontier was now much more closely guarded. After the successful third attempt we were together again and immediately made arrangements for the next leg of our odyssey. While waiting, no education time was to be wasted. I continued going to school, and my father and I read Russian poetry aloud in order to improve my pronunciation. During that time we managed to read Pushkin's epic poem "Eugene Onegin" in its entirety.

About the same time we were visited by two relatives of my father who lived in Kiev. Both were doctors, but there all similarity between them ended. One, a middle-aged, balding man, was a successful public health official, an *apparatchik* (bureaucratic Soviet true believer) if ever there was one. Although quite normal when talking about his wife and children, he sounded like a propaganda speech on any public issue. Not only would he not criticize any Soviet policy or practice, but he would not even listen to any of our complaints. Instead he would look furtively all around and quickly change the subject. Clearly he was the product of Soviet brainwashing, wide-spread persecutions, neighbor denouncing neighbor, and the constant fear of deportation to Siberia. He had lost all trust in humanity and all ability for honest communication.

By contrast, the other cousin was a relatively young man and a bachelor. Unable to get into a university because of his bourgeois background, he worked several years as a coal miner to qualify for admission to medical school. He was totally cynical about the Soviet system, explaining to us how *blat* (a way of bartering goods, services and favors with no money changing hands) functioned in the Soviet Union, and how it pervaded the economy and politics from top to bottom. Here was a clear regression from a sophisticated, capitalist economy, to an older, more primitive, though no less complex system. "It is all in who you know," he said.

He was a handsome, jolly fellow, full of fun and jokes secretly circulating among the cognoscenti. One went like this: "One day, Stalin decided to eliminate the letter 'm' from the Russian language. After all, there is no meat, no meal, no milk and it isn't worthwhile to keep the letter just for Molotov and *makhorka* [the coarse Russian tobacco]."

We had plenty of anti-government jokes to counter with: "An American and a Russian were comparing their countries. 'In my country,' said the American, 'I can approach President Roosevelt and boldly inform him I don't like his policies.' 'I can do the same thing,' claimed the Russian. 'I too can approach Comrade Stalin and inform him I don't like President Roosevelt's policies.'"

So we would banter back and forth, learning the true conditions in Russia and the cynicism of the population in the process. We truly enjoyed this visit and exchanged addresses and promises to keep in touch. But none of it came to pass. We left Bialystok soon after his visit and never heard from him again.

One other event occurred during that time which was to have important consequences for our family. As required by law, we were all registered as refugees from Germany. The Einhorns would not have dared to shelter us unless we did this. Now all of us had to fill out a questionnaire choosing one of three options. Would we like to go east to Russia proper and become full citizens of the Soviet Union, or would we prefer to stay in the newly annexed area, in which case we would have to move to a small town at least 100 kilometers away from any external border? The last choice was to return to German-occupied Poland. Here was a dilemma. None of the choices appealed to us since we were planning to cross over to Lithuania. We opted to return to Warsaw, figuring the Russians could not or would not let us do this, or at least would not do it immediately. By the time they might get around to it, we hoped to be gone.

When all was ready we traveled to Lida, a small town near the Lithuanian border, and settled there to wait for an opportune moment.

It was here that I had my first menstrual period, and soon sprang a pair of very substantial breasts. What awful timing! Here I was, proud of becoming a woman, excited and somewhat scared at the same time, dropping very transparent hints about my new status ("Oh, I am so tired" or "Now that I am a woman...") while nobody paid any attention; even Henry was merely embarrassed and ignored my hints. My mother was so preoccupied that she barely noticed my changing appearance, let alone bought me a bra, which I sorely needed. This was typical of the re-prioritizing caused by the war, which resulted in such an abnormal adolescence for me.

We stayed in Lida several days, spending the first night in beds piled high with pillows. Unfortunately, as soon as the candles were put out the bedbugs came out in force, relishing our fresh, soft flesh. We ended the night on the floor, preferring its hardness to sharing the beds with the nocturnal visitors. The next day we got some blankets and continued sleeping on the floor, to the amazement of our hosts whose time-hardened hides were impervious to the bedbug attacks.

Our little group had to be broken up for the next stage of the trip; the guide could not handle so many at once. We dressed up as peasants, a cap on my father's head, kerchiefs on my mother's and mine and traveled by horse and wagon towards the border, as though going to market. Suddenly, Russian soldiers appeared on the road. "*Stoi!*" came the order.

We did not know it, but at that moment, our hope of escaping the horrors of the Holocaust ended.

The soldiers arrested us all. We were too close to the Lithuanian border to claim convincingly any excuse for our presence there. Besides, the soldiers were not listening. They forced us to board the truck which had been concealed just off the road, suggesting that we had been betrayed and the patrol was lying in wait for us, and drove us to a nearby, makeshift prison.

The prison complex was located on the premises of a rural rabbi's home. The synagogue served as the offices, while soldiers were quartered in the rabbi's home. The prisoners were incarcerated in the barn and the stable, the women drawing the stable. What became of the horses and cows or, for that matter, of the rabbi and his family, I have no idea.

We stayed in our stable for several days. This was my first experience with communal, barrack life. To convert the stable to a prison, the Russians had knocked down the stalls and used the lumber hastily to put together a large, continuous shelf. We threw some straw on it and *voila*, this became our sleeping space. We shared this space with a group of young Polish peasant girls, who were there for some offense unknown to me. They were kind and cheerful, and totally unconcerned about their future. They sang a lot, chattered happily and spent a large portion of the day sleeping. This was not surprising, since they were away most of the night "having a good time" with the guards, and came back at dawn reeking of sweat and alcohol. Even during the day, the guards visited the stable for some heavy-handed flirtation. As a consequence of all this fraternization the girls were inundated with food, which they shared with us good-naturedly. I don't know if they understood we were Jewish, but they commiserated because we were separated from our men, who were in the barn.

The girls' insouciance was a distraction, but frankly added to my sense of unreality. Here we were briefly sharing the same space, but our pasts and future fates were so different. Even in the present we were aliens, meeting for just a handshake, only to be hurtled again along our separate roads.

The days passed in a mixture of boredom and anxiety. We were only allowed out to go to a primitive outhouse some distance from the stable. We were escorted there by guards walking behind us, rifles at the ready, as if my mother and I were dangerous criminals about to make a violent escape. We had to keep our hands on top of our heads, presumably to foil any such attempt. I found this very scary. I wasn't worried about any murderous intentions on the part of the guards, but what if the rifle went off accidentally? My knowledge of firearms was so rudimentary that I didn't even know if that was possible. The guards, who for the most part were kind young men, always acted formally and harshly on these bath-room expeditions. Whether they did this to impress their superiors or out of general discomfort with their roles, I don't know. These brief excursions should have provided distractions from the monotony of our days. Instead I dreaded them and was ashamed to admit it. Besides, I did-n't want to add to my mother's worries. All this time we were never ques-tioned, but we also did not see my father. The girls found out from the guards that he was still there, and with that we had to be contented.

After several days of incarceration, one afternoon we were loaded on a truck and taken back to Lida. Thank God we were together again. My father had fared in his barn as well as we did. Neither he nor we had ever had reason to fear for our lives. Even so, he had been questioned about and admitted to an illegal attempt to get to Vilnius. "We were just trying to join our relatives there," he claimed. "In these uncertain times it is best to be with one's family." Of course he did not mention our further plans or the fact that our Vilnius relations were well-to-do people—all anathema to the Soviets. So, we had these few hours together.

Not knowing what was to come, we hastily reviewed contingencies in case we were separated again. Aunt Sonia's address in Tel Aviv, 79 Jehuda Halevy Street, was the ultimate rallying point. In any town we landed in, we were to find Jewish doctors, a synagogue and the Jewish Council. My parents made sure I also memorized our addresses in Bialystok and in Lida, my grandfather's address in Vilnius, and Dr. Jellin's address in Warsaw (my father's best friend). We sat huddling together, hugging, my mother crying or on the verge of crying all the time, my father and I trying to console her.

With trepidation we felt the truck stop. We had arrived at the Lida jail. My father was whisked away to a cell and just like that, without a chance for a proper parting, he was gone. We were not to see him for 14 months.

Meanwhile, my mother and I were left for several long hours sitting in a long hall. It was a busy place, doors opening and closing, preoccupied men walking briskly from room to room with file folders in their hands. Armed guards were everywhere, but no one paid us any attention. Had they forgotten us? Would the two of us be separated? What would happen next? we wondered anxiously.

After a long wait, an official came out and talked to us right in the hall. "We don't imprison women and children," he informed us, "so we will let the two of you go." "What will happen to my husband?" my mother asked tearfully. "He will be moved to Baranowicze and stand trial there. More than that I don't know myself," replied the official. When all of this would happen he didn't know either.

We walked out of the prison carrying our luggage. Although it was early May, there was still snow on the ground and a nip in the air. It was evening. The town lay dark and silent around us. The guard at the prison door directed us to the center of town, and we trudged along filled with despair. All our plans, our shining hope for safety and for a future, lay in ruins. Defeated and bewildered we made our way to the temporary lodgings where Adek, Zina and Henry awaited word from us. The night was spent crying, mourning, and finally, dispiritedly, making some immediate plans. None of us even contemplated abandoning my father and making another stab at escape. There was no point staying in Lida if my father were going to be moved. The next day my mother and I went to the jail and were told my father was already gone to Baranowicze. With this confirmation we boarded the next train and went back to Bialystok to settle again in the same apartment with the Einhorns.

We resumed our life in Bialystok but everything now seemed temporary and suspended in waiting for what would happen to my father. My mother traveled to Baranowicze every couple of weeks. She was never allowed to see my father, but from time to time we received a postcard on which he was allowed to scribble that he was well and was receiving the packages delivered at the prison gate. When he finally was released, he told us he did in fact receive some of the food, clothes, and toiletries we sent, although a major part of them was swiped by the prison guards.

The business of living, obtaining food for ourselves and for my father and endless discussions about the uncertain future preoccupied the adults in our family. I didn't go back to school but spent as much time as possible reading, mainly to escape the gloomy atmosphere in the house. Henry was the only one who took a hand in my education, and this time I wasn't a bit grateful. I was still reading children's books obtained at the local library, eagerly escaping into the world of boarding schools and innocent romances. Henry felt I was too old and too intelligent to waste my time on such trivial things. Under duress I made my first foray into literature. Henry's choice was rather unfortunate: Joseph Conrad's *Typhoon*, a novel about a ship in a storm. I found it at once depressing and incomprehensible. The detailed description of maneuvering the ropes and sails to weather the storm was utterly boring, so much so that I missed the drama of battling the elements for survival. But at Henry's urging I finished the book and was allowed to proceed to Tolstoy, Sienkiewicz and Prus—the latter two Polish writers of great renown. My eyes were opened to the glories of literature. It has remained one of my favorite recreational activities, and I am an eclectic reader.

My own story was unfolding within the context of larger events. The winter of 1939-40 was quiet in the West, and the inactivity had occasioned the term "phony war." In the East, Russia fought against plucky little Finland, which inevitably surrendered in March 1940. The spring of 1940 saw Germany winning conquest after conquest. Norway was overcome in April. Denmark was occupied almost simultaneously. In May, Holland and Belgium were overrun as the Germans bypassed France's fortified line of defense, the Maginot Line, and quickly took most of France, entering Paris on June 14. Only the bravery of the English people prevented the total annihilation of the Allied forces in France, extricating most of them to England at Dunkirk.

The war boiled down to the Battle of Britain, the so-called "blitz," during which the Germans tried unsuccessfully to break down the indomitable British spirit by random bombing of the civilian population along with the military targets. The battle for the seas proceeded without pause, with Roosevelt sending more and more supplies to England and dragging his reluctant country closer and closer to actual participation in the war.

We knew all this from newspapers (though in Russian-occupied Poland the news was censored and slanted) and from short-wave radios which picked up Swedish, Swiss and English stations. The English stations were making an effort to broadcast to Eastern Europe in order to keep up our morale and encourage sabotage activities against Germany.

Early in the summer rumors about impending deportation to Siberia began to circulate. My mother and I took to spending the nights with local friends, while Adek scoffed at the danger. Finally one night the rumors came true. Soviet soldiers came to all the apartments where residents had opted to return to Germany and picked them up, including Adek, Zina and Henry. When we returned to the apartment that morning, they were gone.

My mother became totally despondent. She had now lost my father, Zina and Adek, and was truly alone except for having me. All her life she had been sheltered and protected by her father or her husband. She needed somebody to lean on and make decisions for her. In desperation, she ran to the Soviet immigration office and begged the officials to pick us up. They missed us by mistake, she argued, intent on reuniting with the rest of the family. The official on duty gravely took our names and address and told her to go home and wait. She ran to the train station, and somehow in all the chaos located Zina and her family, informing them of what she had done and assuring them we would be joining them shortly. She came back to the apartment, packed more supplies for them and delivered them to the train. Then she came back again and we waited.

Thinking back to that time I must say that, to put it mildly, my mother was not at her best under pressure. While she was running back and forth I was left alone in the apartment. Had the officials taken her at her word they might have snatched her up on the spot, leaving me to fend for myself. The same thing might have happened during either of her trips to the train station. But none of this happened. The next day the trains left and no one ever came to pick us up. We were undeniably on our own.

Bereft of all support, my mother was reduced to crying and wringing her hands. Few children have had to grow up so suddenly as I had to at that moment. I rose to the occasion and made the necessary decisions. We presented ourselves at the office of immigration, and announced our desire to become citizens of the Soviet Union without relocating into Russia proper. Our goal was to stay as near as possible to Baranowicze, where my father was incarcerated. On the spot, we were issued Soviet passports with "Paragraph 11." This made us into second-class, untrustworthy citizens, forbidding us from living in major towns (county seats, or towns with populations exceeding 100,000) and restricting us to an area at least 100 kilometers from any external frontier. The latter proved a rather severe limitation, since the area occupied by the Soviet Union was long and skinny, a large portion of it lying in the proscribed zone.

Finally, after poring over a map and consulting with our hosts and few remaining friends (by now most of our friends were either in Siberia or somewhere else deep in Russia), we settled on Slonim, a half-Jewish town of about 40,000 located roughly 30 miles from Baranowicze, with a direct railroad link to that city. Today the city is located in Belarus about 100 miles from the Polish border.

By now the war had been going on for almost a year, and we had had both good and bad luck. We and, amazingly, almost all our family and friends had survived the bombardment of Warsaw—it's amazing how few people died in all that fire and fury. We had moved five times, and smuggled ourselves and our money across a hostile frontier. It was indeed a torturous, confusing and heart-wrenching year. And at the end of it my father was in jail, his fate unknown from day to day. Zina, Adek and Henry were in Siberia, and the two of us were forced to move alone among strangers. Family and friends were scattered, quality of life was deteriorating with each move, and no end to the war was in sight. This was to be the pattern of the war for me—periods of relative calm, though at times in deplorable conditions, alternating with sudden changes and violent events, always unpredictable.

It was as if we were tiny ants trying to live peacefully in our colony, helpless to resist the actions of the giants who controlled us. They might leave us in peace for a while, or they might stamp on us suddenly, killing many of us and dislocating our colony. They might deliberately pick one up from our midst and cruelly crush it between their fingers, or even, on a whim, return it safely to the fold. Those of us who survived had lived with this anxiety and uncertainty for six long years. It colored our lives forever afterward.

CHAPTER 5

1940-41: AN INTERLUDE

U pon our arrival in Slonim, we quickly sought out the Jewish community and rented a room with kitchen privileges from an Orthodox religious family. Since the school year was just beginning, I was enrolled in a Russian-speaking school, and my mother and I settled down to await future developments.

In spite of our continuous anxiety over my father and Zina's family, the next 10 months were probably the most peaceful and serene of the entire war. Life in the small town where we now found ourselves was much easier than in Bialystok. Ordinary necessities of life were easy to come by so that our lifestyle, though modest, was comfortable enough.

The room we rented was large and warm. Food was readily available from the baker, the Jewish butcher, the grocer, or the local open market. There were plenty of friends to make among the refugees from the West or the local Jewish population. The owner of the house we lived in, a professional Torah copier, lived with his daughter and two grandchildren. Before the war, most of his scrolls were sold in America, making him a prosperous and respected man, but now his income had dried up, hence the necessity to take in strangers like ourselves. This was my first encounter with life in the *shtetl* and with truly Orthodox people, and I found it fascinating. Evidently the old gentleman held some hope for me, for he was willing to talk to me in his broken Polish. Yet he allowed me to

65

become the resident *shabes goya* (a non-Jew who turns the lights on and off on Saturday), a clear sign that my salvation was impossible, and thus I could be allowed to continue sinning.

His life was closely circumscribed by Talmudic rules. He prayed and studied the Talmud every day, and continued making a new Torah copy for "when the war is over." How unvarying was his ritual of study and work. How reverently he handled the tools of his trade: the pens, the ink, the scroll itself. How sure his stroke, never an ink blot in sight, and how beautiful the result! His life was a revelation to me, to be respected but not emulated.

He did not seem to concern himself with the details of running the house. This was his daughter's responsibility.

His dissociation from the world outside was almost total. Once his granddaughter, who was younger than I, came home from school with a question: "Is it true," she asked me "that the earth revolves around the sun?" "Of course," I replied, surprised she was ignorant of so obvious a fact. From the other room, the grandfather yelled, "Don't listen to such *nareshkeit* (nonsense)! Of course the earth is at the center of the universe! After all, the Bible says so." I retreated to our room, more aware of the old man's limitations and though no less respectful, certainly less admiring. Now I think people who have such faith and certainty have an easier life, but a less interesting one.

The daughter, on the other hand, was a model of a small-town Jewish housewife, what is known as a *balyboste*. The house was spotless, the linen always mended and pressed, delicious food always prepared on time, and the children guided firmly and lovingly to grow up into exemplary Jews in their turn. To accomplish all that, she worked from morning until night, her hands never still, her mind constantly reviewing and planning a list of chores.

We arrived early in September, so I had a chance to witness the preparations for the winter. Our landlady cooked vast numbers of pots of fruit and sugar, reducing the contents to preserves to be used on bread throughout the year. Several days were devoted to making noodles of various descriptions. First she kneaded the dough, then she rolled it out into a large, thin circle, folded the circle into a long flattened tube, several layers thick, and then her knife would start flying, producing very thin spaghetti, remarkably uniform and fine. She never once nicked a finger as she gradually fed the dough into the knife space. She could do all this while talking, without even having to look at what she was doing. Sometimes, instead of long spaghetti, she would cut the dough into flat, fine squares, or gently rub it against a flat sieve making the tiny *farfel*. Then several large tables were set up in the yard, covered with white tablecloths, and the noodles were spread out to dry in the sun. Once dry, they were stored in large jars for the winter, when eggs would be much more expensive. There was a big cellar for apples and root vegetables, but all the produce had to be inspected before storage to eliminate wormy or imperfect specimens.

Our landlady raised her own chickens, and after the kosher butcher had killed them, she dressed and koshered them (i.e. salted and soaked) in the prescribed manner. On Friday she baked *challahs*, twisting the dough into ribbons and brushing the tops with egg yolk to make them golden and shiny. She never rushed, never complained, never lost her temper, and just went all day long from chore to chore. I admired her skills, and marveled at how hard yet satisfying her life was. The pattern so clear, every job done well, just as it had been for centuries. How different from the way my mother had lived!

Of course, this was not quite possible under our new circumstances. My mother had to shop and cook for us, but she continued to do it on a day-to-day basis, buying from tradesmen who came to the house, and preparing the easiest possible dishes. We seemed to eat chicken cutlets at least five times a week. I didn't complain, knowing how unfamiliar even this simple task was for her, and how she disliked working in the kitchen under the watchful and critical eye of our landlady, who was forever checking that we didn't inadvertently break some law of *kashrut*.

As often as she could, my mother escaped from our quarters and joined one of her friends for a good, long gossip. All her friends were refugees; she disdained the local Jews as her inferiors. The feeling must have been mutual. I frequently overheard our landlady commenting on my mother's laziness, lack of homemaking skills and her choice of friends. My mother's best friend at the time was Anna, a tall, good-looking blond who lived in one room with her brother and her lover. I am sure now that the one room was just a matter of the need to economize, but at the time, it was a source of endless speculation into all the exotic possibilities and permutations of this unusual triangle. In time all three of them became our friends, and the two men became almost like uncles to me. Of course my mother had other friends, but this odd family group stuck in my memory. My mother's friends and their conversations didn't interest me much at the time. I lived a separate, parallel life, much of it in my head, not unusual for a teenager.

Of course my main occupation was school. My schoolmates were local Jewish children, ranging from children of Orthodox, usually uneducated parents, to those from more assimilated and more successful families. I became a frequent guest in two homes, Hannah's and Galya's.

Hannah's father had been a successful businessman, owning real estate and several factories. Their home was virulently anti-Communist and they, like ourselves, were living by selling off their possessions and foreign currency. They shared our fears and our uncertainties. Hannah was the only one of my school friends who knew my father was in prison in Baranowicze. Everyone else was told he had been in the Polish army and we didn't know his whereabouts. Galya's mother had been married to a doctor, but they had been divorced for some time, and her mother lived with her family and worked as a nurse.

Both girls were good students, great readers, and, like me, avid fantasizers. This was the time to talk about love and sex, as these concerns were entering our imaginations.

So I had a triumvirate again, a shield against the world. Right now, however, that world was benevolent enough. With no effort I was an an "A" student in school, enjoying all the little privileges that went with it. I was fond of most of my teachers. My classes were not particularly challenging. I usually managed to finish my homework before leaving the building, by doing work for one class while paying partial attention to another.

My teachers, most of whom came from Russia proper, considered my academic achievements praiseworthy, and I was singled out as an example to other children much as if I was a *Stakhanovietz* (a Soviet term for an overachiever) in a factory. I was not universally loved by my classmates either, although I often provided some help to the slower students. Human nature, I guess!

The only teacher I really disliked was my gym teacher. He was Jewish, a lawyer, and a refugee like myself. One would think that would forge a bond between us, and he would treat me decently. Unfortunately, he liked to fondle young girls, and I was one of his favorite victims. I was still short, but was now fully developed, plump and with an impressive bosom. I was not overly athletic, but I was not clumsy either. Whenever we exercised, he would walk around correcting the posture or the performance of the students, which gave him ample opportunity to touch us. Oddly enough, he rarely found anything wrong with the performance of boys or flat-chested girls, concentrating his attentions on well-endowed girls. When we practiced broad jumps, he would stand on the far end of the mat we had to leap across, with his arms extended and his hands cupped just right to grab our breasts.

I suffered agonies of embarrassment, but never confessed my misery to anyone. In an effort to avoid the class I feigned an increased frequency, duration and severity of my menstrual periods. Unfortunately, I had to apply to the gym teacher to be excused from the day's torture. A sadistic man, he clearly enjoyed my discomfort on those occasions, and interrogated me closely, commenting on the frequency of the requests. Of course, both of us knew what was going on. He was getting a high from tormenting me. How I hated this man!

Early in the spring of 1941, my mother's aunt by marriage came from Moscow to visit her own relatives who lived in Slonim and, of course, she also visited us. She gave us another glimpse into life in the Soviet Union. Her husband (my mother's maternal uncle) was a chemical engineer of some renown. He lectured at a university and had written several technical books. She was a physician. The couple was childless. Just the two of them occupied a four-room apartment in the center of Moscow, though she confessed the rooms were very small. Still, it was an unprecedented luxury of privacy in Russia. They even had a maid who cleaned, cooked and stood in lines.

I suspect this was her most time-consuming occupation. In Russia, the aunt said, people often did not go back to the office after lunch, instead spending the afternoon in the interminable lines. For many people it became a reflex action; when they saw a line they joined it before even asking what it was for.

But it was my aunt's coat which, for me, became symbolic of the shortages in the Soviet Union. That garment had been turned inside out for the second time. In other words, when the original outer side wore out, the coat was remade so that the wrong side was now out, but after some time, this became so worn, that, by comparison, the original right side came to look good by comparison, and so the coat was remade again.

This is why our teachers, most of whom came from Russia proper, were so happy to be living in the former Poland. We still had goods from before the war that were well-made. We had artisans and merchants with

the skills and desire to produce good clothes, good shoes, and good furniture, despite all the regulations and taxes. We still had abundant food,
since for the right price you could buy almost anything on the black market.

Our aunt was staying at the house of her cousin, a wealthy and elegant
woman of about 40. My aunt confided to my mother that the cousin had
a lover, and expressed her disapproval over this relationship. One day we
were invited for dinner to the cousin's home. Here was a home similar to
our pre-war apartment. Somehow this made me envious in a way my
friend Hannah's home never did. The dinner was ostentatiously rich. One
dish followed another, all beautifully served by a uniformed maid. To
think that some people still lived like this, and flaunted it in the faces of
refugees like ourselves! Inviting us was neither kind nor sensitive,
although, very likely, our hostess had not given the matter any thought.

But the biggest surprise was the lover. Sitting right next to our hostess,
on the other side from her husband, was none other than my gym
teacher. He blanched when he saw me, but recovered fast. He was so
happy to see his favorite student, he proclaimed. What a coincidence! I
saw his uneasiness and reveled in it. I let him wonder whether I would
dare to mention his behavior in public. Of course I had no intention of
saying anything. I would have been much too embarrassed and besides it
would just be my word against his. He could always contrive to turn it
into a joke. He avoided me most of the evening but when we were leaving, he said with a meaningful look, "What a nice person you are. See you
in school tomorrow." From then on, he never touched me, was as friendly as possible, and excused me from gym any time I asked with no com-
ments.

In Slonim, my afternoons were free, with one exception. One day a week
I went to Madame for my French lesson. Madame was an ancient Russian
lady, an aristocratic refugee from Imperial Russia, where she still lived
mentally and emotionally. Her little house overflowed with mementos:
faded, sepia photographs of gone and forgotten officers in fancy uniforms and ladies with large hats and gentle smiles, fans and dance cards.
Invitations to balls, shawls, and little knickknacks jostled for space on
round tables covered by long, lacy tablecloths. We always had tea, which
we drank from dainty porcelain cups. I was taught how to pour the tea,
how to hold the cup, and the conversation appropriate to this activity.
Obviously, the French lessons had to be accompanied by deportment
instruction since, in her eyes, I was sadly lacking in social graces. I grew

very fond of the old lady and her reminiscences. Her French was as impeccable as her appearance and her posture. She lived alone with a parrot and a poodle, struggling to make ends meet. She had a great deal of dignity, but it was all very sad.

All my intellectual energies went into reading. Slonim had an excellent public library, of which I became a steady patron. With little direction I devised a simple system for myself. Upon encountering new authors, I simply read everything by them available on the shelves. Thus, I read all the works by Molière, Tolstoy, Shakespeare and other luminaries familiar to me. Books written by Nobel Prize winners usually had lists of other winners in the back. This became my source for new authors, and led me to extensive readings of books by Scandinavian authors, including those gloomy, dark stories of Sigrid Undset, Selma Lagerleff, Knut Hamsum and Bjorn Bjornson and such exotics as Rabindranath Tagore. I was becoming self-educated without knowing it. My patience for these long, difficult works seemed endless.

I soon got some help in my endeavors. A young librarian noticed my efforts and began talking to me and giving me advice. Soon we became good friends, and would take long, rambling walks on Sunday, discussing the latest books I had read. She too was a refugee from western Poland, and was all alone, having become separated from her family. In spite of my youth, I was more her intellectual match than most of her peers in Slonim. But our discussions were confined to books; she did not burden me with her problems and I reciprocated her restraint. She did, however, allow me entry into the proscribed stacks, which included many of the authors I was reading, some of them quite innocent. Any book which "advocated" (read: did not condemn) capitalism, religion, or "prurient" sex was barred to the general public. There were more books in the forbidden stacks than in the open ones.

I did not participate in sports or other extracurricular activities at school, but there was one activity sponsored by the Young Pioneer organization (entry rank of the Communist Party) which I could not resist: a variety show. It was to be the last one in my life. It was all in Russian, and consisted of songs, dances, skits and poems. Poetry recitation was and still is very popular in Russia; renowned poets draw enormous crowds, but poetry is also recited in coffee houses, at parties, and at a variety of meetings. The Russian language is melodious, so it lends itself naturally to poetry, and even though this national pastime was exploited by the Communist Party for propaganda purposes, the beauty of the language overcame this handicap. Some great poets like Mayakovsky sold out and followed the party line, gaining fame and fortune. Others, like Pasternak, didn't and their work was forbidden. The dissident poets themselves were poor, shunned by society, or even exiled to Siberia. Mayakovsky must have been consumed by guilt. In the end he committed suicide.

I acted in a skit and recited a poem. The show was presented at the school, and was such a success that the administrators decided to send it "on the road." We performed at un-exotic locations such as a local hospital, an orphanage, and an old folks home, but we also went to a prison camp and a voting place.

The prison camp was located some distance out of town. We went there by truck. The assembled prisoners looked neither happy nor healthy. Although they worked on an agricultural station, they looked thin and underfed. We did not get to see their quarters, but their clothes looked dirty and ragged, their hair long and unkempt, their demeanor one of apathy and resignation. We presented our show outdoors on a hastily erected stage with the prisoners sitting on the bare ground.

One old woman drew me aside and told me she was there for stealing some corn from the Soviet cooperative farm. Her children were hungry. Her sentence was several years in the camp. I looked at her in amazement: she had young children? Her hair was gray, her face wrinkled, her mouth had the collapsed look of many missing teeth, her back was bent from arthritis and years of hard, physical work. "How old are you?" I asked. "About 40," came the answer. Suddenly I believed her story, which might have come straight from *Les Miserables*.

The prisoners enjoyed our show. Perhaps they were ordered to applaud, I thought cynically. On the way back, our troop, flush with success, sang and joked all the way, but I felt depressed by the vast misery we had just glimpsed. The thought that anything like that might happen to me did not even cross my mind. To me the prisoners were oppressed human beings. I pitied them. Still, they seemed so utterly alien, I could not even imagine what their lives and their feelings might be. I had no premonition of my own future.

By contrast, the performance at the voting station was just plain silly. A vast hall was commandeered for the purpose, and profusely decorated with hammers and sickles, crossed on a red field by garlands and flowers. Upon arrival, the voters were offered a generous buffet of sandwiches, cake and fruit. If you looked closely, you could see some of the women secreting some of this bounty into capacious purses. Then they watched our show, this time enlivened by several folk songs and dances. Appreciation was expressed by the crowd joining in the singing with enthusiastic clapping. Some voters, too sick to make it on their own, were brought in by buses, cars and even ambulances. Laggards were rooted out of their homes by an army of door-to-door party hacks. After eating and being entertained, the voting came.

One might think that all the hoopla was designed to put the voters into a benevolent mood so they would vote for the party candidates, but such was not the case. There was only one slate. In theory, the voters had only the choice between voting or abstaining. As it turned out, they did not have that choice either. No wonder the Soviets could proudly claim 99 percent turnout. One of our jokes concerned the dismay of the authorities when the turnout was found to be 102 percent. The whole thing was just an empty propaganda exercise, cynically engineered by the party for the benefit of the populace who no longer believed in anything.

Such was my everyday life. On the surface, my mother and I played our traditional roles. I was the child, going to school, reading and playing with my girlfriends. She was the mother, shopping, cooking, cleaning and supervising my activities. But underneath, our roles were reversed. I was the strong and decisive one, and she the weak and lost one. She clung to her traditional values. In her eyes my schooling was all-important. I understand now that it gave her a feeling of normality and reinforced my place as a child in her mind. Nothing could be allowed to interfere with my education. Thus, she never allowed me on her trips to Baranowicze, where once a month she continued to deliver packages and letters to my father.

But, in reality, it was I who decided what we would sell next to provide for ourselves and finance the packages. I arranged the sale through Hannah's father. My mother was an impulse shopper. It was not easy for me to talk her out of some frivolous purchase or persuade her to return some gloves or stockings we did not need, explaining over and over how limited our resources were. Thus, I did the money managing and participated in planning the packages. We did not have furniture, books or clothing to sell on the black market, but we did have all those $100 bills sown into my mother's corset, and jewelry and gold coins secreted in a double-bottom suitcase. However, I felt our wealth had to be used sparingly, since there was no telling how long it would have to last.

By now, we had heard from Zina and knew of her family's hardships. When they got to Siberia, Adek was arrested for reasons unknown, and was sent to a prison camp there. Zina and Henry were free to arrange their own lives, though forbidden to leave the area—this was called free exile. Henry worked as a lumberjack and Zina had lost so much weight that one day her skirt fell off in spite of the string she kept it up with. She had to carry water to the hut they shared from one kilometer away. In the winter, the hut was so cold that her eyelids froze together at night. Food was hard to come by, and sanitary facilities non-existent. We did what we could, sending food, clothing and soap to them. Fortunately, after Germany went to war with Russia, their status changed abruptly from "hostile capitalists" to ordinary people, and they were allowed to move to the Caucasus, where the climate was more benign. There Henry supported his mother by driving a truck. His love affair with automobiles dates from that time. Eventually, Adek was released from prison and joined them. They were able to get in touch with Adek's sisters in Moscow and, through them, with their son Leo, already in America at that time. Right after the war, Leo was able to bring them to America.

Later that year, an incident took place which illustrates clearly my mother's childish nature. On July 23, 1940, the Soviet Union illegally annexed Lithuania. They also annexed Estonia and Latvia, a situation that wasn't rectified for 50 years—all of which cut off the exit valve out of Europe. There was now no point in keeping the border between Russian-occupied Poland and Lithuania closed, since as far as the Russians were concerned it was all the same country now. As a result, it became possible simply to board the train and go to Vilnius. Now my mother was able to satisfy her craving to see her father and sister Niuta (Solomon and Abrasha and their families were long since gone). She arranged to have food delivered to me by our usual tradesmen, who instructed me carefully in simple cooking skills (which I knew already anyway), and off she went. She stayed away for four weeks. She came back full of stories of her sister's social life and new husband, though somewhat chastened by her father's scolding for leaving me alone. I would not dream of leaving a 13-year-old child of mine to fend for himself in peacetime, let alone during a war. Anything might have happened: sickness, a new outbreak of fighting, bombardment, fire.

What did happen in my mother's absence was a new wave of deportations. Fortunately, I heard the rumors beforehand, and took the precaution of not sleeping at home. Most of our friends were refugees, capitalists or professionals—undesirables anyway, and thus potential victims of deportation themselves, so it was not easy to find a safe shelter. I ended up with my friend Galya, reasoning that a nurse would not be judged a potential danger by the NKVD (the Soviet counterpart to the Gestapo). In fact, the police did come for my mother and me one night, and our landlords told them we were away.

It is questionable whether I would have survived if deported to Siberia alone. My mother's action was the height of irresponsibility and truly inexcusable, but at the time, I took it in stride, being already accustomed to the role of the adult in the family. Sadly, I had learned not to count on her.

About that time, I pointed out to my mother that we had no visible means of support, a dangerous and suspicious situation in the workers' paradise. In response to her claim that she lacked any marketable skill, I suggested that she embroider commercially, a skill every well-brought-up girl from my mother's generation was supposed to have. After my making the necessary inquiries, my mother joined an embroidery *artel* (work cooperative). It was a piece-work, cottage industry. My mother was given a stack of handkerchiefs, blouses and *rubashkas* (men's embroidered shirts), all made of fine, white linen, with the pattern stenciled on, and a supply of silk yarn, to be worked on at home and returned upon completion. She proved a very slow and clumsy worker. Half the time, stitches had to be taken out and redone. Her earnings would not keep us in bread, but at least she became officially employed.

Uneventful for us, the year was also relatively quiescent on the world stage. Hitler's original plan was to subdue western Europe before turning east, but failing to conquer Britain, the Nazis engaged in mopping-up operations in the East in preparation for the great adventure in Russia. Hungary, Romania, Bulgaria and Yugoslavia were either invaded or became willing allies. In the fall of 1940, Italy attacked Greece. The Italians, having lost all their Roman war talents, bungled this operation disastrously, embroiling Hitler in the Balkans and forcing him to postpone the invasion of Russia, originally scheduled for mid-May 1941.

Meanwhile, Rommel was having some success in Africa, where Hitler again had to come to the aid of his Italian allies. The Anglo-American lend-lease program was helping Britain to withstand the "blitz," feed its population, and allow it to begin stockpiling arms and equipment for future actions. The war seemed to be at a standstill, but both sides were gathering material and energy for the next violent explosion.

CHAPTER 6

BARBAROSSA

We always seem to remember exactly where we were and what we were doing when a momentous historical event descends upon us. June 22, 1941, was a hot and sunny summer day in Slonim. The school year had just ended, and with my mother's permission I went alone to the river. A pair of shorts over my bathing suit, a book under my arm and a towel to dry with and lie on were all I needed for a pleasant afternoon. The area was completely safe and the little grass patch by the river secluded. The river was shallow with no strong current, posing no danger for even a novice swimmer. I was in the water, cavorting and enjoying the lovely coolness, when I heard my mother's voice calling me from the top of the little escarpment, "Klara, Klara, come right out! The Germans have just invaded Russia!"

Operation Barbarossa had begun. Barbarossa, "red beard," was the sobriquet of Emperor Frederick I of Hohenstaufen, who had ruled Germany 700 years before. Hitler was obsessed with numbers and historical symmetry, so this was the code name he gave the invasion of the Soviet Union.

I scrambled out, hastily threw on my clothes, and rushed home to consult with my mother, Anna and the others. Some people were evacuating to the East, but we were obliged to stay because of my father's imprisonment and the uncertainty of what the Soviets would do with the prisoners. There was very little we could do to prepare for the upcoming events. This time we did not have connections or the resources to stockpile supplies. There was also very little time to prepare. The speed of the German advance was such that Slonim, about 100 miles from the German border, was to be taken within two or three days. Luckily, we were too unimportant a target to warrant aerial bombardment, but we did spend two days and nights in the cellar, listening to the artillery barrage in the distance. Evidently the Red Army was trying to slow down the retreat, really a rout, and Slonim was one of the places where they made at least a temporary stand. Consequently, though to a lesser degree, our experience of the siege of Warsaw was repeated. We again listened to the shells whistling above us, trying to estimate how far away they would hit. We again huddled in the dark, hoping that the front would hold. We hoped that the barrage would stop, but not if it meant a German victory.

Our landlady was a simple, uninhibited woman. She screamed at each near hit, each time setting off the children's crying, whereupon she would hug them to her as if she could protect them with her body. Between the hits she lamented our fate and the fate of her poor children, beseeching God for mercy at the top of her voice as if he were merely hard of hearing. If only he could hear her voice he would grant her plea. Her father sat quietly, mumbling prayers all the time, totally uncommunicative. The atmosphere in the cellar was heavy with fear and despair. My mother and I sat a little apart. I keenly felt our isolation from the rest of the people in the cellar. We were among our people, but not among friends.

These incredible initial German military successes in Russia reinforced our belief in German invincibility and confirmed all those jokes about Russian inefficiency and stupidity. Within three days the advance German troops entered Slonim. The trap had closed again, this time with no place to run. We knew that we had nothing to fear personally from the *Wehrmacht*. Their business was to fight the Russians. It was who would come later that we feared—the occupation forces.

The Germans had advanced so rapidly that pockets of the Red Army were caught behind the front lines and attempted to fight their way out. This happened in Slonim. Soon after the town was occupied by the Nazis, fighting broke out again. Using loudspeakers mounted on armored cars, the Germans ordered all civilians out of their homes and herded us into several large, open areas in town. We spent the entire day sitting on the ground, with no food, water, or sanitary facilities. We were ordered harshly to place our hands on our heads whenever a detachment of soldiers passed by. All day we heard sporadic fire as the Germans were conducting house-to-house searches for any lingering Russian soldiers. It was a frightening, ominous day with fear compounded by physical deprivation.

Finally, when night fell, we were allowed to return home. Soldiers had gone through the house causing disarray, but no damage or looting had taken place. The next morning, there was another scare. A neighbor ran in announcing the Germans would collect all able-bodied men and take them away. We were safe personally, as my mother and I were alone and our landlord was an old man, but we worried about Anna's brother and her lover. Had they heard the rumor and found a place to hide? Unable to stand the suspense, my mother decided we should warn them. But who should go? Of course, I was elected. After all, soldiers were not likely to bother or even suspect a child.

So, dressed in my best and most childish pink dress I set off on the 10-minute walk. The streets were deserted except for occasional military vehicles rumbling by. I walked fast but did not run, my heart in my throat the whole time. The *Wehrmacht* were still patrolling the area looking for Red Army soldiers and shooting them on sight since they had not surrendered when the town fell. Thus, as I walked I heard occasional bursts of gunfire and cringed each time, although I knew they were not directed at me. A couple of times German soldiers greeted me convivially from the trucks. At one point a passing foot soldier gave me a piece of candy which I accepted humbly, thanking him prettily while at the same time privately wishing him in hell. Hugging the walls whenever possible to make myself small and invisible, I walked resolutely.

Arriving at my destination, I conveyed the news of Germans rounding up men, which turned out later to be a false rumor. They had not heard it, and immediately set about finding a hiding place in the woods behind their house. Anna hugged and kissed me, thanking me tearfully for the risk I had undertaken on their behalf. But unfortunately, the journey had to be repeated. My mother could not be left in ignorance of my whereabouts. And so I ventured out again, retracing my steps in the eerie silence of the streets.

The very next day, my father came home to Slonim.

He had spent 14 months in the Baranowicze jail and was never interrogated or tried in all that time. He spent his entire incarceration in the same large cell, a space designed for 8 to 12 prisoners but occupied by about 35. It was a large room furnished with a stove and a big square table with chairs, and with burlap-covered, straw-filled pallets for sleeping. Prisoners were issued a blanket and a straw-filled pillow, but no sheets. Because they had not yet been tried, they wore their own clothes and did not work. I think my father would have preferred to work, particularly if it could have been in his profession.

The food was crude, but provided in adequate quantities. A latrine visit was allowed once a day, otherwise prisoners used the bucket in the cell. Showers were permitted once a week. The cell, in spite of sporadic efforts on the part of some prisoners, was always dirty and pungent. The crowding meant noise and no privacy all day long. Exercise was irregular, depending on the whim of the guards and on how crowded the jail was at any given time. The attitude of the guards varied; some were kind, others indifferent, still others sadistic and anti-Semitic. One of the doctors from the staff visited the cell every few days and removed very sick prisoners, but since most of the men were in the prime of life and were not being starved, this was a rare occurrence. Every doctor knew my father was a colleague, but if anything it embarrassed them. Certainly it did not gain him any preferential treatment. Probably it was not in the doctors' powers to grant him any privileges anyway.

Uncertainty and the pall of constant boredom tormented the prisoners. Calendars and initials were carved on the table. A chess set had been made out of bread and charcoal, with the board carved into the table. But mainly the prisoners slept and talked. A man who could tell stories, real or invented, was truly valued in such a situation. My father was such a man. He had a terrific memory for books he had read as far back as high school, as well as anecdotes about people's lives. Always interested in people, he had amassed a truly impressive reservoir of stories from his patients and friends, and now was the time to roll them all out. In addition, he was the only professional man in the cell and the inmates all knew it, so he received numerous confidences and requests for advice during that time. Overall, he was highly respected by all his cell-mates.

Of course, some prisoners were removed from the cell, whether to be freed or sent off to Siberia, they never knew. People were just taken out, sometimes to be questioned and returned (never tortured or even beaten), sometimes disappearing for good. Since my father didn't know where we were, he couldn't attempt to send us a message by telling everyone to contact us in the event anyone was freed. He knew we were nearby, since he received our partially looted but most welcome packages once a month, particularly the soap (which was never stolen), toilet paper and any goodies which relieved the monotony of prison cuisine. He also received form letters in which we were not allowed to supply our address, but could write hints like "Klara is doing well in school," or "Zina is visiting Stephen [our code word for Siberia], she writes she lost a lot of weight, but Henry is well," and so on.

New prisoners brought in information on the progress of the war. One time, a Polish peasant was brought in and was asked whether America had yet entered the war. He replied that he had never heard of that king. The Polish peasants' ignorance was truly abysmal. This same man came in so encrusted with dirt that the guards took him to the washroom and scrubbed his entire body with coarse brushes designed for scrubbing floors. "Haven't you ever taken a bath?" they asked jocularly. "Of course I have!" he replied indignantly. "On the eve of my wedding!" No one knew, he least of all, how many years ago that event had taken place.

In all, 105 prisoners passed through the cell during my father's incarceration, some truly colorful characters, others clods like the peasant described above. Common criminals were mixed in with political prisoners. My father, whose crime was to try to leave the Soviet Union, was considered a political prisoner, but it was well known that the "politicals" were given stiffer sentences. My father was the only Jew among the prisoners, who never expressed any overt anti-Semitism. He was also the only formally educated inmate. However, some of the others were self-educated, and many were quite intelligent. As a result, my father became the repository of many true stories, since bored men under stress need to talk, and they knew they could trust in his discretion. Many of the prisoners were there for rather trivial offenses, while others had committed truly horrendous crimes.

There was a man who was in for the theft of a neighbor's plow. This man, a peasant, had been involved in an old feud with another family in their village. At one point, a member of the other clan was getting married and, as usual, the wedding was followed by a three-day-long orgy of eating and drinking. On the second night, when all the participants had drunk themselves into a stupor, the prisoner's clan sealed the house, doused it with gasoline and set it on fire, killing all those trapped in the building, including women and children. Far from feeling any guilt for such action, this man expressed satisfaction over the successful revenge. He was not a vicious man otherwise, my father told us, but life was hard. Hatred ran deep in the villages, but so did loyalties.

In spite of the boredom, my father was glad his case had not come up. He dreaded any resolution, which surely would have sent him to Siberia and separated him much farther from his family. On the day the Nazis attacked, the prisoners heard gunfire and the guards told them the news. A day or two later, the guards opened the cell doors and disappeared. Dazed by this sudden turn of events, the prisoners timidly emerged from their cells. There were no guards, but there was also no food in the kitchen. They walked out of the building and found themselves on the edge of a town already occupied by the Germans.

My father walked around the town, not wishing to ask questions until he came to a synagogue. Here he identified himself and told his story. Our strategy of leaving information for him paid off. He was sent to a doctor's house, fed and given news of us. He stayed for a few days, to gain strength for the journey to Slonim. He was shaved and bathed; given clothes, food for the road and detailed directions, and finally set out. Slonim was only about 30 miles away, but for a man weakened by prolonged inactivity and not very athletic to begin with, it was quite a long journey. No automobile or cart could be hired, not even a horse, which he wouldn't have known how to ride anyway. So he trudged along steadily, keeping to the edge of the road and stepping off altogether whenever he encountered German troops passing him in the opposite direction.

At one point, a troop of foot soldiers marched by, and one soldier called to him jokingly, *"Wohin gehst du Solomon, nach Palestine?"* (Where are you going Solomon, to Palestine?) Dazed with fatigue, my father momentarily wondered, "How does he know my name?" But he quickly realized the soldier recognized him as a Jew and used the name generically. Night came and there were still many miles to go. He could not walk any further; his feet were already swollen and blistered. The night was clear but moonless, and the dark was so deep he could not see his way clearly. He lay under a tree and dozed off, but soon was awakened by animal noises. A pack of wolves was approaching and small mammals were scattering. Clumsily he climbed the tree, which was soon surrounded by the howling wolves attempting to jump up to reach him. Luckily the tree was sturdy, but he spent the rest of the night clinging to a branch and shivering with fear. At dawn, the wolves slinked off and he resumed his trek, finally arriving in Slonim at midday and finding our house soon after.

What a happy reunion this was—the only truly happy event of the war! We soaked his aching feet, plied him with food, all three of us talking at once, kissing, hugging and relating how the 14 months had passed for each of us. We introduced him to our landlord, with whom he immediately made friends, communicating easily man-to-man in his fluent Yiddish.

We stayed in Slonim about three more months, but life was never normal during that time. Stores remained closed and, whereas we were never hungry, the ordinary mechanics of living, the things one takes for granted, came to occupy much of our time and energy. There was no bakery, so bread had to be baked at home. Furthermore none of us, not even our indomitable landlady, knew how to do this, so we had to hire a professional baker. We provided the flour, but she brought her own yeast. The baker was paid in kind, receiving one loaf per baking. She came once a week, so the bread was carefully wrapped in clean linen and kept in a dry place to last for the seven days.

A black market was already in existence. Under the Soviets, many items were not available in stores. There was also a gray, or "soft black" market. You could slip into a store through the back door, usually after hours, and buy items unavailable to off-the-street customers. Now all those stores were closed, but the merchandise was still available to special customers. We needed to replenish my father's wardrobe as well as buy supplies for his little black bag which we had kept while he was in prison.

We found it difficult to resume our previous relationship, and several clashes occurred between us. My father did not approve of one of my friends and told me to stop seeing her. I refused point blank; no one was going to tell me who my friends were to be. I had become independent during the months in which I made the family decisions. Now the genie could not be forced back into the bottle. It took my father some time to understand this and allow me to make my own mistakes, but we never regained the natural closeness of my childhood. I suppose this too was a natural part of my becoming a teenager, but it was exacerbated by our unnatural situation. This doesn't mean that I was ever contrary or obstreperous in a crisis. I was certainly sensible enough to know we all had to pull together at such times. Furthermore, my father came to appreciate my input, as I did not panic and was always at my best under pressure.

My father was a frustrated chemist. He loved to putter in his lab, devising new tests and techniques. Now, with so many necessities unobtainable by normal means, he began to make some of his own. We had a large kitchen into which my mother and I had been admitted only grudgingly. My father, however, had free run of it almost immediately, with all the help our deferential landlady could provide. Downstairs, there was a vast cellar used for storage but still with plenty of room for a primitive still.

My father's first and most immediately successful product was vodka, made from milk or potatoes. Needless to say, in the war-torn Belorussian countryside there was always a ready market for vodka. Two brothers who had served in prison with my father owned a tavern in Slonim. As soon as my father arrived he made inquiries and found them. Not only did they buy whatever he produced (in spite of its somewhat odd taste), but they became our friends and an extremely valuable resource for information. A country tavern, frequented by locals and German soldiers alike, was a priceless asset. Here, deals could be made, bribes extended and gossip and hard information exchanged. As will become clear, the devotion of the owners was invaluable to us. They loved and respected my father and would do anything for him and his family.

Another project of his was to make shoe uppers out of old sheets by suffusing them with chemicals that would make them impermeable to water. This project, in spite of all efforts, proved a failure. The third idea was to make saccharine, sugar being the one product that literally disappeared overnight. This was a much more sophisticated process, requiring bulk quantities of several different chemicals and equipment including large Buchner funnels (porcelain funnels operated by a water-induced vacuum used for product purification and drying). By this time, we had connections with the pharmacist who also supplied my father with medicines. The equipment was assembled, and eventually produced several batches of acceptable product which were instantly snapped up by eager buyers. My father continued to make saccharine in the Warsaw Ghetto and even after the war in Tel Aviv, where it was much in demand by diabetics. It proved to be my father's most successful product and supplemented his medical earnings for years.

I use the plural "we" when describing these activities, and it is not the royal "we." I instantly became my father's assistant and eager apprentice, learning quite a bit about lab techniques and chemistry. Incidentally, this provided me with an occupation to fill my otherwise empty days.

Whether my father did this deliberately or not, it proved one of his peda-gogical successes, since I eventually became a chemical engineer.

If we had been left alone, we would have muddled our way through the war years. But naturally, the Nazis had other plans for us. These plans began to unfold soon after the area was fully pacified. One of the first edicts was designed to curtail commercial contacts between Jews and "Aryans." At first this order included a prohibition against treatment of Aryans by Jewish doctors, but here an insurmountable problem arose. Slonim had a 50 percent Jewish population, but not a single Aryan doctor in the town or the surroundings. Faced with the choice of importing physicians or depriving the Aryan population of medical care, half of the Jewish doctors were reluctantly allowed to treat only non-Jews, and the other half only Jews. My father was on the former list, which proved to be a boon for our finances, since only the peasants paid in much-prized food. But this solution was so bizarre we suspected it was only tempo-rary. In fact, rumors about an impending ghetto for the Slonim Jews were already circulating.

Word went out that there was a new doctor in town. We spread the news as much as we could among our friends. My father hung out a sign for the peasants coming into town and soon he was in business. Since even a primitive laboratory was out of the question, he had to revert to being a general practitioner, not easy since he had not practiced as a clinician for 20 years. My father explained to me the great advantage of being a physi-cian: you could always make a living, since doctors were needed regard-less of economic conditions.

The next order forbade the Jews to hoard food, and threatened surprise inspections and harsh punishments. We looked frantically for hiding places in the house. Bricks were removed and walls rebuilt creating secret spaces, but these were reserved by our landlords who, after all, owned the house. Our friends the tavern owners came to our aid. They kept the food for us and doled it back to us as needed.

Soon we started hearing some truly frightening rumors. In little *shtetls* Jews were being ordered out of their homes, lined up near pits or anti-tank ditches and shot in the back. A Jewish man wandered into town and recounted one such story. He and his family were routed out of their house, herded next to a large pit and shot. The soldiers missed him, but he had the presence of mind to fall into the pit as if he had been shot as well. After the mass grave was full, the soldiers shot into it at random for good measure. But by this time there were several layers of bodies above him, and he escaped unharmed again. The grave was covered with a thin layer of earth, but there was enough air for him to breathe. He lay there, buried alive for a long time. When he judged night had come, he pushed his way out cautiously and silently left the village. He slunk into Slonim covered with blood, a wild man, the desperate sole survivor of his family and motivated by the urgency to warn the Jewish community.

Another story, even more terrifying, reached us soon after. A group of Jews was forced into a closed truck, a hose connected to the exhaust pipe at one end while the other end was placed inside the truck. The engine was then started, killing all those inside by carbon monoxide poisoning.

We could barely believe such horrors. This rumor may have been premature, or prescient. According to my recent research into this matter, the use of trucks for gassing Jews did not begin until December 1941 (at least that is the first documented instance of it), but the method had been previously used in Germany for the "euthanasia" of mental patients. Perhaps it was just in the planning stages during the summer of 1941. Between the mass shootings and mobile gassing trucks, the Special Action Squads (*Einsatzgruppen*) attached to the SS killed 1.2 million Jews in eastern Europe and the western Soviet Union, including 33,000 in Babi Yar near Kiev. This massacre is movingly described in the poem "Babi Yar" by Yevgeny Yevtushenko.

As the summer progressed, more and more stories of mass killings reached our ears. We began to feel terrified and exposed. In a small town where everyone knows one another, there is no place to hide. Furthermore, this was not our hometown, and apart from the tavern owners, we had few connections. We came to the conclusion that we would be better off in Warsaw, although this would mean living in the Ghetto. I believe it was the right decision, for I have heard of no one surviving in a Polish village or small town unless he or she had devoted Polish friends.

Getting back to Warsaw presented a very difficult problem. As far as we knew (and who could keep up with the multitude of new and irrational ordinances appearing every day?) Jews were forbidden to travel from town to town without a police pass. We were also banned from public transportation such as buses and trains, whose schedules were very sketchy at the time anyway. Seeing no other options, my parents did something either very brave or very foolish: they went to the Gestapo offices to request a pass to Warsaw. They just reasoned they had to risk it.

When they appeared at the local Gestapo headquarters, the first person they encountered was a Polish receptionist and interpreter. He looked at them with amazement. Jews just did not voluntarily enter Gestapo quarters! His first reaction was to advise them to leave forthwith, but my father demurred. "We must leave here," he said, "and a pass is necessary. I think the Gestapo officer will be so surprised by my request he might just grant it."

The receptionist frowned and looked at my father closely. "You are Dr. Salamon!" he exclaimed. "I was your patient in Warsaw!" He was on our side, an *amicus curiae* as it were. He pondered the dilemma. "It might just work if I introduce you as someone I know and pick the right officer."

The officer he selected was an older man. He looked stern but listened to the story patiently. Why did we want to go back? All our friends and family were there, as was my father's lab and his patients, my father responded. "What are those two white spots in your hair?" inquired the officer. My father explained how during the Russian Revolution, a Bolshevik had put a gun to his head. "I felt no fear at the time, but afterwards I noticed those two spots." It transpired that the officer had fought the Bolsheviks as well and hated the Communists as much as my father did. Now that they were united in their hatred of the Soviets, my father related his time in the Soviet prison. The officer was most interested in this story and asked many questions. Finally, he said, "All right, I'll write the pass."

My parents returned home in triumph. The document was investigated carefully. My mother noticed that it did not say "*mit Gepäck*" (with luggage). My father went back to the Gestapo, found his friend the receptionist, and the error was rectified. When I think about this story, I marvel at the combination of ingenuity and resourcefulness on my father's part and the plain blind luck involved in getting this pass. To me, this is symbolic of precisely the kind of confluence of circumstances that was necessary for survival.

Now that we had the pass, we needed transportation. We turned for help to the tavern owners. They suggested paying German soldiers to take us to Warsaw in a truck. They knew several supply sergeants who traveled extensively, and offered to ask about one who might be going to Warsaw and was willing to take us. Our pass would serve as a back-up, but they judged it too dangerous for us to travel openly. Any official, inspector, soldier, or hostile Pole (our friends were Ukrainian and no lovers of Poles) could grab the pass and destroy it. Then where would we be?

Several days later, one of the brothers came by to tell us he had found two willing soldiers. The price was agreed upon and the money was to be left in the tavern to be picked up by the drivers after they delivered us. The Germans were the ones who came up with the payment scheme, and we found it encouraging. After all, we were trusting our lives to two unknown German soldiers! The Germans, two courteous young men, came the next afternoon. They helped us into the truck and told us to sit in the back on some boxes. Then they piled more boxes in front of us; they too considered the pass a matter of last resort.

The truck moved off, rattling and shaking as we proceeded slowly out of town. We were stopped several times at various checkpoints. Each time we trembled with fear, but our drivers' papers were in order and no one thought to search the truck. It was already dark when the truck stopped, and one of the drivers came to the back. We thought this was our last moment on earth but we misjudged him. Instead, the young driver inquired solicitously if we were all right, particularly if I needed to go to the bathroom. Fear is a great diuretic—I did. One by one, we got off the truck and went into the bushes. The driver reassured us that we were almost there, and the trip resumed.

Finally, we arrived at the Ghetto checkpoint. Here, the drivers explained why they wished to enter the Ghetto, and then we were ordered out. Our documents were scrutinized, but the three sets of guards, German, Polish and Jewish, were baffled: Jews did not volunteer to enter the Ghetto. After some consultation between them, we were allowed in, and since it was past the curfew hour, our drivers offered to drive us to our destination.

The friend nearest to this particular checkpoint was Dr. Jellin. We directed our drivers to his apartment, where they helped unload our luggage and waited while we rang and summoned the terrified door-keeper. Yes, he said, Dr. Jellin lived in the building. The door-keeper went to get him, and we were greeted joyously and bidden to enter. We took leave of our drivers; if only all Germans had been that humane...

Excited and exhausted, we carried our luggage to Dr. Jellin's apartment where we were exclaimed over, hugged, fed and put to bed.

CHAPTER 7

ADAM CZERNIAKOW

The city we came back to was very different from the one we had left two years before. To give some idea of how the changes came about, I will tell the story of a man who was intimately involved in the affairs of the Warsaw Jews.

Adam Czerniakow was an ordinary man. He was born in 1880, educated as an engineer and married to Niunia. They had one son, Jas, whom they idolized. Czerniakow had a mediocre career, but in mid-life he became interested in politics in general, and in Jewish politics in particular. He ran unsuccessfully for a seat in the *Sejm* (Polish Congress), and although he was not a member of any Jewish political party (Orthodox, Labor or Zionist), he was appointed to the *Judenrat* (Jewish Council) in 1937.

In Poland, the Jewish Council was not elected by the Jewish community, but appointed by Polish authorities. Among the Council's functions were supervision of religious education; welfare disbursements; keeping birth, marriage and death records; and the upkeep of Jewish cemeteries. To support these activities, the Council collected fees and taxes from the Jewish population.

When the war started in 1939, Czerniakow was 59. Soon after the Germans entered Warsaw, they appointed him as chairman of the Jewish Council of Warsaw, a position he maintained until July 1942, although sometime in 1941 the Germans changed his title to Mayor of the Warsaw Ghetto.

Although I never saw him, his name became a household word in our home and the homes of all the Jews in the Ghetto. He was, after all, our main conduit to the Germans. He was the messenger for the German orders and pronouncements. He had some chance to negotiate better conditions for the Ghetto. He also had some power over the Ghetto population. Thus, his skills and his character were of great importance to us.

As soon as the war started, Czerniakow began keeping a diary. He wrote his thoughts down in nine notebooks, although the fifth one, covering the period between December 14, 1940 and April 22, 1941, was lost. Czerniakow made entries almost every day, although some were only one sentence or a few words long. The existence of the diaries was long unknown. They were rediscovered in the sixties and published by Yad Va Shem in Israel. The diaries shed light on both the author and his time.

Czerniakow described the gradual tightening and institutionalizing of the persecution of Jews. In the early months cruelty was sporadic and random. Bearded men or traditionally clothed Jews were stopped in the street, beaten, humiliated and forced to do hard labor, mostly clearing the city of the debris left by the German bombardment. The problem became so severe that in October 1939 the Jewish Council suggested organizing battalions of Jewish workers instead of snatching people from the street.

By October, all Jews were required to carry an ID card (*Ausweis*). In November, armbands featuring the Star of David became obligatory, and Jewish shops also had to be clearly identified with the Star of David. This made the Jews and their businesses marked targets for Polish criminals, hooligans and assorted anti-Semites. Some Jews were exempt from wearing the armbands, underscoring the policy of special privileges granted by the Germans which proved to be quite divisive in the Jewish community. The winter of 1939-40 was unusually severe, contributing to the hardships suffered by both the Polish and Jewish populations. Shortages of food, clothing and fuel developed almost immediately and kept intensifying. Prices for these commodities soared.

Rumors about the formation of the Ghetto in Warsaw started soon after the occupation, but it seems the Germans came to the decision gradually. Throughout 1940, more and more streets were closed to the Jews. Refugees arriving from the outlying towns were permitted to live only in the Jewish district. Then any Jews moving from an apartment were forced to move into the Jewish area, while the gentiles were forbidden to move there. The area designated as the Jewish district was larger than the eventual Ghetto district.

As late as September 1940, Czerniakow said he was still hoping for an open ghetto with the Jews confined to it only at night. Since throughout the war Warsaw had a night curfew, this would not have been too oner-ous. Even before the Ghetto was organized, the area originally reserved for it was reduced, partly at the request of Poles trying to protect their residences and businesses. The peripheral area was inhabited by a mix-ture of Jews and Poles, so that the formation of the Ghetto caused seri-ous dislocations for both groups.

Finally, on Yom Kippur, October 12, 1940, Czerniakow was summoned by the German authorities and handed the order for the formation of the Ghetto. The document started with, "In the name of humanity, at the behest of the Governor General, and in conformity with higher authority, a ghetto is to be established." A map of the Ghetto accompanied this document. Czerniakow was to form a Jewish militia consisting of 1,000 men to keep order in the Ghetto. Resettlement was voluntary until the end of October, after which the Ghetto was to be sealed.

The next three weeks were a period of desperate scrambling for space in the totally inadequate area assigned to the Jewish population of Warsaw. The original 500,000 inhabitants were augmented by an unknown num-ber of refugees. Pushcarts loaded with pitiful belongings were pulled by bearded men, accompanied by wailing women and children. There was a confusion about boundaries. Originally, most of the boundaries ran through backyards, utilizing existing fire walls and minimizing the need for building additional walls. Initially the Ghetto had 22 entry and exit points used daily by 53,000 people with crossing permits.

But the Germans soon realized this arrangement was too lax for their purposes. It was easy for Jews to escape (which they did at the rate of thousands every month) and for food to be smuggled in. In 1941 the number of entry points was reduced to 15, and teams of Jewish militia-men, Polish policemen and German soldiers were assigned to guard them. The borders of the Ghetto were moved several times, each time shrinking the Ghetto area and running borders along the middle of the streets, necessitating the building of more walls financed by and erected by the Jews themselves. The prisoners were forced to build their own prison.

The Germans also established an organization officially known as the "Ambulance Service," but it came to be commonly known as "The Thirteen" because of its location at 13 Leszno Street. Its ostensive purpose was to combat the black market and profiteering, but in fact it was the dreaded "Jewish Gestapo." Its members acted as agents and informers for the Gestapo proper. Once, a German, Dr. Klein, remarked in Czerniakow's presence that there seemed to be a great many scoundrels among the Jews. Czerniakow—daringly—reminded him of Newton's Third Law ("For every action there is an equal and opposite reaction.")

With the formation of the Ghetto, the responsibilities of the Jewish Council, and hence of Czerniakow, expanded dramatically. Auerswald, the commissar for the Warsaw Ghetto, wrote in a 1941 report, "Allow the Jews maximum freedom to regulate their own affairs within the district. Allow cultural activities, theaters, variety shows, coffee houses, etc. Allow a trade school system. The Jews represent a danger of epidemics. Isolate them, exploit their labor, prevent smuggling, but best of all, move them out of Warsaw."

In his diaries Czerniakow recorded the daily details of his administration and his life. He wrote about his attempts to feed the hungry, educate the children and house the homeless. He wrote about fighting a rear-guard action with the Germans: always trying to get some favor in a steadily deteriorating situation. He was offered a visa to Palestine in 1940, but refused and castigated Jewish leaders who fled the inferno. His greatest efforts were on behalf of children. He visited orphanages and gave the little living skeletons soup and chocolate. His greatest emotional exertions were on behalf of these helpless children and against the rich. "Damned be those who have enough to eat and drink, and forget about these children," he wrote.

Yet Czerniakow lived a distinctly privileged existence. Although they had to move twice, he and his wife always had an apartment and enough food. Once they went away to Otwock, a mostly Jewish resort near Warsaw for several days' vacation. This was an unheard-of privilege for others in the Ghetto. The Czerniakows attended concerts, plays and operas composed by Bizet and Offenbach, since Jews were allowed to attend or perform only works by Jewish writers and composers.

Contacts with Jews in other cities was minimal. Czerniakow's son Jas lived in Lwow and was never heard from after early 1941. This was a cause of constant anguish to Adam and Niunia and frequently mentioned in the diaries.

Early in 1942, rumors of wholesale deportation of Jews from Warsaw began to circulate, but Czerniakow refused to give them credence. He continued to place his faith in an irreducible core of human decency and rationality possessed by even the Germans. After all, in the Warsaw Ghetto there were 50,000 Jews producing uniforms, shoes, mattresses, furs and furniture for the German war machine—surely this slave labor was of value to the German economy. Thus, in spite of the rumors and the hard information about the disappearance of Jews from Lublin, Krakow and other towns, as well as his knowledge of Treblinka, which was being built by workers commandeered from the Warsaw Ghetto, Czerniakow continued to delude himself and to hide his knowledge from his people to prevent panic and chaos.

Twice he was arrested, beaten and released without any explanation. Each time his release was celebrated with offerings of flowers from his grateful "subjects." Periodically he would order the Jewish police to confiscate luxury goods (mainly food) from shops and take it to orphanages. He interpreted for us the German ordinances and symbolized for us rationality, order and hope. I know that his name was spoken with utmost respect in our home and the homes of our friends.

On July 22, 1942, Czerniakow was summoned by SS Major Hoffle and given his orders. All Jews, irrespective of sex and age but with certain exceptions, were to be deported to the East. The first contingent of 6,000 was to be ready at *Umschlagplatz* [the station for deportations] by 4 p.m. of that day. The exceptions included council staff, Jewish police and the workshop workers, all with their families—in all perhaps 100,00 to 150,000 people. Still, Czerniakow tried to bicker and expand the number of exemptions. On July 23, Czerniakow was recalled to Hoffle's office and given new instructions. He was to implement the orders and kill Jewish children himself. If he refused, his wife would be the first to go. Left alone in his office, he closed the door, wrote two notes and took a cyanide pill, refusing to preside over the destruction of his people.

Chapter 8

LIFE IN THE
WARSAW GHETTO

Morning came and with it the need to face the new reality and establish some viable pattern of life. The Jellins assured us we could stay with them as long as we wanted, and were most helpful in explaining the existing situation and helping us to re-establish ourselves.

The first challenge was to find a place to live. Although the tortuous walls encircling the ghetto were 11 miles long, the area was only about 1.5 square miles, already somewhat less than that in 1941. The wall was so long because of its many zigzags. Upward of half a million Jews lived in this space. It was no Manhattan. Most buildings were four or five stories high. This was not just a residential area, as it included factories, hospitals, offices and shops. The best estimate of population density was seven people per room, three times the population density in the rest of Warsaw, but by no means uniform.

Dr. Jellin and my father put their heads together and came up with a solution to the apartment problem. Like most Jewish doctors in Warsaw, both had been partners in several clinics. One such clinic stood on the corner of Nalewki and Swietojerska Streets, across from the Krasinski Garden. It was within the Ghetto boundaries and, at the moment, stood vacant. Those of the remaining partners who could be reached were contacted and all agreed to an equitable proposal. For a minimal monthly rent paid to the partners, we could use the facility and protect it from squatters.

The clinic was on the second floor and consisted of a very large room as one entered, which had served as the waiting room and office area. There were also three smaller rooms accessed individually from the large one. We immediately telephoned Cesia, Aunt Zina's former maid who was holding our belongings. Somewhat reluctantly, she agreed to return some of them. The most important part, the lab furniture and equipment, she didn't care about. But she was stingy with our personal belongings, the sale of which she claimed she had been living off for the last two years. But since we now had room only for the bare essentials, a deal was struck with the understanding that the remaining furniture belonged to her from now on. Cesia's boyfriend was in the smuggling business and owned a truck. He also knew whom to bribe, and when the right combination of German soldiers and Polish and Jewish policemen guarded a certain gate, he delivered our goods.

We were able to recover three beds, two chests of drawers, one wardrobe and several tables and chairs, although none of it was our best furniture. Thanks to her basic honesty, or perhaps her ignorance, Cesia also sent us our best Rosenthal china and our sterling silver, as well as a complement of everyday china, tableware and kitchen utensils, clothes and even several fur coats. She kept back the most valuable ones. Best of all, the lab equipment arrived intact, including a large supply of reagents and all three of my father's microscopes, which were the single most valuable possessions we had. Also received were a sufficient quantity of lab furniture and glassware. Even my father's library was sent over.

Cesia's attitude was characteristic of decent, honest Poles. She wanted to do the right thing but, I am sure, after two years she came to consider our belongings her own—perhaps she had given us up for dead. Furthermore, she too lived with uncertainty about the future and wanted to protect herself. We were grateful that she was honorable and helped us to get a new start, but we did not ask her for further help and she did not volunteer any. In fact, we never got in touch with her again. Considering the constant barrage of anti-Semitic pronouncements by the Germans and, no doubt, many of her neighbors and friends, it would have been hard for a simple woman like Cesia to remain sympathetic to Jews. I don't know if she ever was—we never spoke to her about those topics.

Within a week we were settled in, occupying one room as our living quarters, designating the second one as the lab and the third for storage. As many doctors as we could reach were notified that the lab was open, and gradually more and more patients appeared. Business was not as lively as before the war, since many people could not afford medical care. But, in spite of doing a large volume of pro bono work my father managed to make a living for us, albeit more modest than before the war.

Panna Fela, the younger of my father's pre-war assistants, showed up within days of our arrival. Her family's situation was quite desperate. One of her brothers was a soldier in the Polish Army and disappeared in 1939. She had several sisters, all scrambling for work, and totally unemployable parents. She came back to us as a sort of general factotum: a part-time lab assistant and a maid. We paid her no money, but we fed her and every day we sent a meal for her family. She was more than content with that arrangement, and worked hard and willingly, becoming almost like another member of our little family.

The Ghetto was a model of inadequacy. Here, insufficient space was combined with insufficient food and lack of gainful work, which in turn caused a maximum amount of suffering, just as it was intended by our "masters." I want to stress that, even in the Ghetto, I was partially shielded from the worst suffering. I could not help but see it and hear about it, as it affected some of our friends, neighbors and relatives, and our people in general, but I did not personally experience severe hunger, sickness, or physical maltreatment at the hands of the Germans. I was never taught to ignore suffering or to harden myself against the sufferers. Rather, I was kept busy and focused on my own responsibilities, chief of which was to become an educated person. If, therefore, this story doesn't say enough about the suffering in the Ghetto, it is because I only observed it without experiencing the worst of it.

My parents spoke of the war as something to be lived through, giving me hope that what seemed interminable at the time would indeed end some day. They were always making plans, amassing supplies, getting us vaccinated and keeping the family as safe as possible in such precarious times. My father in particular, as a man of intellect, wisdom and action, was a truly worthy role model. Here was a man who had come to Warsaw 20 years earlier practically penniless, and now had connections, a position, and enough wealth to keep us in the upper brackets of our Ghetto society. I learned from his experience the value of education and the need to guide one's children to the right path. I admired my father and later emulated him.

One would think that a man so conservative in his politics might not approve of women in the professions. Virulently anti-Communist and anti-Socialist, he admired rigid rules and structure. He supported Jabotinksky, the founder of the militant Zionist Revisionist movement, Haganah. Jabotinksky's followers later formed the Irgun Zvai Leumi. To give an indication of my father's conservatism, he considered Richard Nixon to be liberal. But as for women's liberation, I suspect his politics were altered by his love for me. Years before the birth of feminism, he was a confirmed feminist. Women, he claimed, should all have a profession, even if they chose not to practice it. It liberated them from dependency on men. A curious anomaly in my father's pantheon of opinions.

After we arrived in the Ghetto, the boundaries remained more or less static, with some major adjustments, needless to say not in our favor, occurring between October and December 1941. As a result of those changes, the "Little Ghetto" became more isolated from the main, northern part known as the "Big Ghetto." A single pedestrian overpass connected the two sectors. The twisted boundaries were the result of negotiations, mainly between the Poles and the Germans, and were designed to keep the most elegant and prosperous streets out of the Ghetto. We understood that they were always subject to further manipulation as we suffered attrition to our population. During the past two years the Jewish population of Warsaw had been augmented by the arrival of Jews from the surrounding areas, forcibly resettled by the Germans. This process was now complete, although small groups continued to arrive almost until the end. We had very few births and many deaths because of the severe living conditions.

The shortage of food was our biggest problem. German rations allowed us between four and 22 pounds of bread per month, in proportion to a person's usefulness. Jewish policemen had the highest allotment, as did other Ghetto officials, after which came the workers in the German-owned factories. The destitute on the bottom of the heap received the smallest amount, being judged expendable right from the beginning. Other rations were distributed irregularly and included potatoes, sugar, jam, and butter. I don't believe there were any meat rations, and egg rations were one per month, but even that was often skipped. Once, a large load of potatoes arrived, but they proved rotten from frost and turned to black, stinking slime upon cooking. In all, the Germans allotted 13 groszy (less than a dollar in today's currency) per day to feed one Jew, about one-third of the amount allotted to Poles. The official calorie allocation was under 200 per day for Jews, 600 for Poles and over 2,000 for Germans.

The Ghetto residents could not have survived without smuggling. Smuggling was our lifeline. Food was smuggled in, and everything we possessed—currency, clothes, furniture, and works of art—was smuggled out. Smuggling was a dangerous occupation, but most profitable to its practitioners. Since they were not in it for charity, it follows that prices were exorbitant and could only be afforded by the more affluent part of the population. Warsaw, as an old city, had labyrinthine alleys and many buildings connected to each other. When the Ghetto was first formed, smuggling was easy, because the boundaries ran mostly through rear courtyards in an attempt to utilize existing fire and separation walls. Soon, however, the Germans began to re-organize the boundaries, running each wall as much as possible down the length of a street to minimize smuggling opportunities. The 10-foot walls, topped with coils of barbed wire, were now more conspicuous, reminding us constantly of our status as sub-humans to be quarantined away from the normal population. But this was our city and we knew it very well. In addition, fewer than 100 Germans, Poles and Jews were assigned to guard the walls. Patrol frequencies, though subject to change at any time, could usually be figured out.

Food came in through every available conduit. It was thrown over walls and carried through secret cellar passages linking the Ghetto to the outside. Trucks would come in when guards could be bribed, and the poor Jewish children brought food in, rushing the gates or squeezing though minute holes in the walls like veritable moles. There was a story about a man who gave his daughter a hole in the wall for her dowry. In use 24 hours a day, the hole provided a good living to the young couple! At one location there was a drain pipe. The top was outside the Ghetto, the bottom inside. All sorts of pourable foods came in this way: flour, sugar, and milk. Infinite ingenuity operating against endless cruelty and repression was the order of the day.

To understand the complexities and hence possibilities for loopholes in a divided city, it is necessary to realize that prior to the war Warsaw had been a unified, dynamic city. Although most Jews tended to live in one area, they owned factories or worked in offices and factories all over the city. After the German invasion, Jewish businesses outside the Ghetto were confiscated, and were now under German or Polish management. But many of them still employed Jewish workers, who at times even secretly ran the businesses for incompetent bosses. By the summer of 1942, less than 10,000 Jews were employed outside the Ghetto, compared with 53,000 who commuted before the number of gates was reduced.

One gate was located across the street from our apartment, and since the windows of our room faced the street, we were able to observe the activities at the checkpoint. We even owned a pair of binoculars, and I came to recognize the faces of some of the guards. Watching the gate was as compelling as rubber-necking is at an accident site. All of us would run to the window in any spare moment and sit there, hypnotized by what was going on. This was human drama unfolding before our eyes, and the high stakes involved made it even more fascinating. It was almost as if it were our duty to see the evil and the devastation and to bear witness. In the morning, I saw the work battalions marching out to their jobs. At the same time, trying to take advantage of the distraction, the children, increasingly skeletal and ragged as time progressed, would rush through. Sometimes they all made it. Sometimes some would be caught, beaten and turned back. Sometimes shots would ring out; one could see little puffs of smoke, and then a little corpse or two sprawled in the street.

Occasionally, a German guard nicknamed "Frankenstein" would be posted at our gate. Then the word would go out: stay away! Frankenstein liked to shoot at people randomly, even when they had legitimate passes or were just walking by in the street. On those days, the whole area became abandoned. Even residents of apartment houses such as ours avoided the street.

During the day there was little activity, except on the rare occasions when the German and Polish crews were both open to bribery. Then the checkpoint got very busy. Trucks came roaring in, each one viewed by us as a triumph over our enemies. People would eat tonight! Fake work groups walked out unchallenged, sometimes even accompanied by a Polish policeman. We knew that on "the other side" people would melt away one by one and proceed to their hiding places, never again to return to the Ghetto. We could tell they were not workmen because they were too well-dressed and looked fat from the layers of clothing they wore.

On those days, children also passed unimpeded. It was all part of the deal. All day long, while on the "Aryan side," the poor children did menial work, begged, or even stole anything that could be converted into food. Often they carried out some meager possessions which they attempted to barter for food for themselves and their starving families. It was all based on the supposition that even anti-Semites would not extend their hatred to starving children, that they would find a spark of pity in their souls. It worked sometimes, but the children often had to contend with true Jew-haters, assorted Polish hoodlums who preyed on these most pitiful victims and the *Junacy*, an informal designation of uniformed youth groups, usually ethnic Germans.

In the evening the entire process was reversed. The worker groups came back and this time were spot-searched for contraband. Since it was impractical to search so many people, sometimes whole battalions would come back intact. At other times, some of the workers were pulled out of the ranks and searched perfunctorily or thoroughly, all according to the whim of the guards.

Jewish policemen worked for the Jewish Council to enforce laws passed by the Germans. We generally preferred them, because they used less violence in carrying out their duties. I regret to say, however, that some of the Jewish policemen were as bad as their German and Polish counterparts, either because they had not been bribed, or because they attempted to appear super-diligent to their "colleagues." Gradually, all the guards tended to become brutal through their power, as they became increasingly inured to death and suffering.

The children, like the "workers," returned to the Ghetto with food concealed on their persons if they were lucky. As they did in the mornings, at night they ran in large groups past the guards hoping that all, or at least most, would get in safely. The lucky ones would eat tonight, and tomorrow the whole process would be repeated. I looked at them and tried to imagine what it was like to live this way, but I couldn't, as I was still protected personally from experiencing the worst horrors of the Ghetto. Still, I could not be protected from seeing them.

Western Poland was ruled by the General War Governor, Hans Frank, and he appointed commissars for various Jewish districts. For the most part, the Germans did not enforce the Ghetto rules. In fact this was the only advantage the Ghetto brought us: a lower level of contact between the Germans and individual Jews. Less exposure also meant less random cruelty and abuse. We seldom saw Germans walking in the Ghetto streets. Occasionally they came to inspect individual facilities. At such times they were invariably accompanied by their Jewish minions. When a German was seen in the Ghetto, Jews had to bow and get off the sidewalk so that the *Übermensch* would not be "contaminated."

The "Jewish Gestapo," who worked for the German Gestapo, was a stain on our community, but certainly one to be expected under the circumstances. In every lawless, chaotic situation—war, revolution, repressive regimes, depression—the scum of society tends to rise to the surface and flourish at the expense of the general populace. Certainly our condition qualified as such a case. Persecuted by the Germans and many Poles sympathetic to the Germans on the Jewish issue, and governed by an inexperienced and powerless council trying to cope with steadily deteriorating living conditions, we were bound to produce our share of scoundrels, informers, extortionists and underworld figures who degraded and corrupted the Ghetto.

Ghettos represented the last organized life of Jews in Poland. In spite of the criminal elements described above, the vast majority of the population and Jewish officials acted responsibly and in a manner designed to minimize trouble. Throughout the entire duration of the Warsaw Ghetto, as far as I know, no irresponsible acts were performed by Jews which could have affected the whole community— truly something to be proud of. I am excluding smuggling from this category, since it was essential for the Ghetto's survival.

Nevertheless, it was a very imperfect society. The gap between the richest and the poorest was even greater than that in the United States. Although the Ghetto's rich people would not necessarily be considered wealthy here, the poor were so much poorer. At the top of this pyramid were the nouveau riche, the smugglers and criminals who lived it up as ostentatiously as possible. They were the ones frequenting the coffee shops and nightclubs, where because of the curfew they had to pass entire nights. It was reputed that in such places, hidden away in cellars, the decor was fabulous and the choice of food and drink almost as large as before the war. ("Gather ye rosebuds while ye may ...") My mother and her friends, who had been addicted to cafes before the war, had neither the time nor the heart to enjoy themselves while others were starving.

Next on the ladder were the "old rich," particularly if their pre-war apartment was within the area that became the Ghetto. These people retained all of their belongings, making life more luxurious and providing valuable possessions to exchange for food. Those who had to move into the Ghetto, on the other hand, could usually bring along only a fraction of their belongings, and were forced to rent space in someone else's apartment.

My grandfather's friends, the Rowinskis, belonged to this "old rich" category. Of course, they tried to conceal it for their safety. Mrs. Rowinski had a sweater whose buttons were actually diamonds disguised with cloth. They invited us for dinner several times, which was extraordinary in itself at the time. It was almost a pre-war-style meal, served on matching china and flatware by a maid in their dining room. Some stores in the Ghetto carried luxury foods such as sardines or chocolate, and they availed themselves of these delicacies.

The Rowinskis owned a factory which made knit underwear and socks. It was located right in the apartment house they lived in and owned. They had other real estate as well. The factory had been confiscated and taken over by a German named Schultz. But the Rowinskis were lucky. Before the war, they had sent their son to study textile manufacturing in Germany, and there he made many German friends, among them the very Schultz who now owned the family business. Evidently, Schultz was a decent man who not only protected the entire Rowinski family but let the younger Rowinski run the factory while he himself attended to raw materials, procurement and product sale. All this made the Rowinskis one of the wealthiest and safest families in Warsaw, a circumstance which was to prove quite important to us.

My friend Zula's family was also among the lucky ones, though not nearly on the Rowinskis' scale. They still occupied their apartment on Orla Street, although they now shared it with two tenant families. Thus each family had a bedroom, a rare luxury in the Ghetto, and shared the kitchen and bathroom. Zula's mother Ruta and her family kept possession of the living/dining room combination. Zula's father had been a successful leather merchant with a warehouse located within the bounds of the Ghetto and which had escaped looting and provided the base of the family livelihood.

Ruta's relative Freda, the special friend of my childhood, shared in this wealth. Her husband, a doctor, had been drafted during the mobilization of 1939 and never came back. He survived the war, and some years later visited us in Tel Aviv. But now Freda and her son Robus were alone and dependent on their sister's largesse. Robus, who was two or three years older than I, had to grow up very quickly to take care of his dreamy, impractical mother. He became a successful, bold merchant. I think he was young enough to view his activities and the risks they entailed in a spirit of adventure. He dressed vaguely like a Hitler Youth, carried false papers and walked out of the Ghetto regularly to arrange sales of portions of the leather goods. I admired him greatly as a heroic figure, but could never emulate such bravery.

Ruta was the chairwoman of the social committee in her apartment house. These organizations constituted the backbone of the very rudimentary and imperfect welfare system in the Ghetto. They collected food and money from the tenants and ran a soup kitchen in the building for the neediest residents and for as many street children as they could feed. For many, this was the only meal of the day. Panna Renia, my father's other lab assistant, was now married and living in Ruta's building. I don't know what her husband did but she was now a lady, with a maid, elegant clothes, and red nails. She became an active and proud benefactress of the soup kitchen.

The Germans taxed us periodically as a community, demanding money from the Jewish Council, often as ransom for individuals or groups. We also taxed ourselves internally to run our meager institutions. The process involved delicate negotiations in which the individuals who were assessed frequently pled poverty in an effort to minimize their payments. Like the Rowinskis, we grew secretive about our wealth, such as it was. What we had for dinner was not discussed with friends and neighbors. So many of them were falling on hard times that we could not possibly sustain them all, though several impecunious relatives were never turned away from our door, and often left with food and money.

The poor Warsaw residents were several rungs lower on this ladder. They still had their apartments, but had never accumulated possessions which they could sell. Fela's family belonged to this group. Without her job with us they might have starved to death, as many people did quietly in their apartments. Social committee members who inspected the apartments in their buildings would frequently come upon skeletons lying in their filth as the situation in the Ghetto deteriorated steadily. Czerniakow mentions an example in his diary: The corpse of a six-year-old boy was found in an apartment, partially decomposed and abandoned by his mother, who did this because the Community Authority refused to bury anyone without payment. Her own extremities were already swollen from starvation, and she was expected to die soon. Two more corpses were found that day at the same address. The inspection also found the community toilet to be a sanitary menace, increasing the risk of disease. In poor tenement buildings, individual apartments did not have bathrooms. Bathrooms were located in the hall, one to a floor, and shared by several tenants who also shared the responsibility for their cleanliness, resulting in a most unsanitary situation.

At the bottom of the Ghetto's social strata were the refugees, forcibly resettled there by the Germans. They often arrived with just a suitcase, no place to live, no connections, no job, and no skills for living in a large, complex and dysfunctional city. If they were lucky, they had relatives in Warsaw to turn to. Most did not, and lived in refugee centers or on the streets. This group contributed most heavily to the high attrition rate in the Ghetto. One out of every 10 Jews died of starvation or typhus during the less than two years of "peaceful" existence of the Warsaw Ghetto. The suffering of these people was truly unimaginable. They begged in the streets, sang folk songs or some tuneless inventions of their own, snatched parcels from passersby or gave up and sat or lay down on the cold pavement, quietly desperate. In the morning, there were always corpses lying in the street, sometimes covered by newspapers. Some were practically skeletons, barely covered with rags. We all got used to walking around them as we went about our business.

How different was my new life. I was no longer the child who only two years before had not yet seen a dead person. Our "masters" were teaching us a lesson in callousness. The axiom is known to every doctor, nurse or other practitioner who must deal directly with death. If you let pity overwhelm you, you lose the ability to function. Pity must lead to constructive charity, but your heart must learn to stand apart. Thus, my father treated many patients for free. My mother cooked for and fed a second family on a daily basis. We helped several relatives in need, but we walked past the corpses, averting our eyes.

The Ghetto was losing people in yet another way—people crossing to the "other side." What had begun as a trickle eventually assumed gigantic proportions. Towards the end, the rate stood at about 4,000 per month. The Germans complained about this to the Jewish Council, claiming the escapees were carrying with them typhus infection. Even if it wanted to, the Jewish Council was powerless to stop the exodus. Often, its own members participated in it.

Leaving the Ghetto to live on the "Aryan side" was not a simple matter. First, one had to have false papers. If one planned to work, the papers had to include a birth certificate, library card, driving license, work papers and letters written to one's address on the outside. In short, one had to own the paper trail characteristic of 20th-Century life. If one rented a room in an apartment, one had to withstand the onslaught of curious neighbors. Who was the new tenant? What did he do? Where did you meet him? A suspicious and anti-Semitic neighbor might denounce you to the authorities and collect a bounty if he or she were right. I know a man who survived by moving every few months, and staying aloof from neighbors and landlords who did not know he was Jewish. He spent his days walking around the city, while he was believed to be at work.

A Jew living outside the Ghetto could be spotted in many ways. In spite of frantically learning about Catholicism and its practices, he might not know some prayer or custom. He might accidentally reveal his under-standing of Yiddish or knowledge of Jewish customs. He might be recog-nized by a previous acquaintance. A man might be betrayed by his cir-cumcised penis, as unlike the custom in the United States, only Jews were circumcised in Poland and the rest of Europe. Supposedly, a very expen-sive operation could be performed reversing the results of circumcision. I heard of several men who underwent this procedure successfully. Clearly, a Jew on the other side had to be on his guard all the time. At best he led a nerve-racking life, cut off from the solace of being with his people.

People were often stopped in the street by Germans or Polish policemen for no apparent reason. Every such incident, although routine for a Pole, was fraught with danger for a Jew. Unmasked Jews were summarily shot on the spot or taken to the Gestapo to be tortured into revealing hiding places of other Jews. No wonder wealthy Jews preferred to find a secret place and deal only with their landlords, as did the family of Anne Frank. Sometime in the spring of 1942, the Rowinskis left the Ghetto and went into hiding, although their son stayed behind, protected by his job.

My family fit somewhere in the middle of the economic hierarchy out-lined above. Because of our history, we had neither a fancy apartment nor a fashionable address, but we did have some of our possessions, our con-nections and my father's profession to sustain us. I did not go hungry. Our food remained nutritious and wholesome, though we lacked such luxu-ries as fresh fruit, cake, or chocolates. If meat was unavailable, we got our protein from eggs or cheese. On days when there were no potatoes we made pancakes, *kasha* (crushed grain), or noodles. We always seemed to have bread and flour in the house. Everything else was *ersatz* (substitute). Herbal tea replaced real tea. Chicory took the place of coffee. There was a joke that Hitler commissioned a scientist with a task of making butter out of feces. After a while, went the joke, the scientist reported having solved the consistency problem and stood ready to tackle the flavor issue.

Electricity and gas became intermittent. They were available only three times a week for several hours at a time. We adjusted by cooking franti-cally during such times. In the winter, the large front room and the last room in the back served as storage areas for fuel, flour, root vegetables, canned goods and cooked food. One of our favorite foods became *cholent*, a rich stew consisting of lamb or beef, potatoes, barley and lima beans. On Fridays, religious Jewish women used to prepare a pot of these ingredients, seasoned them, poured water over them, sealed the pot tightly and placed it in a hot baker's oven to cook slowly overnight—a sort of giant slow pot. On *shabbes*, after prayers, the women would retrieve the pot from the baker, providing a hot, delicious meal on a day when no fire could be lit. We made the *cholent* on a gas burner on any day gas was available, using pork in place of lamb. Our ancestors must have been turning in their graves!

We purchased a free-standing, Franklin-type stove. On gasless days we could re-heat meals or cook very simple ones on its single burner top. Hot water was always simmering on the stove for drinking and washing dishes, clothes or ourselves. The little stove was also the only means of heating our quarters, which is why we all crowded into a single room— and even that was inadequate. When Fela came early in the morning, the room would be freezing. I would be allowed to stay in bed for half an hour while the temperature rose to bearable. The cavernous front room and the toilet remained icy all winter, so I bathed once a week using a small bowl of warm water placed in front of the stove.

My mother did most of the cooking, learning as she went along. Normal cooking skills did not prepare one for coping with shortages of various ingredients, and preparing reasonably tasty meals became a real challenge. Fortunately, hunger dulled our sense of taste. Though we were not starving, our appetites were always normal, and everything tasted good. The building we lived in was occupied by lower-middle-class merchants, artisans and blue-collar workers. Here too a soup kitchen was organized and my mother attempted to join in, but came back disillusioned. These Yiddish-speaking, babushka-clad women were too alien to her; she continued to contribute financially to the kitchen but withdrew from active participation.

As ever, in times of relative peace my job was studying. My intermittent schooling in Bialystok and Slonim had kept me far behind my peers in Warsaw. Their schooling had continued, though with some interruptions, in small clandestine groups organized by Jewish teachers. They were now covering material appropriate to the third year of *gymnasium*, equivalent to American ninth grade.

I could not join in. My parents decided, however, that I was bright enough to catch up in a single year. Accordingly, 1941-42 was to be devoted to this effort. Two tutors were hired for me. The general tutor, a young man, came to the house every day for two hours and covered math, history, geography and Polish language and literature. My prodigious reading the year before in Slonim came in very handy. I was all caught up in literature and history, requiring only some systematizing of facts and ideas already in my head.

My father coached me a little in science, but that was difficult to do without a lab. Three times a week I went to the home of my other tutor for Latin. It was November before all this was arranged, so I had about seven months in which to cover three years of Latin. Walking in the street I kept my Latin book and notebook hidden under my coat, since the Germans forbade Jewish children to study beyond the fourth grade, except for vocational training. Obviously, my study regime kept me well occupied, focusing more on preparation for final exams than on the conditions in the Ghetto. My parents thus managed to salvage a modicum of normalcy and childhood for me in the midst of the pervasive misery surrounding us.

On the other hand, my activities also kept me solitary. My former close friends had become distant through the two years we were apart, and now our different lives continued this separation. Zula and Chris remained best friends, but the girl closest to the three of us, Bronka Miedrzycka, took my place in the triumvirate. Those three lived close to each other, Zula and Bronka in their pre-war apartments and Chris in a different apartment. None of my friends came to visit me. I would occasionally visit them, but not on a regular basis.

Once more, I was an outsider looking in, caught between two opposing choices. Did I want to become one of the clique, immersing myself in its frivolous interests, or remain my own person, friendly with the group but solitary, with an invisible line written in the sand? The feeling of being part of the group and yet apart from it had gnawed at me for two years. In Bialystok I had no desire to become part of my class, yet something in me yearned for the sense of belonging even then. In Slonim, I acquired several friends yet still remained the essential outsider, a child brought up in a big city separated from my friends by a different history and upbringing. I remember trying to fit in, but every once in a while something would slip out: maybe a mention of having gone to the opera, or to the theater, or to Paris, and suddenly a gulf would open between us. I understand now that they felt strange around me, and instinctively distanced themselves. All through my later life, I was to feel it even more strongly whenever I mentioned surviving the Holocaust. People sympathized or felt morbidly curious, but at the same time did not want to feel too strongly, and therefore distanced themselves from me emotionally.

In June 1942, I went to the homes of individual subject teachers and was tested, in writing and orally, in all the subjects which I had prepared. Collectively, I was judged very adequately prepared and ready for the next grade. I even received a written document to that effect, but, of course, this disappeared into the maelstrom which was to follow. Meanwhile, our community was constantly fighting rear guard action against the increasing persecution and the resulting deterioration. Every new rationing system cut the monthly allotments, ostensibly due to widespread shortages in the entire German Reich.

Soon after our arrival, the Ghetto boundaries were adjusted several times to exclude the Jewish cemetery, the Great Synagogue on Tlomacka Street and some of the best areas on the edges of the Little Ghetto. The Ghetto also lost the *Umschlagplatz* (reloading and railway station), where supplies for Ghetto businesses were stored. It was to become the site of deportations from the Ghetto later on.

In December 1941, a possible deportation of 120,000 Jews from Warsaw "to the East" was mentioned for the first time. Suddenly, the earth shifted beneath our feet and the very existence of the Ghetto was threatened. All of us tried to dismiss this horror from our minds, but the exodus to the "other side" intensified. It was at this time that our friends, the Jellins, sent their little daughter Gabrysia outside the Ghetto to be brought up as a Christian by a friend of Mrs. Jellin.

As our Christmas present, in the spirit that it is better to give than to receive, the Germans requisitioned all furs owned by Jews along with new, unused underwear and a certain type of warm boots particularly popular in the mountains. They gave us four days to surrender these goods, which officially were being "donated" to help the German war effort. For the next three days, smuggling out of the Ghetto rose to a fever pitch as people tried to sell what were, for some, the only things of value they still owned. The best furs were hidden in the Ghetto while the least valuable pieces, old fur hats and collars, were surrendered. We stood in long lines to perform this duty and felt obligated to turn in something, since our "donations" were being registered. It meant, however, that no furs could be worn in the streets, a real hardship during the cold Polish winter. With the help of young Rowinski, our furs were smuggled out and stored by one of his trusted Polish employees. While we were at it, we also sent out our Rosenthal china and sterling silver, anticipating that these might be requisitioned next. This did not happen, but these saved treasures helped support us later on. Incidentally, the estimated value of the furs collected by the Germans was 50 million zloty, the equivalent of about 40 million kilos of bread on the black market, and this did not include the smuggled-out or hidden furs, probably worth much more.

The only good thing that winter was news of the war. Sometime during the fall of 1941 the German offensive in Russia, having penetrated almost to Moscow, became bogged down. In 1942 we heard a lot about a town called Stalingrad. We did not know it at the time, but Stalingrad proved to be the turning point of the war. From then on the Germans were to suffer more defeats than victories. For us the shining moment was the entry of the US into the war in December 1941. Germany had declared war on the United States on December 11. We rejoiced at Hitler's stupidity in engaging so powerful an opponent. Once America entered the war, the issue of German defeat was never in doubt. It was just a question of time! We never lost faith, even when the strange-sounding Pacific islands fell to the Japanese one after another. Having a view of America as all-powerful, we were sure it would prevail, but would it be in time?

A spirit of determination pervaded the people in the Ghetto. All but the weakest of us strove to survive and outlive our enemies. That was all the victory we could think of, but that was the thought that kept us fighting. Suicides were unheard of in the Ghetto.

Our people had an inventiveness which could match the fabled Yankee ingenuity. Condoms were made from baby pacifiers, and carbide lamps from metal cigarette boxes. We too had such a lamp. I did much of my studying by this light. The lamp stood on the table, making it easy to read and write, but the light did not reach the corners which remained always in the shadows. We sat around the table, I studying and my mother mending, as she became very adept at this important activity, while my father would be reading the newspaper or studying and planning the next new product to attempt in his lab.

Right from the beginning, small manufacturing concerns sprang up in the Ghetto, doing brisk business with the "Aryan side" and even the Germans. Small Jewish firms, licensed for export by the Germans, manufactured electrical, mechanical and photographic equipment as well as toys, cosmetics, and even uniforms. The needle trade in particular had always been a source of income for many Jews.

In Poland before the war there was a sewing machine in almost every Jewish home. There had been one in ours, though I am not sure my mother knew how to use it. From time to time, an itinerant Jewish seamstress would come to the house and make sheets, towels and nightgowns out of big bolts of cloth. In other homes, seamstresses would be hired to make children's clothes twice a year. Our maids bought their dresses from Jewish hawkers advertising their wares in the courtyards. Many Jews were skilled in the various segments of the garment industry.

Some enterprising Germans decided to take advantage of this labor pool. They obtained the necessary permits and opened workshops in the Ghetto. There was the Toebbens workshop, which manufactured clothes, particularly uniforms; Schultz (the "big Schultz" as it was known), which made mattresses and furs; Waldemar Schmidt, which made shoes often from straw; and Bromberg's metal goods factory which made furniture. By July 1942, these workshops employed about 50,000 Jews, comprising half of the Ghetto's gainfully employed residents. The German firms paid starvation wages for long hours and hard work. Since some of the supervisors were German, not even the prospect of a meal was enough to entice the more prosperous part of the population. One of Fela's sisters got a job at Schultz, marginally relieving the family's problems. None of our friends was tempted by such jobs, which at first were filled by the poor. Even without the wealthy, the available pool was quite large, allowing the Germans to be quite choosy. Only the young and healthy were selected, and only those with appropriate skills; the poor skeletons in the streets and in the refugee centers need not apply.

When we arrived in the Ghetto, another scourge was already afflicting the population. The typhus epidemic began from a few cases appearing soon after the Ghetto was sealed. The danger of epidemics had been the spurious official excuse for establishing the Ghetto in the first place, and now this danger was actually materializing in spite of the quarantine.

Typhus is really a cluster of related diseases; the principal one in the Ghetto was of the epidemic variety, transmitted from one human to another by infected lice. We believed at the time that rats were the original source of the infection, transmitting it to lice, so rat extermination became a high priority in the Ghetto. We learned to shake our coats out before entering the apartment and then search them carefully for any lice. In the crowded streets we tried to walk without brushing against anyone, particularly the dirty-looking beggars, distancing ourselves from them as if they were lepers. We attempted to do it casually, as if by accident, so as not to hurt these poor people's feelings, but I am sure they knew what it was all about. It may be that we were confusing our typhus with the endemic typhus, a somewhat milder variety with similar symptoms, carried by the combination of rats and fleas. Perhaps both were present, raging side by side, indistinguishable from each other. A louse found on one's clothes gave rise to instant panic. We searched for bites, and if we found one, prayed the louse had been healthy.

The epidemic typhus victim is infected by scratching the lice bites, thus rubbing the louse's infected feces into the wound. The lice themselves die after a couple of weeks whether they infect a human or not. The incubation period lasts two weeks, after which the patient experiences headaches and general malaise, followed by a high fever lasting for about a week and a rash covering most of the body. A healthy person, carefully nursed through the disease, has a good chance of survival although the recovery might be quite protracted and accompanied by depression and weakness even following an uncomplicated course of illness.

How different was the situation in the Ghetto, where crowding, filth, poverty, cold and hunger had already lowered the victims' resistance. Typhus struck the rich as often as the poor. In fact, the poor may have been struck less often, having developed a better immunity to the disease, but the rate of recovery was much higher among those better fed and hence in a better physical and mental condition.

Fela's mother and one of her sisters succumbed to the disease, as did Aunt Cyla's mother. Cyla's mother was by now an old lady. She died in spite of devoted nursing by Cyla's sister and medical care from my father. Cyla's sister also caught typhus but survived, though at the end her hair had been shorn since it was believed that shaving a person's head helped speed recovery. Her body was emaciated to skeletal thinness and she looked to be at death's door. She improved with time, though she never regained her former looks or vitality. Typhus probably killed as many people in the Ghetto as starvation, but since the majority of the victims died of a combination of both, it is useless to attribute the deaths to one or the other cause. Instead, one should rightly attribute them to the real culprits: the Nazis.

Sometime late in 1941, limited amounts of anti-typhus vaccine were smuggled into the Ghetto. This material came from Switzerland, at the secret request of Jewish doctors in Warsaw. The vaccine was available only to the rich. My parents paid about 200 American dollars—a vast sum which could have kept us fed for months—to have the three of us vaccinated. Czerniakow writes of being inoculated twice. It seems to have been pretty effective, though the vaccination itself induced mild fever and headache which passed after a day or two.

It always amazes me how some people can claim that the Holocaust never took place in the face of a vast volume of proof. Life in the Ghetto was extraordinarily well-documented. Many Jewish scholars kept diaries. Some of them were smuggled to the "Aryan side." Some were buried and uncovered after the war. The Germans themselves were not ashamed of their handiwork. They filmed Jews building the 10-foot-high walls isolating the Ghetto, trading in the streets, sitting in cafes, attending concerts, plays and nightclubs, and dying or dead in the streets. At one point they planned to film Czerniakow as a host at a ball. What surrealism! The hall was filled with flowers, and Czerniakow dressed in evening attire when, at the last minute, Commissar Auerswald nixed the plan. A professional comedian replaced Czerniakow in the propaganda film.

The Ghetto had an official newspaper, *Gazeta Zydowska*, and a number of underground leaflets which were printed and distributed clandestinely. All through the spring of 1942, there were published and verbal reports of radical changes in other ghettos in Poland. The Krakow, Lublin and Lwow Ghettos were being liquidated and their Jewish Councils arrested. Where were these Jews taken? Our sources were silent on this point. No one wanted to believe the awful possibility. No one dared to verbalize it. We learned later that rumors of Jews being gassed were suppressed by our Jewish Council for fear of outbursts and their consequences. After the war, many people blamed Czerniakow for being untruthful with us, but his diaries indicate clearly that he was deluding even himself to the last.

Late in the spring, rumors of an imminent deportation of Jews from the Warsaw Ghetto began and intensified through May and June. A figure of 120,000 being permitted to stay was mentioned. Suddenly it seemed wise to be employed by one of the German-owned workshops in the Ghetto. Surely, it was argued, these workers were performing such a useful service that they and their families must be spared. In the end, this was not so.

Concurrent with the rumors about deportations, new place names began to enter our language. Belzec and Sobibor near Lublin were already in operation, and a new place, called Treblinka, near the Bug River, was being rushed to completion. Jews from the Pawiak prison in the Warsaw Ghetto were sent there to build the camp. At one point that spring, Czerniakow was ordered to provide more strong, young men to work there.

The rumor mill was wild. At this same time, there were also rumors of emigration becoming possible to the United States, South America and Palestine, allowing families to be reunited. Husbands or wives would be allowed to join their spouses, parents, children and so on. The war had broken out so suddenly that many families separated by a business or vacation trip were frozen apart by the hostilities.

Early in the spring, my father realized the advantage of being connected with one of the German-owned workshop and, through the intercession of young Mr. Rowinski, attached himself as factory doctor to the little Schultz factory (not to be confused with "big Schultz", which employed over 20,000 people). He spent part of each day there and became acquainted with a Mr. Rozwadowski, an Aryan occupying a high position at the plant. Rozwadowski was the trusted employee who was holding our china and silver, sent "outside" the previous December. Like all Polish employees, he was involved in smuggling, and some of our food as well as hard information on the political situation came from this kind and honorable man.

At the same time, plans were being made for me in case conditions should remained unchanged. Having caught up to their level, I was to rejoin my friends at their secret school, but my father felt this would not occupy me fully. Besides, summer was coming and with it the traditional summer vacation — a strange concept in this hard new life.

My father felt that I needed a trade with which I could support myself in any eventuality. Sometime in the future, when the war was over, I would go to college. This was a given, but for the time being I was to learn some useful trade. Opportunities in the Ghetto were limited. After several long discussions, we decided to investigate watch-making and watch repair. I was not enthusiastic about this prospect. The thought of spending long hours bent over the tiny mechanisms with a loupe in my eye was not attractive, although understanding how a watch worked piqued my curiosity. There was no denying, however, the wisdom of learning something and not wasting my time. I agreed. A master of the trade was located. He interviewed me, found me suitable and agreed to take me on for a small fee until I was skilled enough to earn my continuing instructions.

In the middle of July, Czerniakow asked Commissar Auerswald about the deportation rumors. Auerswald claimed he had no knowledge of it. Within several days however, a new official, *Sturmbannführer* Hoffle, an SS Major, appeared on the scene. On July 22, the ax fell.

CHAPTER 9

DEPORTATION

Killing Jews had been the logical outcome of the virulent anti-Semitism articulated by Hitler in *Mein Kampf*. Up to 1939, the Nazis' goal was to force Jews to emigrate, leaving all their worldly possessions behind. Mass killings began soon after the invasion of Russia, when millions of Jews fell into Nazi hands. But the January 1942 Wannsee Conference marked a turning point in Nazi persecution of Jews. At Wannsee, the "Final Solution" was enunciated. This differed from previous policy in a crucial way. The new goal was not just to kill Jews, but to kill all the Jews in Europe, 11 million in all, including the Jews in Great Britain.

The proposed genocide differed from previous ones. It was a deliberate, state-planned policy that was executed coldly, systematically, and efficiently on a heretofore unprecedented scale. Unlike the Inquisition, the policy gave the Jews no option to convert. For the first time, the persecution was not religious but racial, or perhaps it would be more correct to call it biological, since it branded people with even a small fraction of Jewish blood as Jews.

At first the slaughter yielded handsome profits for the Nazis, who collected clothing, jewelry, gold teeth and other Jewish belongings. Body parts such as hair were sold to be made into felt and mattress stuffing, and human ashes were used as fertilizer. In a sense, this was a modern and grotesque cannibalism. Commercial concerns which manufactured the ovens and Zyklon B also made money on the operation. Each camp had to be self-supporting. But in the long run, the killings made no sense even from the Germans', or purely economic, point of view. Slave laborers were being killed off in spite of an acute labor shortage. Trains which could have been carrying supplies and soldiers were instead requisitioned for ferrying Jews across Europe to the killing factories of Treblinka, Majdanek, Sobibor and Auschwitz, among others. Hitler's insane hatred of the Jews took precedence over any logical, sensible considerations.

We learned of the deportations on July 23, 1942. On that day Adam Czerniakow committed suicide, and orders for "resettlement," as the deportation was euphemistically called, were plastered all over the Ghetto. The order exempted workers in German workshops in the Ghetto, the Jewish police, and the Jewish Council and their families, about 120,000 people in all. But it also meant that between 300,000 and 400,000 Jews were to be deported at the rate of 6,000 per day. The placards urged Jews to volunteer and present themselves at the *Umschlagplatz* where they would board the trains. We were told working camps with better living conditions than in the Ghetto had been readied for us in the East. All those who showed up at the train depot on their own were promised three kilos of bread and a kilo of marmalade, a generous offering to starving people. The offer had many takers. An elderly couple, my father's distant cousins whom we had been helping for the last eight months, came to our house that day and announced their decision to go. We listened sadly as they told how they were exhausted from their daily struggle to survive and had no material or emotional resources left.

We too believed the resettlement story. But we viewed the promises of a better life as a propaganda ploy designed to paint a rosy picture of what we expected to be a brutal deportation to hard labor concentration camps. The Nazis were trying to talk us into going peaceably, while we were determined to resist the move with all the means at our disposal. At that point, the "other option," the thought that we were all going directly to our deaths, was still too terrible to contemplate, but while no one articulated it out loud, we felt it in the pits of our stomachs.

A giant hand had shaken the kaleidoscope of our lives and a new pattern emerged. It was a pattern more terrible than any of us had ever known, more terrible than any human mind could imagine. The next three months were the most horrendous time in my life. Even after all these years, just thinking about it brings unbearable pain and despair to my soul. My mind recoils from the thoughts and tries to obliterate them.

The deportation affected our lives from the first day. Except for the workers, there were no more privileged people as the inexorable quota of 6,000 lives per day pressed upon all of us. From the beginning the Germans were not consistent in respecting the I.D. papers and passes of workers' families, so all of us were at risk all the time. The Ghetto became a ghost town. Except for groups of workers marching to work in the morning and some scurrying around in early evening, no one ventured into the streets. Even that was gradually changing as the big workshops began housing their workers in buildings adjoining the factories, eliminating the need for traversing the empty streets. Where just a few days before crowds bustled, traded, begged, gossiped, or just went about their business, now ghostly silence reigned. But, in the warren of cellars and along the rooftops, secret passages were being forged, allowing some minimum communication to persist. Even so, from that point on the streets belonged to the Germans.

On the first day of the deportation, my friend Chris's stepfather was picked up by car as usual to go to his protected job at the Italian consulate. Though he was Jewish, his working papers were in order. At the Ghetto checkpoint, however, he was ordered out and taken to the *Umschlagplatz*. The Italian consul himself intervened and sent an official car to the *Umschlagplatz*, but to no avail. On that first day the SS, who were running the operation, were determined and rigid; no amount of persuasion would sway them. Thus, a man we considered so well-protected was gone.

We heard later that Chris' mother "married" a Jewish policeman. During the deportation there were no single policemen and no single workshop workers, as they all faked marriages to try to save somebody's life. But such methods became less and less effective as the easy deportation fodder ran out and the Germans came looking for the hard core of workers and people in hiding. Chris and her mother soon obtained some false papers and crossed to the "Aryan side." That was the last I heard of them until after the war.

Our lives became totally isolated and reduced to a struggle to survive one day at a time. Paradoxically, the struggle for food eased. As more and more apartments stood empty with their doors wide open, the inhabitants gone to the workshop dormitories or "to the East," the supplies they left behind became available to the night foragers. Besides, food was not a high priority: surviving the day was.

The myth of work camps in the East did not last long. The evidence of the awful truth began to pile up fast and thick. Peasants living in the vicinity of Treblinka began to notice the smell of roasting flesh, which spread miles from the camp in all directions but particularly, of course, downwind. Jews who helped to load the trains at *Umschlagplatz*, most of whom were members of the Jewish police, began to recognize particular railroad cars, often marking the cars themselves to find out how long before these same cars returned. To their horror and amazement, they found that cars loaded in the morning returned the same day. The turnaround took only several hours, making it obvious that the disembarking station was quite close. Put all that together with the knowledge of a new camp recently built at Treblinka and the destination was not difficult to guess. But what was happening at Treblinka? Was it a trans-shipping point? Certainly there was no room there for the mass of humanity that was being sent there.

The final proof came from several young men who, independently of each other, escaped from Treblinka and courageously made their way back to the Ghetto just to bring back the terrible news. Arriving at Treblinka, each train was met by officers who carried out a selection. About five to 10 percent of the victims, all able-bodied men and women, were selected to live and work. The rest were led off to the "showers." Here men were separated from women and children, herded into separate rooms, ordered to strip and jammed into gas chambers equipped with fake shower heads. The young men and women sorted the clothes and belongings, sometimes recognizing those belonging to close friends and relatives, unloaded the death chambers of their grisly contents, stripped the naked bodies of gold and hair and fed the crematorium ovens operating day and night. The sorters and handlers did not last very long themselves. Exhausted physically and emotionally, overwhelmed with horror, despair and sorrow, they soon became oven fodder themselves, replaced by a new supply of ever-available fresh workers.

The time for deluding ourselves was over.

My father, as I indicated earlier, had wisely secured a job at the small Schultz workshop. This entitled him and us to be exempt from deportation. At the very beginning, we trusted in this arrangement. My father would leave for his job in the morning and come back in the evening, always bringing back some food which had been smuggled into the Ghetto by Mr. Rozwadowski, our friend and principal supplier. This went on for about 10 days after which we experienced a crude and cruel awakening. Early in the morning before my father went to work, our building was surrounded by the Germans. Everyone, regardless of papers, was forced to march to the *Umschlagplatz*.

Umschlagplatz was a place of ultimate despair. Here people were condemned to death. It was only a matter of time. Depending on the number of people caught in the net, and the availability of trains, one might be there for a few hours, a few days or leave immediately. The building, located on Stawki Street, was in a sort of no man's land— outside of the Ghetto, but out of sight of the Aryan side. The rooms and halls were jammed with people, still trying to hide in order to postpone their ultimate fate, measuring the reprieve not in days, but in hours. There was no food, no water, and hardly any sanitary facilities. The heat was sweltering.

On the day we were there, there were thousands more victims than could be accommodated by the day's transport capacity. We arrived terrified and bewildered and were pushed into a large hall. We found bedlam. We were in a large open space. Some people paced nervously back and forth, silently or moaning loudly. Others sat dejectedly propped by a wall, their vacant eyes staring at the scene as if it were some impossible nightmare. The sounds of wailing mixed with the cries of the children asking for food and water. We were overwhelmed by the noise and the suffocating heat, the stench of fear, sweat, urine and feces—as some people lost control of their bodily functions. Many of the denizens of this hell seemed no longer human. Certainly collectively, we were no longer a society, just a mindless crowd. Each of us suffered in isolation, abandoned.

But even here, my father did not give up. We knew that there was a functioning hospital on the grounds and, after several hours of panic, my father managed to get there and telephone young Mr. Rowinski, apprising him of our plight. He also met several colleagues who gave him permission to bring us to the hospital proper. Although the hospital was periodically raided by the SS to fulfill the daily quota, on that day it was relatively safe as the *Umschlagplatz* was overflowing.

My father came back to the hall my mother and I were sitting in, and led us out into the open. Here too people were milling around and collecting near a fence surrounding the facility, trying to make contact with somebody or trying to bribe somebody to let them out. We ran to the hospital entrance and were admitted to its comparative haven. It was cooler there and much less crowded. Water was available, but most importantly, people there had some hope of rescue. Here we waited, our hearts in our mouths. Would young Rowinski come across on his promise of help? Would he prevail to get it to us on time? After several interminable hours, the impossible happened. Help came in the form of an ambulance driven by a German medic. We were hustled in. Other unfortunates looked in awe at our incredible luck. Some tried to get into the ambulance with us. But the German driver would have none of it. He was sent for us. That day we would be the only ones snatched from death. We could not jeopardize our luck by pleading with him for the other lives.

He drove us to the workshop where young Mr. Rowinski met us and took us to his parents' apartment on the Aryan side. Since it was now dark and past the curfew hour, we spent the night and the following day there, luxuriating in the safety, the plentiful food and the cleanliness. Here our shattered nerves had a brief and welcome rest, but we knew we could not stay for very long. We had to leave and face the horror outside again.

By now the pattern of the "Great Action" was firmly established. In the first few days, the human quota had been obtained from the population at large and consisted of volunteers, vagrants, inhabitants of refugee centers and other places where large numbers of helpless, unprotected people congregated and were easy to round up. After that, every morning a group of SS men and their auxiliary Ukrainian and Lithuanian minions surrounded a different small section of the Ghetto, several city blocks in size, and announced the "selection" on loudspeakers in the courtyards. The inhabitants were ordered out of the apartments, but as fewer and fewer complied willingly, the soldiers had to comb the apartments for their victims. The need for the tedious search infuriated the soldiers, so that the whole process was conducted amidst rage, shouting, dogs barking, resistance, gunfire and moaning; in short the bloody confusion of a battle, but with one side powerless to defend itself and the final outcome in no doubt.

It was by now clear that our papers identifying my father as a worker for Schulz and my mother and me as his dependents would be no help.

Our apartment was totally unsuited for hiding. Having been designed as a clinic, it lacked the cubbyholes, closets and other storage places which could be turned into effective hiding places. Its location on the edge of the Ghetto was also a disadvantage. As the number of Jews in Warsaw dropped, the Germans began to tighten the boundaries, with whole streets being turned over to the Poles. We hoped we were safe for a few days since the building had just been raided, but even that was no guarantee. My father made inquiries the very next day. We planned to move as soon as he found us a place.

Disaster struck again before we had a chance to move. Two days later, while my father was away at work, I looked out the window and saw a contingent of SS men and auxiliaries approaching our building along Nalewki Street. I grabbed my mother, and we ran down to the courtyard, yelling: "They are coming! They are coming!" Other tenants followed us, and soon we were a group of 15 or 20 terrified people, blindly running deeper and deeper into the second courtyard and then a third, hoping against hope for some miracle. At the end of the building, we ran into a one-story-high wall, separating us from safety. But how to get to the other side? There were three or four young men among us who could manage it, but the women and children, the old people? The Germans were in close pursuit, just a few minutes behind us. From the distance we heard their strident yells, their shots and the screams of the unfortunate victims they found. I spotted a couple of mattresses lying nearby on the ground: "Throw these over on the other side and we can jump onto them," I shouted to the nearest young man. With a possibility of a concerted action, we turned from a mob into a team, this sudden change perhaps the biggest miracle of all.

One young man climbed onto the shoulders of another and lifted himself onto the top of the wall. Briefly he surveyed the other side of the wall— another courtyard, silent and empty. Next, the two mattresses were thrown over to provide a cushion for our falls. Hastily, with the help of the last young man still on the ground, people were lifted to the top and jumped. My mother went over and then it was my turn. I was lifted to the top. The drop looked terrifying, but the greater terror lay behind me. I closed my eyes and jumped.

Shaken but unharmed, I stepped off the mattresses, making room for the next unlikely acrobat. Thus our whole group escaped capture. We scurried out of sight and landed in somebody's apartment where we spent the rest of the day. For a second time in just a few days, we escaped death by a combination of enterprise on our part and tremendous luck granted to us by whoever is in charge of such things.

In the evening we reluctantly returned to our apartment, in order to reunite with my father. He found us a place to live, together with our friends the Jellins. Carrying a minimum of personal belongings in a push-cart, we moved that very night.

Our new quarters, where we were to spend about a month, were located in a second courtyard of an old building. Careful examination revealed several potential hiding places, one of them a small, internal attic which could be accessed only by a ladder. We camouflaged the entrance with a large picture and decided the place would serve my mother and me. When necessary we could climb up, pull up the ladder and then Elizabeth Jellin could put the picture in place before scurrying to her own hiding place. Dr. Jellin, like my father, worked in a workshop as a doctor, so both men were out every day.

At first glance, the Jellins were an incongruous couple. Dr. Jellin was a big man, burly and jolly, with the dark hair and hooked nose which clearly marked him as a Jew in the eyes of the Nazis. He came from a poor, Orthodox family, and like my father had started his education in a *cheder* (Jewish parochial school). He could never shake the sing-song accent acquired in his childhood. A kindly man, he tried to lighten the atmosphere in the apartment by telling jokes and stories every night.

His wife, Elizabeth, was much younger, a slim, elegant creature, quite beautiful and clearly worshipped by her husband. She had come from a highly assimilated family and had a philosophy degree from a Warsaw university, a highly unusual distinction. Her Polish was impeccable and her connections with former, Aryan college friends were numerous. She would have followed her little daughter to the Aryan side long ago were it not for her husband, whose "Jewishness" was a severe liability.

We got along with the Jellins very well. By day we did a little housekeeping, read, talked a lot and waited for the men to come home with some food and news, knowing we had survived yet another day. I now realize that my father's life was much more difficult than ours. While performing his job, he was under constant pressure to report sick workers or their relatives to the authorities, thus endangering them in the next selection. On top of this he must have been consumed by continuous worry about us. Would he find us there that evening when he came home, or would the door be wide open, the apartment ransacked and all of us gone and lost to him?

The workers themselves were also in constant jeopardy. Inspections and selections were frequent. The strongest and the healthiest were exempt, while those who moved too slowly or looked too feeble to be efficient were sent to death. Children were rarely spared. Families were separated casually, with one member having to see a loved one disappear while trying to look unconcerned in order to avoid a like fate. Women wore make-up in an effort to look capable to work. In a movie or art, this would be called surrealistic. Alas, it was only too real.

As our numbers shrank, so did the Ghetto. The Little Ghetto had been lost to us long ago. Poles were already moving into the vacant apartments. One of the two Toebbens factories located in the Little Ghetto had to move. The Ghetto was becoming a series of islands consisting of the workshops separated by a no-man's land and raided periodically by the Germans in search of the illegals, now known as "barbarians" or the "wild ones." Elizabeth Jellin, my mother and I belonged to this group because we were not employed by a German workshop.

We survived two searches, our system working flawlessly. But in the middle of August we went through yet another miraculous event. It was 11 a.m., long past the usual times for an action. Gas and electricity were on, a rare event in those days, and we took advantage of it and did some housekeeping chores. Elizabeth had just washed her hair and her underwear, and, wearing only her robe, went out to hang them on the little balcony. She came back ashen-faced. "He has seen me! I am lost! Hide quickly, so you two may be saved," she cried. But there was no time for that. The young Ukrainian who had seen her immediately ran up the flight of stairs and kicked in the door to our apartment, surprising us all in the front room. "*Raus! Raus!*" he yelled, adopting the German of the occupiers. But now Elizabeth started to beg him for our lives. We are too young to die, she said feelingly in Russian, tears running down her face.

The young auxiliary saw in front of him a beautiful, blond woman. Perhaps she reminded him of someone he knew. Perhaps he was moved by hearing his mother tongue coming from a young woman's mouth. Perhaps, that day, he got out on the right side of the bed. He hesitated for a moment and then smiled. "All right," he said. "I will help you." He left the apartment, partially closing the door. A few moments later, we heard the steps of several soldiers in front of our door. "I already searched here. There is no one there," we heard our rescuer say.

Within a few minutes the soldiers were finished with our staircase and moved to the one across the courtyard. Peeking through the curtains we saw a slowly growing group of victims assembling in the court. One old man tried to run away, and our rescuer lifted his rifle and repeatedly clubbed him, until the bloody, lifeless body was sprawled on the cobblestones.

How do you explain the actions of a man, who, within an hour, saves the lives of three women and savagely kills an old man? This young man and others like him held countless lives in their hands. Yes, they could kill us all, but didn't it enhance their power if, from time to time, they could grant some of us life? Although I feel grateful to this young man for our lives, I question his motives, for I think they owed more to caprice and self-aggrandizement than to genuine altruism.

For that matter, how could we understand the reactions of our own people to the horror visited upon us? I think about my friend Zula's cousin, Robus. He was an adventurous young man, full of bravado and zest for life. He and his mother Freda were attached to the Toebbens workshop. During an early selection, Freda was selected for Treblinka and he for work. Unhesitatingly, he crossed the line and went to death with his mother. (The Germans almost always permitted this.) Mothers, husbands and other immediate relatives often made the same decision, but just as often they chose to live. Early deportees did not know their fate. Freda and Robus might not have. In any case I would not have guessed that Robus would prove so loving and heroic. With his courage, enterprise and connections on the Aryan side, he stood a good chance to survive, but gave it all up to be with his mother. And Freda... What a loss of a free spirit and poetic soul, and what a loss of a dear friend for me.

I believe that extreme, catastrophic demands for such choices do not change us. They just reveal what was there all the time. We don't know what lies behind the veneer of civilized behavior of those around us and of our own selves. It is only when we are stripped of this protection that we find out whether we are cowards or heroes, egoists or altruists, who really comes first in our hearts. It is all part of being human. I admire the people who chose to share death with their loved ones, but I do not condemn those who chose life, knowing the sacrifice to be futile.

One man who chose this sacrifice was the universally admired Dr. Janusz Korczak. He was a physician and an internationally known educator and writer. His life was devoted to children, for whom he wrote charming books. The best known was "King Matt the Great," the story of a heroic boy-king, who tried to reform his country. Korczak, whose real name was Henry Goldszmit, also presented a weekly radio program for young people and published a weekly newspaper for children in the form of an insert added to a Jewish daily. This was the newspaper where my letter to the editor had been published when I was about 11.

Korczak also ran a Jewish orphanage where he applied his educational theories. He was the best-known children's advocate in Poland, and worked on behalf of all, not just Jewish, children. For example, one of his books described the life of poor Christian children in Poland.

During the war Korczak devoted all his efforts to feeding and educating the children in his orphanage. He was forced to move the orphanage several times, using his connections to obtain new quarters for his children in the shrinking Ghetto. Each time, the children marched in an orderly formation, singing as they followed their beloved doctor. It was a prelude of things to come. In August, the Germans came to the orphanage. Korczak was so well-known that even the officer in charge of the action had heard of him and offered to exempt him from deportation. But the old doctor refused to abandon his children and marched at the head of their formation, the children singing and waving the Star of David and King Matt flags. What a picture that must have made! But even that did not soften the frozen German hearts, and the pitiful little brigade boarded the train at the *Umschlagplatz* and went to the gas chambers of Treblinka.

Towards the end of August, there was a brief respite from the deportations. It is estimated that by this time the Ghetto population was reduced to 120,000 people, about 50,000 of them legal. The respite was utilized for a feverish building spree. Like the catacombs in ancient Rome, a secret city was built under the Ghetto and up under the rooftops. Thousands of trap doors and secret entrances led to whole rooms camouflaged by bookcases or armoires. Narrow spaces under false floors, where people lay stacked like cordwood, became hiding places, as did cold, unfired ovens and garbage dumps. Elaborate bunkers, capable of sustaining life for a year or more and equipped with venting and air supply systems, were dug out under the cellars by those who could afford such luxuries. Suicide pills were distributed to avoid the agony of gas suffocation.

The thoughts of the young turned towards defense and revenge. For hundreds of years Jews had been persecuted all over Europe and the Middle East. We were exiled from some countries and suffered pogroms in others. The philosophy we had developed to deal with our tormentors had been, "Bend like a reed, and like a reed you shall survive. Yes, some would perish, but the majority will live." This method had worked, after a fashion, for centuries. Now, when it was failing us, we had no emotional or physical mechanisms for resistance or retaliation. Far away in Palestine, our people were standing tall and fighting the enemy. Here in the dying Ghetto, some decided to stand up and be counted as well. They would rather die fighting for the honor of our people than become sheep led to slaughter. Mostly, these were young people connected to Zionist and Labor movements in Warsaw and usually not responsible for any families. But before their uprising could come to fruition one more terrible action took place, an action we called the "Kettle."

On September 4, 1942, posters appeared in the Ghetto ordering all Jews to proceed the next day to the area bounded by Smocza, Gesia, Zamenhofa, and Szczesliwa Streets and Parysowski Square, an area comprising some 10 city blocks. The gathering, the posters announced, was for registration purposes. We were to bring food and water for two days and leave our apartments unlocked behind us. In the face of this deadline, decisions were made in haste and confusion. Should we stay behind and hide in houses which might not be part of the Ghetto in a few days, hide somewhere in the small designated area, or trust the working papers? What would we take with us if we decided to go in? Trusting his connections, my father decided we would go to the Mila Street Kettle (so named from the main street it contained).

The move was chaotic. As soon as we got into the Kettle, it was sealed off and all existing identification and passes were declared void. This action was a truly diabolical idea. The Germans now assigned a certain number of workers to each official enterprise and forced Jews to perform the selection for them.

The week we spent on Mila Street, in the cauldron, was utterly hellish. Over 100,000 people were jammed into a small area, 10 to 20 to a room. There were no beds for most of us, in some cases not even enough room to stretch out on the floor. The food we brought with us ran out after a couple of days and it was practically impossible to smuggle any more in, so tight was the seal the Germans put in place around us. Each family and each person suffered an anguish of his or her own. Who would get out and who would not? If one could not get a place in the ranks of the workers, where to hide afterwards? And what to do about the children?

Feverish negotiations and efforts to bribe the Jewish foremen who ran the German workshops continued all week. The entire "Kettle" population was like the contents of a pressure cooker, roiling with anxiety and despair. In a way it was even worse than the *Umschlagplatz*, since some had strong expectations of reprieve, others had none, and still others had some hope of escaping so that secret maneuvering, whispered conversations, and suspicions isolated us from each other as we were desperately contending for the available spaces. In the meantime the Germans, no longer hampered by such niceties as checking papers, combed the abandoned areas of the Ghetto. Whoever was left outside of the cauldron was, by definition, a "barbarian" and automatically subject to death or deportation. In all, about 50,000 Jews perished that week, almost one half of the remaining Ghetto residents. One can only imagine the frightful scenes as the victims were pulled out of their hiding places and manhandled to the *Umschlagplatz* and the trains.

My father had some alcohol with him, and made me drink a little of it every night to sedate me. Through young Mr. Rowinski he secured places for the three of us in the little Schultz contingent. My situation was the most iffy, for while my body was fully developed, my face was still childish and my short stature also contributed to making me look underage.

When the day to march out finally came, the workshop workers were formed into military-like battalions and passed a gauntlet of SS men, who checked the condition of the marchers and every once in a while pulled out some unfortunate soul who looked too old or too weak to be a real worker. Knapsacks were pierced with bayonets, sometimes evoking a cry of a young child concealed inside it, whereupon the bundle might be dashed to the ground and the parent allowed to proceed, or both would be pulled out of the line and sent to the trains, depending on the whim of the particular SS man. Babies and toddlers smuggled out were usually heavily sedated, their mouths taped so they would not innocently give themselves away. Some parents found later they had carried out a bloody corpse.

Our group was less than 1,000 strong. I was put in the middle of a row in order to attract minimum attention. To improve my chances for passing as an adult, I was wearing high heels, rouge and lipstick. I must have looked most incongruous in the midst of the raggedy crowd. But no one noticed this farcical aspect in the midst of the monumental catastrophe taking place all around us. I tried to make myself as inconspicuous as I could, keeping my eyes down and not making eye contact with the

Germans surrounding our brigade. All around me I heard shouting, sudden cries and shots as we slowly shuffled by.

Finally, we made it out of the Kettle, our own family intact but many in the group leaving behind loved ones. On that day, foundations were laid for life-long tragedies of mourning and despair.

I later became friendly with two women, Sonia and Niuta, both of whom left their little daughters in the Kettle. Of course, they left them hidden, expecting to get back to them later, but they were never able to do so. A "kind soul" told Sonia some time later that her little girl had been seen wandering in the street crying for her mommy. The child was too young to understand the gravity of the situation and must have left her hiding place. Sonia told me that this picture of her beloved child never left her head and tormented her day and night. Niuta cared for her husband's small niece who had been hidden on the Aryan side. The child's parents were shipped to Treblinka, and Niuta was bringing her up as her own. The husbands of both women had been in the Polish Army, went east in 1939 and were never heard from since. So the women struggled alone, trying to support and save themselves and their babies. When I knew them they were both consumed by sorrow and guilt. They should have gone to death with their little girls, they thought. Images of their children dying alone, frightened, hungry and thirsty, perhaps with no one to comfort them, while they themselves were surviving, never left their minds and their hearts.

The tragedy formed an insoluble bond between the two women. They shared their feelings and found some solace in shared grief, but they really did not care whether they lived or died. Sonia in particular became my friend and opened her heart to me. If their husbands survived, she told me time and time again, how could they confront the two men and tell them that they survived while their daughters did not? Their daughters were not torn out of their mothers' arms, but left behind callously (or so it now seemed to her) while their mothers were saving their own, worthless selves. I felt helpless in the face of this tragedy, but I could see then that even the end of the war would not bring a surcease of sorrow to many of the survivors.

When we left the Kettle we did not go back to our previous apartments, but to a house on Leszno Street adjoining the Schultz factory. There my father was assigned a tiny apartment, and my mother and I immediately reverted to the "barbarian" status. By now, all the workers had real working skills in operating the various knitting machines. My mother and I would not last a day before some German supervisor would spot our inadequacies and send us off to Treblinka. It was high time to go to the other side, no matter the risks involved.

We spent about a month in these quarters. There were no major new actions during that time. In fact they were not to resume until January 1943, but we could no longer kid ourselves that this was the end of the slaughter. It was only a matter of time until the Germans decided to liquidate the Warsaw Ghetto altogether, as they had already done in most of the other Polish towns. It was the time for "*sauve qui peut*" (save yourself if you can), as they say in French.

To call the area a ghetto was a misnomer, for this was now a large no man's land, punctuated by islands of life in and around the workshops. The cauldron area was searched immediately after we had left it, and now stood empty and forlorn. There was no legitimate traffic in the streets, which were deserted except for the Germans or groups of workers being marched to perform some task. Low-level selections in the workplace continued uninterrupted, periodically culling out those faltering from hunger, fear or indifference to life. During the day, the living quarters might be inspected at any time, rooting out the few "barbarians" who had managed to elude all the previous nets.

We had a hiding place in our apartment, but outside help was needed to hide and later release us. The walls of Warsaw buildings were very thick. In the kitchen, a cupboard had been built into the wall under the window, a foot deep and about six feet wide. It served as a natural cold storage area for perishable foods, since it was vented to the outside. There were two shelves inside with just enough room to accommodate my mother and me lying one on each shelf. My father would then drag a heavy kitchen table, laden with dishes and pots, in front of the cupboard to camouflage it. Luckily, my father always had advance notice of a possible search, so we did not have to spend all our days hidden away. But we did spend several interminable ones lying there, unable to move in almost total darkness, several times hearing German or Polish voices as the apartment was being searched.

To the discomfort of cramped muscles was added the need to go the bathroom. Wetting myself was a sign of loss of self-respect in my eyes and I fought it successfully each time. Perhaps the severity of the physical discomfort helped to distract me partially from the awful fear of being found.

My father was usually unable to come during the day and check up on us or give us momentary relief. When he did come in the evening, we would drag ourselves out, crying from the pain as our cramped muscles revived.

On the good days we just suffered from boredom, hunger and anxiety. One day, somebody gave my father the Polish translation of *Gone with the Wind*. For the next few days, I was able to escape my own reality and live with Scarlett through the American Civil War. I was just of an age to dream about romance with a handsome, mysterious, dark stranger, but had little opportunity to indulge in such pursuits. I deliberately tried to lose myself in daydreams, to distance myself, at least temporarily, from the dreadful reality.

The Civil War itself seemed pretty mild compared to what we were going through, with chances of human contact between adversaries abounding both during and after the conflict. I could not even imagine a kind German anymore. As for the war, it stretched into the future seemingly without end. We had already gone through so many moves, miraculous escapes and bizarre twists and turns that the future seemed totally murky. It was impossible to foresee what might still happen to us.

My father explored several possibilities to leave the Ghetto through his contacts with the Polish workers at the Schultz workshop. His wonderful personality was yet again coming to our aid, for even under those terrible conditions he was liked and respected by the Poles at the factory. Finally we settled on what seemed the best possibility for us. Our Polish friend Mr. Rozwadowski had two aunts, one a working widow with two barely adult sons and her sister Olga, an almost blind, elderly spinster. The family was barely getting by on the widowed aunt's earnings. Olga was unable to keep house, making life extremely difficult for all of them. They lived in Konstancin, a small resort near Warsaw. The boys and Mrs Rozwadowski commuted to Warsaw daily, she to work and they to school. We would pay reasonable rent for one of the bedrooms, and my mother and I would take care of the housekeeping as well as serve as company to Olga.

At first only my mother and I were to go to test the arrangements. If all proved satisfactory to both sides, my father was to join us. He still felt reasonably safe in his job, so it made sense not to burn our bridges, but I am sure now that there was an unspoken agenda underlying my parents' decision. My father felt that on the Aryan side he represented a liability to us. My mother was a blonde (though rapidly going gray) with blue-eyes. She spoke very good Polish with a slight Russian accent and, super-ficially, could pass very easily for a Pole. I had light brown hair, a straight little turned-up nose and spoke perfect, unaccented Polish. To this day, when I meet Poles they remark on the purity of my accent, a Polish equiv-alent to Oxford English.

My father, on the other hand, was very dark with black facial hair which required two shaves a day, and a sing-song accent he was unable to get rid of. Where we were acceptably petite, he was just short, and Poles tended to be blonde, tall and usually handsome. Of course there are plen-ty of short, dark Poles, and they must have been challenged frequently during the war, but it was easy for them to prove their Polishness. They spoke the right way, knew all the prayers, had all the right papers, were known to many relatives, neighbors and co-workers, and—as a final resort—could prove they were not circumcised by just dropping their pants.

The subject was never articulated in my presence, but I am convinced my father was trying to buy us safe time by not joining us until he had no choice.

The arrangements took several weeks, with Mr. Rozwadowski acting as an intermediary between the two parties while carrying some of our pos-sessions out of the Ghetto in his briefcase, a little at a time. At last, all was ready. We had our false I.D. papers adorned with our pictures, my false name being Barbara Lozinska. We dressed like a woman and girl spending a day in the big city, and received instructions on who would meet us as well as an admonition not to talk in public places. We made our tearful farewells and took our places in the column of Poles returning home from work. Thus, in the center of the protective column, we walked out of hell.

CHAPTER 10

OUT OF THE GHETTO

Walking out of the Ghetto in October 1942 presented immediate dangers. Young hoodlums congregated near the Ghetto gates, preying on the escapees, extorting money from them until these poor souls were penniless, threatening them with exposure, often following them and repeatedly forcing them into house entrances. If the tormentors were sufficiently anti-Semitic, they might inform on them to the nearest German in a uniform.

The closest check point to the Schultz workshop was on the corner of Leszno and Zelazna, a short distance from the factory. My mother and I walked out with the contingent of Poles employed at the factory, but two blocks away we were met by a Polish policeman in uniform. This was part of the arrangement with Mr. Rozwadowski to protect us from the extortionists, and it worked perfectly. No one bothered us as the tall, powerful man led us to the tram. We boarded, the policeman paying our fares, and traveled to our train station. There, he procured tickets for us and stayed with us until we met Mrs. Irene Rozwadowska. We had never met, but she had instructed us through her nephew exactly where to go in the station and described what she would be wearing. We had also described ourselves so well that we recognized each other readily, even though the station was teeming with evening commuters. The policeman left us and Mrs. Rozwadowska instructed us to follow her, but to sit apart from her on the train in case some acquaintance of hers was nearby. She gave each of us something to read so we would look inconspicuous and busy. Once we got off in Konstancin some 40 minutes later, we followed her to the villa. Just in case we got separated, she gave us a little map of how to get to the villa.

The journey went without any problems. My hands were slippery with perspiration, so strange and frightening was the experience. I had spent the last three months in almost total isolation, fearing for my life every minute throughout. My only contacts had been with other Jews. Even before the war my only significant contacts with Aryans had been restricted to our maids. To find myself now amidst all this normality was bizarre. I literally had to pinch myself to make sure I really was sitting on a train, pretending to read and surreptitiously listening to conversations around me.

Even though the Poles were also suffering and in the middle of a hostile occupation, the topics being discussed seemed so odd and trivial to me. Prices of food, what was playing at some cinema, the sickness of a neighbor, plans for the weekend, what to wear to a party—all commonplace and casually normal. These people were speaking my language, yet sitting on that train I experienced the greatest culture shock of my life. I cannot even say that I envied them, since they appeared to me like creatures from Mars.

While watching the commuters on the train, my thoughts kept going back to the Ghetto, to my father, to my people suffering the ultimate horrors. At the same time here, just a few blocks away, people were living normal, albeit difficult lives, going to work, children going to school, openly shopping in stores, cooking meals in well-lit kitchens, taking walks and doing all those things that most people take for granted, and of which we had been deprived for so long.

Konstancin was a sleepy little town, a whistle stop on the train route. It was dark when we arrived, and there were few street lights, but I could just glimpse gracious villas, each surrounded by a garden, wide streets, shaded by enormous trees and, although there was no curfew here, an almost complete absence of people. People we did meet nodded to us or called out a greeting, as people do in small towns. Before the war, Konstancin had been a bustling resort similar to the Catskill resorts near New York, but now the heavily Jewish crowds were gone and only the year-round inhabitants remained.

The villa where the Rozwadowskis lived, like most others, was three sto-ries high and subdivided into several apartments. We climbed one flight of outdoor stairs leading directly to their apartment. Here we were final-ly greeted openly and graciously by our hostess, while her sister Olga, a very emotional lady, hugged and kissed us, tears flowing down her face. "Thank God you reached us safely," she exclaimed. "You must be hungry and exhausted after your ordeal."

There was some stew waiting for us, prepared the previous night by our hostess, and now heated hurriedly. Irene's two sons came in soon after, and we all sat around the kitchen table, eating bread and stew and drink-ing hot tea. Just then I thought I had died and gone to heaven. Irene pro-claimed that we were all too tired for any serious discussion that evening, so the talk was kept light and simple. After dinner we were shown to our room, washed up and slid between the miraculously clean, white sheets. A new phase of my life was about to begin!

The next day we had a discussion to set down the parameters of our life with the Rozwadowskis. It was decided that it was safer for us to stay hidden, in spite of the false papers we had, since we were not sure how much scrutiny we, or our papers, could bear. The villa was sturdily built, with good insulation. Still, whenever everyone was out we would have to be quiet and not run the water or flush the toilet. This did not present any problem, since Olga only went out to do the food shopping. However, she had to do this in several stores, lest the increased quanti-ties of her purchases be noticed. Small towns are like that, and during the war everyone was so focused on food that anything to do with it was very noticeable. So Olga would go out every day for an hour or two, tap-tapping her cane as she went.

We were not to go near the windows, particularly when they were open. Most of the time in the winter, the windows were closed. But even so, someone might see an unfamiliar silhouette through the curtains. At night, the blackout drapes were closed, so it was safe for us to move any-where in the apartment.

Irene and the two boys, Lutek and Bolek, went out every day but Sunday, but Olga was always around, except for shopping. On Sundays, Lutek and Olga always attended a mass, while Irene and Bolek went only occasion-ally and under duress.

The Rozwadowskis gave us the biggest bedroom to compensate for our enforced confinement. It was a light, airy room furnished simply with two beds, a chest of drawers, an armoire (there were practically no built-in closets in Poland), and a round table with four chairs. I got to know this room very intimately, since my mother and I tried to keep out of the family's way. We had to stay here whenever visitors came as well.

The two sisters moved into the boys' room, and Lutek and Bolek slept in the main room, one on the couch and the other on a folding cot. This, along with a large, eat-in kitchen, a walk-in pantry and a bathroom, completed the apartment. All the rooms were large with high ceilings and big windows, modestly but comfortably furnished. But since one always wants what one can't have, I soon yearned to be out in the open, in the streets and gardens which I could glimpse so tantalizingly through the curtains.

Irene was a reserved, somewhat formal lady, but we soon learned of her essential goodness and kindness. The stony veneer was probably a combination of her high-class upbringing and basic shyness. The family had originated in Russia and escaped to Poland after the Bolshevik Revolution.

After the death of Irene's husband, the family fell on hard times, becoming "shabby genteel," as the British say, meaning aristocracy fallen on hard times. Working in a doctor's office in Warsaw and thus acting as the sole breadwinner of the family weighed heavily on Irene's mind. Whenever possible, she turned to her nephew for support and advice. I suspect that he also helped her financially from time to time. Before we came there, she also had to do all the housekeeping after coming home in the evening, since Olga's attempts at cleaning usually resulted in more damage than help.

Hiding a Jewish family presented a great danger. If found out, the hosts might perish along with the refugees. But for our hosts, the benefits were enormous also. Irene could now put up her feet at night, knowing that the cooking and cleaning were done. Olga's life changed even more, as she acquired day-long companions. I became her special friend and read aloud to her for hours every day.

It must be said that the Rozwadowskis were not motivated by material reward and reasons of convenience alone. They clearly had no anti-Semitic feelings. In fact, they felt sorry for their Jewish compatriots and sincerely wished to do their share to save somebody's life. They were totally scrupulous in their financial dealings with us, charging us the going price for the room, paying their share for the food, and bringing receipts for any little items we requested.

Olga in particular was the dearest of women, kindhearted and altruistic. Her goodness helped us to feel human again. She had been an actress in her youth and proudly showed me her pictures from the past and told me the stories of her successes, both professional and romantic. Indeed, she had been a beauty then, and one could still see traces of it in her ravaged face. Her past was very important to her. She tended to live there and talk about it a lot. I got to hear some of her stories many times, since her memory was far from perfect. But she had a willing audience in me, both because I was very fond of her and because her stories distracted me from the miserable present times.

Deeply religious, she bore her affliction of near blindness with dignity and resignation, telling me how grateful she was to God for the comfortable home and the food He provided, and now for the joy of our company. Since the housekeeping was not too onerous, it took only a small part of our time. While Olga shopped I spent the time studying and reading. When she came back, she heard my compositions and grammar and asked questions about history and geography, turning everything into a story. Only then would we both joyfully turn to my reading aloud whatever romance we were currently reading. From her I acquired my taste for romantic novels, which I still enjoy reading when I am tired, dispirited, or just before going to sleep as they are an excellent soporific agent.

For my studies, I used Lutek's and Bolek's old high-school books. Lutek was studying to become a priest, which did not stop him from flirting with me. He occasionally took me out for little walks in the evening, just around the block or in our villa's garden. We soon became good friends, arguing many philosophical questions and amicably disagreeing on many issues. He was deeply religious, and I was inclined to be a cynic just then. Lutek and Olga were the two most religious members of the family, believing in a very personal God who looked out for them, whom one could beg for mercy, or even bargain with. I never argued with Olga, but in my discussions with Lutek I had no such reservations. How could God permit the slaughter I had just witnessed? How could anyone summon enough blind faith to say God knew best under such circumstances? Of course, these discussions never led to any resolution, but helped me to vent my anger and disillusionment. I think Lutek understood this and was willing to absorb my feelings. Towards the end of our stay, feelings between us began to turn romantic, and some smooching accompanied our rare walks.

Bolek disapproved of this development on the grounds of safety and out of fear for Lutek's conscience. Bolek was much less religious than his brother and much more practical. He was studying engineering at the Warsaw Polytechnic Institute and helped me with math at night. I think he was rather impressed with my ability and fond of me, but he repeatedly cautioned both Lutek and me not to get involved. There was no future in it and a possibility of great emotional damage. It is a measure of my trust in these people that I never felt I was endangering my family with my actions. Indeed, such an idea never occurred to Bolek. Nevertheless, I now realize I was being very foolish. Probably I could not help myself. Teenage romances are so irresistible and, in light of the political atmosphere, the feeling was reinforced by a sense of urgency to experience life before it was too late.

After some time, it was decided that my mother should occasionally surface, lest friends and neighbors become suspicious of the eternally closed door to the bedroom. She was introduced to guests as a distant relative with an ailing daughter spending time with the Rozwadowskis. Since my mother had a very similar upbringing to that of the two sisters, she made a very plausible relative: another cultured, impoverished lady, who spoke with a slight Russian accent. One friend, on being introduced to her and hearing the name Lozinska, asked if she was related to Bishop Lozinski, with whom he was slightly acquainted. My mother replied demurely that she did not think so but that it was possible, particularly if the Bishop had come from Russia.

I was never allowed to join the company, ostensibly because of my "illness." Privately I thought then—as I do now—that at least some of the neighbors suspected the truth about us, but were decent people and good friends who would never put the Rozwadowskis in jeopardy.

Several times while my mother and I were in the bedroom, we overheard conversations outside concerning the fate of the Polish Jews. Some visitors loudly expressed their sympathy for the Jews and strong disapproval of German policy and actions against the Jews. Perhaps these were meant to be signals to the Rozwadowskis and to us that we were among friends, but we could not be sure and the stakes were much too high to respond to any such overtures.

We communicated with my father through Mr. Rozwadowski, whom Irene saw sometimes in the city, although Mr. Rozwadowski never visited in the eight months we were there. My father continued to send our clothes as well as his own. We learned that he soon became satisfied that we had found as safe a haven as it was possible to reach in these danger-ous times. Still, he hesitated to join us. His position as the factory doctor and young Rowinski's friend made for relative safety. By now he even knew Schultz, the German owner of the workshop. Hiding with us would strip him of his position and limit his options.

My mother's personality, placid and content, was well suited to pro-longed inactivity and to coping with the constant danger without show-ing any anxiety. My mother had her daily duties which kept her physical-ly active and pleasantly occupied. She was proud of how clean the apart-ment was, taking pleasure in the secret knowledge that it was actually her work that friends of the Rozwadowskis complimented our hosts on.

Cooking demanded a lot of imagination, since the choice of available foods was severely limited. Root vegetables such as carrots, parsnips, potatoes and turnips were readily available and relatively inexpensive. Lamb and pork, the only two meats we could afford, and even then in limited quantities, were used to provide flavor and some protein to our meals. When we first arrived, fall fruits were still on the market, and my mother put to good use the knowledge she had acquired back in Slonim, putting up some jams for the winter. She cooked endless stews, using herbs to vary their taste. Bread was also sufficient, but milk, butter and eggs were luxuries we rarely indulged in. I know my mother derived a great deal of pleasure from putting on the table tasty, nutritious meals, a difficult job under the circumstances, and she enjoyed our appreciation of her efforts.

Mr. Rozwadowski sent us some goodies from time to time. Anything extra which came into the house was shared by all of us equally. In all the time we were there, not one angry word was exchanged between us and our hosts, not just because we were cautious, but also because they were such genuinely good people.

In January 1943 Himmler visited the Warsaw Ghetto and personally ordered the deportation of 8,000 more Jews, but this new action proved very different from the previous ones. Not one Jew went peacefully. Most stayed in the carefully prepared hiding places while some resisted force-fully. The Germans could win easily in street battles; they had the overwhelming force and supplies. But the guerrilla warfare in the cellars, staircases and corridors inside the buildings favored the Jews, who knew the terrain intimately and had nothing to lose. After a few days the action was discontinued, but it was a further blow to the sense of security of the remaining denizens of the Ghetto.

After this, my father finally lost his faith in his personal luck, and came out to join us sometime in February of 1942. He came dressed as a worker, his face adorned with a long mustache he had grown especially for this purpose, a worker's cap on his head, and earmuffs helping to hide most of his face. Back in the Ghetto, he went into hiding during the action, moving from place to place, one night sleeping in a child's crib, always in grave danger. He was very pessimistic about the viability of the Ghetto remnant and, after the brief joy of reunion, very depressed over the situation.

My father brought with him the Ghetto mentality. His first thought after inspecting the apartment was to equip us with a hiding place. The pantry, located in a little hall off the kitchen, provided the only suitable space. He built a false, shallow closet so that the door to the pantry opened onto shelves designed for storing food. The pantry was pretty bare anyway and served no useful purpose. In order to get to the hiding place, the shelves had to be removed, after which the partition could be swung open enough to allow three people to sit on chairs. There was an electric light, but we dared not use it, lest someone open the door and see the light through chinks between the partition and the other walls.

We used this hiding place a number of times, effectively convincing our hosts' visitors that there was no one but the legal residents occupying the apartment. It was uncomfortable, dark, and boring. We could not even sneeze, let alone talk. But it was never scary, as it was used only when friends came to visit, never the police or the Gestapo.

One of our greatest fears concerned the Rozwadowski boys' involvement with the underground. If either of them was ever caught, not only he, but his whole family and, by extension, ourselves, would be doomed. We would have preferred if this danger did not hang over our heads, but we accepted it. The two young men were Polish patriots and very anti-German. Surely they had a right to risk their lives in a cause with which we identified as well, at least with the anti-German part of it. It was a subject never discussed openly, but we all knew about it, in part by dint of the underground newspapers the boys brought home.

These provided us with the best source of news, which at that juncture was not very good. The Allies made some advances in Africa, but that seemed very distant and irrelevant to us. The Americans had not yet begun to retake the Pacific islands they had lost to Japan, although some sea battles seemed to go their way. The Pacific war theater also seemed remote and unimportant, merely distracting U.S. armies, supplies, and energy from the more pressing war in Europe. The Eastern Front also seemed bogged down, a stalemate with much loss of material and life on both sides. Much to the chagrin of the Russians, who were taking the brunt of the fighting, the much-vaunted "Second Front" was not materializing. The oppressed peoples in Europe were also greatly disheartened by this lack of action.

The only bright spot on the horizon was the ever-increasing severity of Allied bombing in Germany. At least the German population was beginning to suffer losses of their homes and loved ones. Shortages were developing. The German armaments industry could not compete with that of the Americans, who were rapidly getting their act together. But even this was a double-edged sword, for the more shortages the Germans suffered, the more they squeezed the occupied countries.

News from the Ghetto was sparse. Everything there remained quiescent, the inhabitants believing that their resistance in January had bought them their lives. Nevertheless, they spent the time between January and April fortifying the bunkers, training their little fighting force, and buying as many weapons as possible from the Polish underground.

On April 18, news of an imminent action reached the Ghetto and triggered the final Ghetto uprising. The outcome was never in doubt. For the fighters, it was a matter of vindicating their honor in their own eyes and in the eyes of the world. The gallant fighting force held out for over a month, longer than all of Poland managed to hold off Hitler. Few of them survived. Those that did survive got out through the sewers, and went on to fight with the partisans, or hid on the Aryan side. The Germans were forced to burn the entire Ghetto, house by house and street by street, in order to flush out the Jews from their hiding places.

At the end, many fighters committed suicide rather than fall into German hands, scenes which must have been reminiscent of the Massada. In all, between 50,000 and 60,000 Jews were rounded up and executed, while German losses measured in the hundreds. Still, it was a complete reversal in Jewish philosophy and attitude toward the tormentors of our people.

It proved to be the stuff of legend, a vindication of our national character, a source of pride mixed with sorrow. When the Ghetto was completely destroyed, the Germans dynamited the Great Synagogue on Tlomackie Street located outside of the Ghetto to signal their victory and the end of Jewish life in Warsaw.

My father warned us that the Germans were just regrouping and would never swallow the insult that Jewish resistance represented to them. The day our hosts told us about the uprising was a black day for us, as were the days to follow. Irene brought us news from her nephew, tactfully trying to play down the catastrophe. Lutek and Bolek, however, supplied us with the Polish resistance accounts, which were more explicit and lauded the Jews for their fighting spirit. When it was over, officially there were no Jews alive in Warsaw, and more than ever we felt completely alone, although we knew that there were many others hidden like ourselves.

In addition to this sorrow, another worry was overtaking us that spring of 1943— money. In 1939 and 1940, we had sent the bulk of our savings to Uncle Solomon in America. The war had now lasted close to four years, and the end was still not in sight. In those four years, my father had been able to work and support us only a quarter of the time. The rest of the time we had been living off the savings we had not shipped out, and at this point we were down to less than $2,000, my mother's diamond engagement ring and the diamond lavaliere she had inherited from her mother, which was concealed in the heel of my father's shoe and may have been irreparably broken. The heel of the shoe had been hollowed by a shoemaker and then reinstalled by him with the jewels in place. Such a hiding place would survive almost any search, no matter how intrusive. My father was careful to wear these precious shoes only in crisis situations to preserve the precarious integrity of this hiding place. Ironically, the lavaliere now resides in my safe-deposit box and still rarely sees the light of day. I hope, someday, to give it to my granddaughter.

We had lived modestly, at times austerely, through the past years, spending only on essentials, but one's judgment of what is essential is relative. Our definition of essential included such expenditures as my education, vaccination against typhus and sufficient and nutritious food, as well as all those expensive moves east and then back to Warsaw. I believe our resources could have stretched out another year or a little more. We scoured the newspapers anxiously, trying to judge the progress of the war, but at the time it seemed most unlikely that we would win this life and death struggle.

It was clear that, kind as they were, the Rozwadowskis could not house and feed us for free. They were barely surviving as it was. We made no secret of our dilemma. Was there any work we could do in the room? Could my mother get a job outside? If so, doing what? She seemed untrained for anything except housework, and few people were hiring housekeepers just then.

In June 1943, Mr. Rozwadowski sent word of a possible solution to our problem. The scheme seemed very problematic to us, but by then we were getting pretty desperate.

Some wealthy Jews living in South America were trying to get their relatives out of Poland. They undertook to support those relatives until the latter could get back on their feet financially so that the immigrants would never be a burden to the state. The papers were drawn up and confirmed by the governments of the various countries. They were called "promessas" (promises), and were really a sort of permission to immigrate given by a certain country. Thus, a Venezuelan promessa might say that a Joseph Greenbaum and his family, currently residing in Poland, would be admitted to Venezuela as immigrants and that a Moses Greenbaum, citizen of Venezuela, undertook to provide for them as long as necessary. The big difference between these papers and ordinary immigration certificates obtained, say, from the United States or Palestine, was that the South American papers were issued not to individuals, but to entire families, naming only the head of the family and not specifying the number of family members.

There were about 100 such promessas issued and sent to Switzerland, which was acting as a go-between in the matter. By 1943 the German government was experiencing all sorts of shortages and looking for ways to buy supplies abroad, using their Swiss connection as one of the links with the outside world. The deal was to be an exchange of the Jewish families named on the promessas for trucks and gasoline, supplies which although not strictly classified as armaments were still vital to the German war effort.

This was a cynical deal, since at the time of the negotiations the Warsaw Ghetto, where the families in question had lived, was no longer in existence, and the few survivors were scattered in death camps or hidden somewhere in Poland. No matter—the promessas contained no photographs, and any Jews would do.

The German authorities designated a safe house in Warsaw—the Hotel Polski. No one was to be harassed in the hotel or its vicinity. This promise was scrupulously fulfilled during the proceedings there. The job of collecting the families named in the promessas was assigned to a crew consisting of members of the German and Jewish Gestapos. The Jewish Gestapo were also in hiding, but maintained contact with their bosses and helped them to root out other Jews. These scoundrels saw their orders as a potential windfall. Since no legitimate family members could be found, they decided to sell memberships in these families. To maximize their profits and surely not to save more Jews, they packed these "families," assigning about 30 or 40 members to each promessa and doing their job very carelessly indeed. Some "sons" were clearly older than their "mothers," and people with all sorts of accents, backgrounds, educational levels, or even countries of origin were assigned to one "family." Clearly, however, the Jewish Gestapo believed in the scheme, since they inscribed themselves and their wives and children as family members, and eventually came along.

Years later, in 1996, when we revisited Poland, I had an argument with our Polish guide in Warsaw about the legitimacy of the Hotel Polski affair. He was the only Pole I had met who had even heard of this scheme, which, in his opinion, was a gigantic Gestapo hoax designed to capture a large number of Jews hidden in Warsaw. He was too young to remember these events, and must have heard the stock explanation ascribed by the Poles to any German plan: Everything the Germans did was designed to harm both Jews and Poles. Events, however, argue otherwise in this case. I do believe that some exchange negotiations had taken place and that the authorities ordered the assembly of a contingent of Jews, should the exchange talks prove successful, without looking too closely into the methods of this assembly. They acted in good faith because the goods that they were exchanging for Jews were so sorely needed.

My mother was chosen as our family representative. Because of her quasi-Aryan appearance she could travel with the least amount of risk. After two days she sent word that the plan appeared legitimate, but that we could not afford places on a promessa. However, a list was being compiled of families with relatives in Palestine who would be willing to take them in. Places on this list were cheaper, because there were no official papers. We would be going under our own names, and we really did have relatives in Tel Aviv, namely Aunt Sonia and Uncle Maniek, who no doubt would be happy to have us. My mother had consulted with the people in the hotel, and recommended that we take the plunge. In fact, we did not have many options left. Gambling on the war ending before our money did was just too unnerving and risky.

Accordingly, the next day we bid farewell to our hostesses and departed. We never saw the Rozwadowskis again. We knew that we were to be replaced by the elderly Mr. and Mrs. Rowinski, friends of my grandfather. We found out later that they survived the rest of the war in the apartment, and later moved to Israel where my father met them. There was never any mention of young Mr. Rowinski, so I have to assume that he did not make it.

Lutek perished in the Warsaw uprising. Years later, I heard Bolek emigrated to Belgium, but I was unable to get his address and contact him.

I had spent these last eight months communicating only with my parents, the two sisters, and Bolek and Lutek. Except for a few clandestine evening walks, I had not left the apartment for the entire time. Emerging that morning nicely dressed and going to the city with Irene Rozwadowska felt very strange. My father traveled with us, but insisted that we pretend not to know each other. He was dressed again as a working man and felt it was safer for me if he was not part of our group. Nothing unusual happened on the trip. My recollections of it once again focused on my instinctive amazement that life for other people went on serenely, while we were experiencing such dangers and upheavals—the same feeling I had had on my way to Konstancin. Of course, this was a naive observation. You really cannot tell what people think and feel when you travel with them on a train.

We took the tram and got off a few blocks from Hotel Polski. Here, Mrs. Rozwadowska showed me the way to the hotel and left after hugging and kissing me. She did not want to be seen in the vicinity since she was taking in another Jewish family. My father joined me, and together we entered the hotel.

How exhilarating to see Jews all around me! All of us had come out of some kind of isolation. Even those who had moved around had gone under false identities. We were overjoyed to be able to speak freely, exchange stories, and just be ourselves without fear of offending anyone. I realized that, nice as the Rozwadowskis were, we had felt obliged to present a cautious front to them, seldom articulating our true feelings in their presence.

We were also all buoyed by the hope of an exchange. We were taking a terrible risk, but every one of us had taken risks before. We were a group of survivors. We would not have gotten this far without enterprise, daring and luck. This time, however, a miracle was being dangled in front of our noses, and its sweet name was Switzerland.

That is not to say that there was no sadness. Never again in my life would I experience unadulterated joy without a memory of those who did not survive. I did not meet anyone I knew at the hotel, but I heard tragic news about many of my friends and others. We heard that my friend Zula and her family had been taken to Treblinka. It was hard to accept that these good, vital people were no more, but the thoughts of their terrible suffering and death were so painful, I tried to blot them out at the time. Even being able to grieve openly was a luxury to us. Now that the days of hiding were over, I really understood the oppressive effects of secrecy and isolation and, in spite of sadness and grief, the presence of companions in misery helped to lift somewhat the continuous depression I had felt for the past eight months.

My parents arranged for our names to be put on the Palestinian list, and were able to purchase a few necessities from the Polish merchants who were freely trading inside the hotel. We had arrived dressed for a day in the city, and although we hoped for a speedy rescue, it was expeditious to provide ourselves with a change of clothing and some extra underwear, as well as a few toiletries. The hotel was jammed with people, but I don't think anyone minded, so great was our need for togetherness and a sense of belonging— a sense of being among our own. Our stay there was very brief, a mere two days. Sleeping on the floor was a small price to pay for the feeling of community we received in return. One contingent had already left, and we were to be the second and final group. I heard later that Jews who lingered in the hotel after we left were rounded up within hours and sent to Treblinka.

We left by buses, and boarded passenger trains, all signs of German good faith. The train was full, but each of us had a seat. The Germans were polite. The windows were not boarded up, although they were curtained, and we were instructed not to show our faces at the stations we would be passing. The trip, we were told, would last two days and a night, and we were issued sufficient food for that length of time. All this, we consoled ourselves, was very different from the treatment on the death trains, where the victims were jammed into cattle cars so full there was no room to lie down, and transported without light, food, water or sanitary facilities, and even with insufficient air to breathe. Many died on the way, particularly if the trip was long.

We left early in the afternoon, and now came the final good sign: we were traveling into the sun! We were traveling west! We were not going east towards the horrors of Treblinka, nor south towards that other frightening place called Oswiecim (Auschwitz). By nightfall, we heard German spoken at the stations and saw the German names of the towns we were passing. Sometime during the night we passed Berlin. The city loomed huge and ghostlike in the darkness, closed in upon itself, no streetlights, nor lights in any windows. Obviously, a blackout was being enforced in preparation for air raid attacks. In fact, as we were moving away we heard the sounds of distant sirens. The Allies were utilizing night bombardment, denying their enemies the peaceful hours of sleep and increasing the tempo of the encroaching chaos.

The next day we continued west, and in the daylight were able to observe the ruins, the great holes in the ground. The devastation visited upon the Germans by almost unchecked Allied air force was staggering. We rejoiced at this evidence of German suffering, and "our" success, greedily counting all such ruins and cheering at the sight of each.

At the same time on this long train ride, we were experiencing a reality check. Our exuberance was fading and fear was creeping in again into our minds. Where were we going? The cognoscenti among us saw no veering south towards Switzerland, not even after we passed Berlin during the night. Where were we going? What was to become of us? We hoped we would at least end up in France in one of the spas converted into camps for foreign citizens from the West, and reputed to have a "hotel-like" atmosphere. We told ourselves that we might be stopping someplace where we would await the final arrangements for our exchange. But in our hearts we feared the worst. Finally, the second day came to an end. So far all the German statements had proved true. Late in the evening, the train pulled up at a tiny station, and we saw a name dangling from the roof of the covered platform: "Bergen-Belsen."

CHAPTER 11

BERGEN-BELSEN

A totally chaotic scene met my eyes. It was June 1943, and we had been traveling through silent, dark countryside, debilitated from the 36-hour trip and the uncertainty of our fate at the end of it. Suddenly, bright flood lights were lit in the little station, the doors of the train were opened, and strident German voices were yelling *"Alles raus!"* (everybody out) and *"Mach schnell!"* (hurry up). Uniformed SS men with gleaming, highly polished boots, leading ferocious dogs on leashes, seemed to be everywhere. The barking of the dogs only added to the general confusion of sounds, orders, and the frightened people trying to obey them unconditionally.

We descended from the train, which up to now had been a safe refuge, and were ordered to march along a road stretching before us. No information was given, but several open trucks appeared to transport the aged and women with small children to wherever we were going. The road passed through a forest looming all around us in the dark. I have walked this road only twice, each time filled with fear, so I remember little of it. Certainly it seemed interminably long, but was probably only a mile or so in length. We were allowed to walk at our own pace, not in any formation. The laggards behind were picked up by the trucks and taken to the camp, with the trucks periodically returning to pick up the next batch. Our family had practically no luggage, but some of the other people were lugging heavy suitcases, barely able to manage without the trucks.

Emerging from the forest, we passed two barbed-wire gates and found ourselves in a vast enclosure. This, evidently, was the camp proper. Some in our group were familiar with the name. People said it in the same breath with Dachau, Buchenwald, Mauthausen and others. All these terrible names evoked equal dread. Walking along the road, we could see only a small part of the camp, but it appeared to be surrounded by a double row of barbed wire punctuated by wooden watch towers placed at regular intervals, from which search lights were continuously playing over the entire area.

Overwhelmed with fatigue, I had no time to ponder the implications of the unfolding events. The feeling of dread descended on me again.

Since it was late at night, the place looked ghostly and deserted. The road we had walked on continued inside and became the main road of the camp, a broad, unpaved, dusty, hard-packed thoroughfare which would turn into a sea of mud when it rained. On both sides we saw barracks, some brick and others wooden, some arranged into little formations, others placed haphazardly here and there at crazy angles. Some of the barracks were quite close to each other, while others had quite a bit of space around them. Barbed wire was everywhere. It separated the camp into enclaves and rose high on each side of the road we were following.

Finally, our crowd was ordered to turn left, where there was yet another guarded barbed-wire gate, and we entered the area designated for us. We were told that things would be sorted out tomorrow, but, for now, we were just to occupy the barracks in any order, and we were counted off, so many per room.

Inside the barrack, things were quite disorganized. The wooden hall was filled with three-tiered bunks made of rough wood, with slats supporting straw mattresses covered with burlap. A smaller version of these mattresses was made of the same materials and served as a pillow on each bed. Originally, one blanket had been placed on each bed, but these soon began to disappear as early arrivals grabbed two or more per person. We were lucky enough to find a blanket each, and spread it on the mattress as a sheet. The bunks were arranged so that two were adjacent to each other, like marriage beds, reducing personal privacy. An aisle about three feet wide separated the double rows of bunks from the next row, and this defined the space we lived in. Naturally, being young and agile, I was assigned a top bunk, and this remained my situation throughout our incarceration, although the person sleeping next to me changed as we moved from barrack to barrack.

Since the kitchens were closed for the night, we were given water, allowed a trip to the nearby latrine and bedded down for the night.

Exhausted from the trip, the unaccustomed walk, the fear, and the strangeness of my new home, I fell asleep immediately.

The next day, plans were made for our life in the camp. The previous night's quarters proved only temporary, since men and women were to sleep in separate parts of our enclosure. Thus, in effect, we occupied two adjacent areas, each consisting of a number of barracks, one area designated for men and one for women, and separated by yet another fence of five or six horizontal rows of barbed wire, equipped with yet another gate, locked but unguarded at night, and wide open during the day, allowing men and women to mix freely.

In the morning, we were each issued an enameled metal bowl, a mug and a tin spoon, and received a generous ration of hot, ersatz coffee (about a quart per person), accompanied by a slice of coarse black bread that seemed to contain more chaff than flour.

That first morning we wandered around, bewildered and feeling deeply betrayed. Most of us were running from desperate conditions, facing the danger of death on a daily basis. Now we had dared to hope for a miraculous escape, and our hopes were being shattered again We had hoped for Switzerland, or at least Vittel. The latter camp was a former spa in German-occupied France reserved for foreign nationals, and with a reputation for comfort and good treatment in its hotel-like setting. But Bergen-Belsen! Did it mean the exchange had fallen through or, worse, had never been contemplated? Had we fallen into a clever and deadly trap? People who had arrived from Hotel Polski several days before us had, so far, been treated better than the rest of the inmates of the vast camp. However, though rumors abounded, nobody knew anything.

Around noon, men in striped, loose, pajama-like trousers and shirts with striped caps on their heads delivered the main meal of the day: a quart of hot turnip soup, into which an occasional piece of meat, fish or potato had wandered inadvertently. The large, steaming garbage-can-like containers arrived at the gate of our compound, to be distributed by our own, internal authorities. In the evening, we received another portion of the "coffee," twice a week supplemented by a quart of bread soup.

We were the second contingent from Hotel Polski. The first one, which had arrived a couple of days before us, had already managed to establish a pecking order in the group, and our contingent was not given any choice in the matter of self-governance. Like all other camps, we were ruled by kapos (short for *Kameradpolizei*, or "comrade police") who had a limited power over us, since they could always be overridden by the Germans. Nevertheless, their power was considerable since they were in charge of food distribution, bunk assignments, designating who was sick and who was well, and most other important details of our daily lives. Furthermore, like in all other camps, these positions were occupied by the most brutish, cruel, and cold among us; in our case the kapos were the members of the Jewish Gestapo who had included themselves in the promessas.

In general, the Germans promoted such arrangements, since they reflected their own hierarchy and best ensured order in the camp. That it also resulted in additional, unnecessary suffering and oppression did not, of course, concern them. Our "leaders," like all others of their ilk, kept a significant part of our food for themselves and always looked well-fed and strong. In fact, they were able to exchange some of that food for luxuries for themselves and their families.

It is amazing how things happen in a moment of transition. While most people react like sheep, there are those who watch for times of flux and take advantage of them in order to secure advantageous footholds for themselves. Once things settle down to a routine, they are entrenched in positions of authority, and always prove extraordinarily difficult to dislodge. This happens in every uprising, every revolution, and every other sort of upheaval. The individuals who come out on top are, in most cases, the scum of the population. The same thing happened in our camp.

I was to stay in Bergen-Belsen for 22 months, and the general conditions remained pretty constant throughout that time. But my incarceration breaks down into three distinct periods according to our moves to different barracks in different areas of the camp.

The first period lasted for about three months. At that time we were a large group, consisting of about 3,000 people listed on the "promessas," about 250 people on the Palestinian list, and a group of 350 people from Lwow (which the Germans called Lemberg), a city in eastern Poland. We were heartened by the arrival of this group several days after our own arrival, because they had individual, legitimate papers issued in their real names. These papers, though similar to the promessas, were completely authentic. In fact their holders had not been living in the Lwow Ghetto, but had had separate, much superior quarters in a building outside of the Ghetto, where they had all been living together since the beginning of the German occupation in 1941. In our minds, the legitimacy of their papers gave us all an added cachet. Of course, they probably felt the reverse, but were too tactful to point it out to us. They came with a lot of luggage, and, no doubt, other less visible resources, and fared a little better than we throughout our ordeal.

In time, I made some good friends among this group, which included more educated people than our motley crew. For now, we settled down to a routine, which remained constant and tedious.

Each day started with an *Appel* (roll call). Regardless of the weather, all but the most grievously ill had to stand in formation and wait for a German officer to come into our enclosure and count us. The decision of who was to be allowed to stay in the barracks and not participate in the roll call was made by one of our own physicians, designated by the Germans to be the official camp doctor. The inhabitants of each barrack had to form in front of it, sometimes standing ankle deep in mud. Once the German group arrived, there was no talking, the total silence punctuated by the barking voices of the non-coms or soldiers counting us off. On good days, this procedure didn't last very long, a half hour or less. But, if the numbers did not agree in a previous section or in ours, or if the Germans were in a bad mood, we might stand there for several hours, becoming half-frozen, while the coffee which might have warmed us was also getting cold.

The roll call was a great hardship and, as we grew weaker, became an ever greater one. Besides the need to stand immobile for long periods of time in inclement weather, it was also our main contact with the Germans, providing an opportunity for them to beat us with the whips they always carried, or knock some hapless soul to the ground for some trivial, or even non-existent, infraction of a rule. The barracks might be inspected as well during a roll call, and had to be in a spotless condition, the beds made up neatly, the floors clean and uncluttered.

The roll-call was followed by the so-called "breakfast" (i.e. the coffee), after which we were free for the rest of the day. This was the essence of our "special" status: we did not work and we continued to wear our own clothes. Not working was our main blessing. It meant that we could lie about and conserve energy, a most important godsend given our starvation diet. It also meant that our daily contact with the Germans and their kapo minions was limited, on most days, to one encounter a day, the often brief, impersonal meeting during the roll call.

Not working, like most things in life, also had a down side. It doomed us to prolonged periods of inactivity and tedium, giving us plenty of opportunity to dwell on our misfortunes, the most immediate of which was constant hunger. Hunger is my most persisting memory of the camp. I got up hungry, went to bed hungry, and experienced pangs of hunger all the time in between. The extent to which people's minds dwelled on food was enormous. Women wrote down recipes for the most elaborate dishes. Memories of special meals were shared with friends in such minute detail that one could taste and smell the food. When one is hungry, it is difficult to try to forget it and focus on other topics. Anything that does divert you from the hunger is much appreciated, provided it is not something even worse.

Thus, storytelling was again in great demand. Memories were exchanged, books not just summarized, but acted out dramatically, often without great attention to accuracy. My father, who was a bottomless well of stories, would often devote long afternoon hours to telling *War and Peace, Crime and Punishment* and other remembered classics, analyzing the characters and inviting discussions by the group gathered around him. I attracted a younger crowd. I too had an excellent memory, but did not have as great a store of books in my memory as my father. My storytelling tended towards romantic or even gothic stories, with plenty of melodrama thrown in.

Wearing our own clothes was mainly a morale booster. It set us apart very visibly from the rest of the camp and reminded us of our privileged status, keeping the hope of a rescue alive for a very long time. However, when winter came, my only summer dress proved vastly inadequate. For a piece of bread my parents bought me a black wool dress which, like much clothing made during that period, proved indestructible. In my current life, my clothes occupy five closets. I wonder whether I am subconsciously making up for the 22 months when my belongings consisted of two dresses, one sweater, and two changes of underwear. I lacked such items as nightgowns and coats. During the summer I slept in my underwear; in winter I dressed up for the night, putting on all the clothing layers I possessed in the hope of staving off the pervasive cold and dampness. As for the absence of a coat, the blanket played this role in the winter, emphasizing my bedraggled appearance. Shoes were also a troublesome item in my wardrobe. By the end of the 22 months, my only two pairs were falling apart, in spite of the very limited amount of walking and exercise available.

During that first period, the distribution of food other than soup and coffee remained quite disorganized. The Germans issued our bread ration once a week, but our leadership, claiming that we could not control our appetites, issued it in daily portions which were often quite uneven. Favorites of barrack leaders got larger pieces, and troublemakers were shortchanged to "teach them a lesson." Other items, provided at irregular intervals, consisted of jam, blood sausage, sugar, toilet paper and soap, but we rarely saw any of these, given the regime we were living under.

When we first arrived in Bergen-Belsen our group was, for the most part, in good physical condition. Because the contingent from Lwow had never lived in the Ghetto, they had always been fed adequately. Its members were mostly business or professional people, men and women of substance who had fared relatively well all through the war. There were a number of children among them, though few very young ones, as Jews tended to avoid having children even during the "better" parts of the war. The much larger Warsaw contingent consisted of people who had spent the last year or so on the Aryan side and, while suffering some privations, had been able to afford to purchase life's necessities. All of these families, or family remnants, could afford to plunk down several thousand dollars to be listed on the promessas, so they still had ample means to survive.

As an indication of this general good physical condition, I need only mention that some people were still interested in sex. A minor scandal erupted when the Germans searched the barracks before the gates separating the men's and women's compounds were open, and caught several men in the women's section, one of them visiting a female friend who was not his wife (the wife slept in a different barrack). The guards had such a good laugh about it, sex offenses not being the reason for the search, that no one was punished. The offenders were merely warned, and thereafter took care to confine their amorous activities to daytime hours. The only baby born in our camp may have been conceived during those activities, right after our arrival, though the timing made it also possible that the infant had been conceived just prior to our arrival in Bergen-Belsen.

One day I ran into Cesia, a schoolmate from my pre-war school days. She had even been with me in Brok, our last vacation before the war. Cesia was an only child and had lost both parents in the deportation. She was living with and under the protection of an older man, perhaps as old as 35. He was an uneducated, coarse, even brutish man, and I felt Cesia had committed a misalliance, even though they were not married. We visited each other several times in our respective barracks, reminiscing about school, our mutual friends and teachers, and that glorious summer in Brok. She told me her lover disapproved of our friendship; he felt it was making her discontented. Indeed, the difference in our situations was pretty blatant. With all the horrors we had lived through and might still have to suffer, I still remained a teenager, loved and sheltered as much as possible by my parents, whereas she was already a woman who had to fend for herself with very few resources other than her youth and physical attraction, which she was exchanging for a measure of security and companionship.

Several weeks passed. We had all gotten used to our routine, and apart from the starvation diet we shared with the rest of the camp, the Germans were not treating us too badly. Dissent against our leadership was getting ever louder and more widespread, when all this nonsense was quickly knocked out of our heads by the arrival of Colonel Z. (I am not protecting his privacy; I just don't recall the name, but it started with a "Z.") He was a high-ranking Gestapo officer from Berlin. We were told he had come to authenticate our documents and interview all the family heads. Thereafter, several heads of families were summoned every day and made the trek to Colonel Z.'s office, located outside our enclosure in the administrative section of the camp. He asked the names, ages, occupations, educational backgrounds and other details of all the members of each family. Several times, he summoned—seemingly at random—an entire promessa family.

When my father's turn came, he reported that Colonel Z. was cold, polite and not at all forthcoming during the interview, keeping meticulous records of all the information gathered. This was all very disquieting. We felt that the authenticity of the "families" could not bear the close scrutiny they were now receiving without giving away the essential fraud: that the people within each "family" clearly had very little in common. Besides, anyone knowing anything about the recent Jewish history, as Colonel Z. clearly had to, would find the existence of such large, intact families not just suspect but downright impossible. The questioning lasted for several weeks, after which Colonel Z. departed without any hint of his findings or their possible consequences. We consoled ourselves, thinking that the whole exercise was a typical German formality. If there were to be an exchange or a prospect of one, what did it matter whether the people on the papers were legitimately related or not, as long as the papers were authentic? If the exchange plans had fallen through, or had never existed, it mattered even less.

At the end of September, Colonel Z.'s inquiries bore fruit: orders came for the departure of all the promessa people. The next morning they gathered their belongings and marched out, again with trucks ferrying the young, the old and the disabled. Suddenly, from 3,600, our group shrank to 600. The Lwow contingent and members of our Palestinian group were staying on. Speculations on the fate of the departed and those staying on began immediately. The picture was very unclear. We had privately rated the Lwow group as having the best papers, followed by the promessa family members, with the Palestinian group on the bottom of this heap. Now the middle contingent was removed, at least temporarily. Was this good for them? Was this good for us?

We were to find out part of the answer six months later, when the previously mentioned baby, conceived so ambivalently, was born with no equivocation. Bergen-Belsen is located in northwestern Germany, between Hamburg and Hanover, near the town of Celle. The mother was taken to a hospital in Celle for the birth, and remained there for over two weeks. Ironically, in those days, new mothers were not discharged from the hospital after 24 or 48 hours. During that time, the mother made friends with a nurse and sent some letters to friends in Poland. Two weeks after she came back, a bunch of replies were delivered by a German medic who happened to be the nurse's boyfriend. One of the letters had been sent to Krakow. The answer, in code, informed us that the promessa contingent had been executed at Auschwitz, a fact confirmed after the war. By this time, the speculations had died down, as we became more and more preoccupied with our own miseries.

The camp felt ghost-like after the departure of this vast majority of people. Cesia and many of the friends I made during those three months were now lost to me. The only up side of this departure was that all the members of the Jewish Gestapo were gone, none of them having been on the Palestinian list. We wandered through the deserted camp, collecting and appropriating the best blankets and other odds and ends left by those departed. Several days later, the announcement came: we were to move to new and smaller quarters within the camp. Thus, the first phase of my stay in Bergen-Belsen came to an end.

❧   ❧   ❧

Our new quarters consisted of three large halls, constituting the middle half of a very long, single-story brick building. A single hall separated us from the camp's main road, which we could just see through two sets of barbed wire, one separating us from the inmates of the single hall, and the other separating them from the road. On the other side, away from the road, there were two more halls, standing sometimes empty, and sometimes housing some of the camp's prisoners. About 200 of us lived in each hall, which was probably designed for 50 or so persons. The bunks were crowded even closer together, but even so, some people had to double up due to shortage of beds. At one point, my neighbors on the adjacent bunk (arranged like twin beds put together), were a married couple. I dressed and undressed under a blanket, but many others lost the need for such niceties. I learned that privacy is a relative term. If you really want it, you learn to achieve it under the most crowded conditions simply by turning inward and turning the outside world off.

We now also had much less outdoor space than before. In front of our three barracks there was a space as wide as an average street, where we formed up for the roll calls and walked around in good weather, or just used to go from barrack to barrack, to visit friends and hold meetings. A smaller space was available behind the barracks. Men, women and children were no longer separated for the night, but curfew was strictly observed. During the night we were confined to our individual barracks. Three months of the camp diet proved long enough to suppress the earlier sexual appetites, but having the men with us was a comfort. I should also mention that no one was tattooed in Bergen-Belsen, and since this was the only camp I was in, I do not have a tattoo.

Our first crisis was political in nature. Now that the Jewish Gestapo members were gone, who would the Germans designate as our leaders? We were afraid they would import some thugs from another part of the camp to rule over us. As soon as we moved to our new quarters, meetings were held in the three halls and a unanimous decision was made. We would select our own leaders and ask the Germans to allow us this choice. It was not difficult to select our representative. He was Mr. Solowiejczyk, an engineer by profession, fluent in German, well-spoken, erudite, and experienced in social leadership and organization. At the same time, we decided to ask the Germans to appoint my father as the official doctor of our section. Although there were two other doctors in the group, two brothers from Lwow named Schwieger, they were rather haughty and snobbish, and as a result were passed over by the group. In the short time we had been in Bergen-Belsen my father had already endeared himself to many people.

Asking for this privilege of choosing a representative was a very risky enterprise. Either Mr. Solowiejczyk and my father, or all of us, might be punished for such a presumption, but the alternative of being ruled by brutish kapos was grim also. A letter outlining our request was drawn up and sent to the camp commandant, Josef Kramer. The next day during the roll call, Kramer showed up in our enclosure and called for Solowiejczyk and my father. We stood in formation while they talked quietly. There was none of the usual German blustering and anger. Kramer must have been impressed by both the arguments and the demeanor of our leader, because he granted our request. Thus, through both luck and our own endeavor, we became "special" in yet another way: we managed to win 100 percent democratic leadership for our group. Mr. Solowiejczyk remained our leader to the end, and my father remained the official doctor for the 600 of us.

This was important. First, it meant that the food distribution became an honest process, immediately improving our nutrition, albeit slightly. We also elected leaders of the three individual barracks, and section supervisors. This group became our council and helped to govern our camp, but always subject to recall by new election if they did not serve us well. The council diverted a small amount of food for the sick and for small children, collected money and valuables from those who still had some, and negotiated with venal German non-coms and medics for additional food and medical supplies for our group. In this capacity, my father was in charge of the latter negotiations, and his efforts in negotiating or begging for medical supplies provided such basic medical necessities as aspirin, sulfa drugs, vitamins in very limited quantities, bandages and antiseptic salves.

It was up to each individual how to consume his food ration, and there were long, earnest discussions whether it was better to eat our daily piece of bread all at once or divide it into two or three portions. There was a general agreement that it should be divided evenly over the week, but some people were so hungry they lacked the will to do it and gobbled it up all at once. They argued that this way they were full at least once a week. Families went through an additional agony, with parents often battling their own hunger in an effort to give their children a little more. My father tried that with me, but I wouldn't accept his sacrifice, and took over our family food distribution, making sure that he got his share.

Having our own, honest leadership boosted our morale. As usual, we also attempted to read more into Kramer's consent than was there, and saw visions of a move to Vittel, France, before our eyes. With no real information, and living under such terrible conditions, we had a tendency to careen between high hopes and deep despair at the slightest provocation.

We adapted quickly to life in our new quarters, where we were to stay for over a year. Our basic routines remained, depressingly, the same as before. But now, with less space to move around, with winter coming, and with the cumulative effect of prolonged near-starvation, we had a hard time keeping our spirits up. We didn't get much snow, but a lot of rain, drizzle and gray days with a cold, penetrating wind, making for plenty of misery in our unheated quarters. On my high perch, I frequently had to collect eating bowls from my neighbors, and use them to catch the rain dripping from the leaky roof. It's a good thing I was small and flexible enough to arrange myself between the bowls at night. The frequently wet blankets and clothes, combined with the inadequate food, resulted in many running noses, flu's and coughs. Tuberculosis came to be the most common cause of death among us. In all, however, during our stay of 22 months, only 12 people died in our enclave.

One of them was a very religious woman from Krakow. We had among us a Hasidic rabbi who ministered to the faithful. He also came from Krakow, and knew the woman very well. In fact, he had been a friend of her deceased husband. In the Jewish religion the highest precept, superseding all other laws, is to save lives, particularly Jewish lives. In accordance with this law, sick people are allowed to eat on Yom Kippur, the highest Jewish holiday, and a day of obligatory fasting. Early in this memoir, I described how my father's grandfather had to eat meat fried in butter, since his doctor proclaimed this diet was necessary for his survival. Our rabbi tried to convince his friend to eat the soup, which was our principal meal of the day in spite of the fact that it was not kosher. But no amount of persuasion could move this woman; she just couldn't get this *trayf* (unkosher) food through her gullet. Subsisting on just bread, she lingered for several months before fading away slowly and inexorably. One feels at once in awe of such faith and exasperated by the needlessness of such a death.

In December 1943, my mother began to suffer severe abdominal pains, nausea, and vomiting, which continued without any interruption, causing her to moan and cry out pitifully. At first, my father and both Dr. Schwiegers diagnosed her condition as an attack of gallstones. She had suffered such attacks before, though never in such acute form. Both my father and I felt desperate and totally helpless while witnessing her agony, able only to wipe her face, hold the bowl for her to vomit into, and try to console her with the hope that the pain would soon pass. Gallstone attacks generally subside spontaneously, but after my mother's pain continued for two days, the doctors came to the conclusion that she was suffering from ileitis. This condition, also known as paralytic ileus, is an

The author's mother, Roza Salman, before her marriage

The author at 6 years old vacationing in Druskienniki, Poland, in 1934

And at 11 years of age on vacation in Brok on the Bug, Poland, In 1939

The author's father, Moses Salamon, in 1946 at his Tel Aviv laboratory

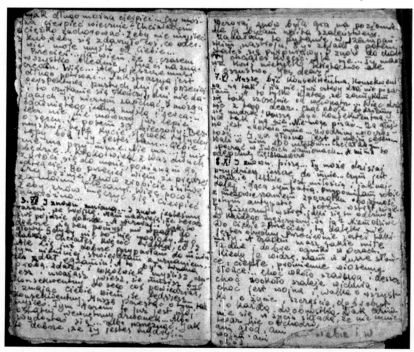

Part of the author's diary written at Bergen-Belsen in Polish, Russian, French, and English

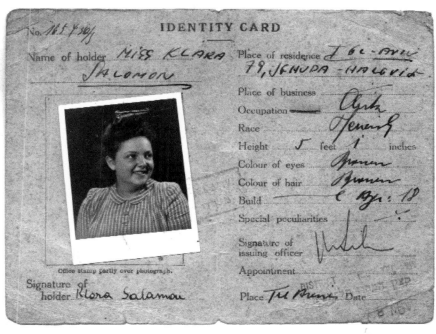

The author's Palestine identity card issued upon her arrival in 1945

The Polish passport issued in Israel for her emigration to America in 1947

The author's "glamour" picture taken in 1954 by her future husband Bert

The author's 1955 wedding photograph

The couple's two sons, Sam (left) and Mark

The author with her favorite Aunt Zina in 1951

The author's son Mark

The author's son Sam

Doing what they love to do, dancing at a wedding in 1989

The author and her top flight physics students and officials at Livingston High School, in New Jersey

The author's grand-daughter, Miranda

Grandson Jack in 1998

obstruction of the bowel, causing the fecal matter to back up and resulting in dehydration and death. Only surgical intervention can save the
patient's life. (President Eisenhower also suffered from ileitis, was operated on, and continued as president, without any ill effects.)

When we realized what was the matter with my mother, my father
approached a German guard and sent word through him to the German
doctor in charge of the whole Bergen-Belsen camp. This German doctor
was a very decent man. Of course, concentration camp inmates were not
taken to real hospitals and operated on following normal, antiseptic procedures, but he extended professional courtesy to my father and made a
rare exception for my mother. As soon as he received my father's note
(relayed by a decent guard), he sent an ambulance for my mother.

Two German medics put her on a stretcher, and the German nurse accompanying the stretcher assured us she would be given the best care. My
mother was only half-conscious from the pain, and not really aware of our
tearful kisses and farewells. She was taken to the military hospital in
Celle where she was to be operated on immediately.

Now came the longest day of my life. We waited for word on the results
of the surgery. Unlike the normal situation, we did not know when word
would come or even if the operation would be performed at all. Anyone
along the chain of people involved, a medic or a doctor, might decide
that a Jewish woman was not worth the effort and shunt her off to some
corner to die in agony all alone. I am sure that my father, being a doctor,
realized that she had little hope because of her poor physical condition
aggravated by pain.

My mother died on the operating table. The German doctor came personally the next day to give us the sad though not unexpected news, and
to extend his sympathy. He assured us that my mother did not suffer. She
had received a morphine injection in the ambulance and died while
under anesthesia during surgery. Her heart just stopped beating. He even
arranged for her body to be delivered to the camp so we could perform
"any rituals that might be required by our religion." His behavior and sensitivity were so rare among our tormentors, I must really stress it. One
simply did not hear of such tact and compassion on the part of any
Germans working in concentration camps.

My mother's body was delivered the next day. Her face looked peaceful,
serene, and somehow younger. We had a mortician among us. He washed
her, composed her limbs, and said the necessary prayers. I did not see

her naked body, but my father did and confirmed the abdominal surgery. The wound was not completely sewn up; she must have died just then. In spite of the kindness extended to us by the German doctor, I nevertheless blame the Nazis for killing my mother, not directly, but by subjecting her to conditions which enfeebled her body, very likely caused the ileitis through the rough diet and made it impossible for her body to survive the operation. We were given one day to mourn over her body. When the two of us were alone with her, crying over her and looking for the last time at her dear face, my father said, "My life is over."

His words filled me with dread even though I did not, at the time, appreciate the full import of them. He was never the same after my mother's death. The next day my mother's body was removed and burned in the camp crematorium. Before my father died in 1972, he told me that since my mother had no grave, he did not want one either. In accordance with his wishes, his body was cremated but his ashes lie buried in a corner of a Jewish cemetery.

I grieved for my mother after her death without fully appreciating what I had lost. I have not written much about my mother. She lived in my father's shadow and did not seem to make as great an impact on my life. Even after she died, while I grieved that her life had been cut off prematurely and needlessly, I did not give her full credit for smoothing my father's and my path by her instinctive goodness, her peace-making talents, her high ethical standards, and her love and compassion. Everybody loved my mother. She was no intellectual, but she had common sense, a lovely musical talent, and, her greatest forte, her "people" talent. At several junctures in my life thereafter, I was to miss her wise and loving advice. I did not know it then, for we are rarely aware of what we do not have, but I might have avoided several wrong turns in my life had my mother been alive. All of life's teachings, from such commonplaces as cooking, shopping and housekeeping, to lessons on relationships with male and female friends and relatives that a mother can transmit to her daughter by example and counsel, I was to be deprived of. I am truly sorry that it is only now, when I am getting old myself, that I fully appreciate my mother and offer her this eulogy.

All the remaining deaths during our stay were caused by respiratory and lung diseases. We did not suffer a single case of typhus in our enclosure, though later it was to ravage the camp.

My father worked hard to convince our people to maintain the highest possible standards of cleanliness in their own, individual interests as well as that of our group. In the morning, before anything else, I went to the large room which served as the common bathroom for both men and women. In these barracks we had several flush toilets, but as the barrack was designed for men only, they had no doors. Privacy could be achieved only by asking a friend to stand in front of you holding up a blanket. The room had two rows of faucets for communal washing, a good half of which were frozen solid during the long winter of 1943-44. There were only 20 or 30 brave souls among us, myself included, who stripped to the waist and performed our daily ablutions all through the winter, and then, shielding each other as much as possible, continued with even more private cleansing. Luckily, none of the women menstruated, a natural condition known as amenorrhea protecting us from losing vital blood under starvation conditions. Needless to say there was no hot water, so all the body washing and the little laundry was done in the ice-cold water, and with almost no soap.

After roll call and breakfast, we made our beds. We were constantly fighting two infestations: lice and mice. Luckily there were no rats in the barracks, though we saw one from time to time outside, but the mice proliferated freely, breeding in our mattresses and pillows. Thus, every day I gingerly handed down to my father all my possessions, one by one, and he shook them out, often dislodging adult or infant mice. To this day I have a phobia against these animals, worthy of the hero of *1984*. Since, as a child, I had no fear or disgust for the mice my father had in the lab, I attribute my adult revulsion to the unhappy associations with the camp.

Even people who had no such feelings against rodents feared them for their disease-carrying capacity. Lice were even more dangerous in this respect, as they were transmitters of the dreaded typhus. During the last year of our incarceration, typhus was king of the camp. It raged unimpeded, killing tens of thousands, though as I said, none in our enclosure. This was probably due to our separation from the other inmates who worked. Our inactivity saved our strength. Perhaps, also, we had built up some sort of resistance to the disease.

To minimize the lice problem we shook out our blankets every day. On nice days they were hung to air on the barbed wire surrounding our camp. From time to time, we also dragged the mattresses out to air them. Grooming ourselves and each other was also part of the daily procedure. Hair was combed with combs equipped with very close teeth designed to uncover head lice. Clothes, especially seams, were inspected daily to make sure lice did not lodge and lay eggs there. Lice and eggs we found were killed by squashing them between our nails, disgusting now, but a very satisfactory sound then. We must have looked like chimps, but our grooming was not social; it was part of the desperate effort to survive.

From the beginning, the various groups in the camp were kept apart. Except for our group, men and women were separated from each other, but otherwise there seemed little logic in the process: some areas were all Jewish, other areas all non-Jewish, still others mixed. Inmates included war prisoners, criminals, political prisoners and Jews. In the mornings and evenings we saw large groups marching to and from work in their striped uniforms—skeletons, routinely harried with whips wielded by the kapos and the German guards. We had no contact with them and wished for none. Their misery touched us, but they seemed bearers of diseases and death. The work they did seemed unfathomable. There were some storage barracks in the camp, and there some of them labored sorting clothes and shoes, but most groups were marched out of the camp, moving rocks and earth, labors invented to keep them busy and miserable, while real work was left undone elsewhere for want of available hands. At least that was the word that reached us.

Our contacts with them were with the men who delivered soup and coffee to our enclosure. They represented some of the camp's elite. They worked in the kitchen, were usually fed better, and improved their lot further by theft and selling their contraband for dollars and jewelry. My father and I had arrived at the camp with about $1,000 and a diamond ring. Incredibly, we were never searched, not even upon our arrival, and gradually we exchanged our valuables for bread during the next 22 months.

On the other side of our three rooms, away from the road, our barrack extended to contain two more large rooms. These were often unoccupied in the fall of 1943, but in the winter the Germans put them to a terrible use. Bergen-Belsen had no gas chambers, and thus no convenient means for killing large numbers of people. Hunger and typhus were efficient killers, but hunger in particular was too slow for Commandant Kramer's taste. The men and women *in extremis*, close to death, could linger for weeks, unable to work and preempting food and space needed for the constant stream of new arrivals. Kramer then conceived a cheap way to speed them on their way.

In the evening, these two rooms were filled with those victims, with about 500 crammed in each, enough so there was no room to lie down. With them would be locked in 20 or so kapos, whose job it was to see that no one came out alive. The kapos were not given guns, but boards taken from the bunks. In the dark, crowded room, they made space around themselves by thrashing around with their weapons, creating such chaos and panic that any victims not killed by the blows either died from suffocation, stamped on each other or otherwise killed each other in their desperate efforts to avoid the bloody boards.

This process, obviously, was not accomplished in silence. Even in the middle barrack where I slept, I heard the screaming all night long, grown men calling for their mothers, for God, for mercy, in every European language. The people in the adjacent barrack also heard the blows as the boards fell against the helpless bodies. After each night of sleepless horror, we watched the bodies being shoveled out of these execution chambers, and carried through our area on wheelbarrows on their way to some mass grave. After two weeks, the ghastly procedure was stopped abruptly and the barracks cleaned out. No one moved into that building while we stayed in these barracks.

Why was this method of killing conceived in the first place? It seemed so inhumane, and at the same time inefficient, which was most unlike the Germans. Further, why was it stopped? The Germans' behavior seemed to us arbitrary and senseless, contrary to all human decency or common sense. At the same time, they tried to justify it with empty and false legalities.

Even though victims were being slaughtered randomly and cruelly, when anyone died in our section, my father was forced to sign a legal death certificate giving normal causes, like heart attacks, as the cause of death instead of the truth: "tuberculosis, caused by starvation and awful living conditions." Once he was called upon to sign several death certificates for people who were not in our section. He had to examine the bodies and sign the certificates claiming death due to some natural cause. The faces of these corpses bore expressions of agony, and since there were no marks on the bodies, my father suspected they died by poisoning; rumors had been circulating in the camp that the Germans were experimenting with benzene as a cheap and effective killer. But why should the Germans need death certificates in the first place? Why keep any records of their atrocities? Evidently that is the way German minds worked. It would be laughable if it were not so tragic.

The status of our group was also totally illogical, though of course we didn't complain since it worked in our favor. After finding most of the papers fraudulent and deporting the bulk of our group to gas chambers, why continue to treat the rest in a somewhat privileged manner? Was an exchange still likely? I doubted it. I think the orders concerning us were just never changed. We fell through the bureaucratic cracks and continued not working and not being subjected to the rule of the kapos. (God once again was playing dice!)

Soon after we moved to the second quarters, my parents bought an English-language book for a piece of bread. By pure coincidence, it turned out to be *Gone With the Wind*, a book with which I already had a strong connection. There were several people in our group who spoke fluent English, and one of them volunteered to teach me using the book as a textbook. He was a friend of my father and we spent many hours discussing English grammar and conversing in English. Paper was difficult to come by, so I did not learn to write in English, a situation which was to be remedied after the war. *Gone With the Wind* really is far from an ideal textbook for learning standard English, but I was a quick learner. By the end of the war, astonishingly, I could speak English fairly well, a skill which was to help me a great deal later on. But, at the time, it was a good occupation for both my teacher and me, and I extended the favor by teaching French to another friend, Alek. In 1947, when I took a course in American history, I discovered I had a very pro-Confederate point of view on the Civil War.

We were always hungry for news from the outside world. We were in a grim, deadly race between the Allied advances and our endurance, with the possibility of deportation to the gas chambers playing like a grotesque wild card in the game. Thus, the exact status of the war and the rate of the Allied progress were of vital importance to us. Some of the workers in the camp were assigned to act as servants to the German officers administering the camp, and every once in a while they managed to swipe a newspaper, although, as you can imagine, this was strictly forbidden. They would then read it themselves and pass it on surreptitiously to other groups. Once in a while, a much handled and studied newspaper, usually days old, would find its way to our enclosure. News of such an event would spread like wild fire. Of course many of us could not read German, but no matter. Those that could would get hold of it and that night, in each of the three barracks, detailed translations and interpretations were presented to the rest of us. Someone would stand guard at the door in case the Germans pulled one of their rare, impromptu night inspections, while the rest of us crowded on the bunks around the speaker and listened, riveted to our seats, to the litany of German defeats.

Of course, the Germans never admitted defeats in their newspapers. Instead, lines would be consolidated or shortened, units would be regrouped, or strategic retreats would be ordered, but if you knew your geography, you could see that they were gradually pushed back in the East, reaching the pre-war Polish frontiers in January 1944 and Warsaw by the end of July 1944. In the West, where our hopes truly lay, we along with the rest of the world waited impatiently for the real second front, with Italy, where the fighting was bogged down all through 1943-44, not qualifying for that title, at least in our opinion. Finally, it came in June 1944. The Allies landed in France. Now more than ever we waited feverishly for quick successes, but it was not to be. We still had 10 months and a brutal winter of suffering ahead of us.

Gaining a view of the world situation based on German newspapers was an art in itself. The grains of truth had to be carefully winnowed from the chaff of propaganda, as the German press was still attempting to convince the German public that they were winning the war. Our experts were very good at seeing the truth. The report would occupy the whole evening. Hidden among the verbiage there was information on increasingly severe shortages; ever more frequent, damaging, and largely undefended air raids devastating the German cities; and losses of manpower and territory. Sitting there huddled in our blankets, in the near darkness, cold, hungry, sick, and scared, we gloated over the German suffering and prayed for the blessed end of this nightmare.

The news reports gave us another idea to pass the time. On several occasions we gathered for rather elaborate entertainment, prepared carefully like reviews. Skits mocking our lives and our guards were written and acted, poetry was recited, songs sung a capella, or humorous stories told. My father excelled at the latter, while I still remembered some poems and recited them most dramatically. Each of those evenings was like a red-letter day. It not only banished hunger and fear for a few hours, but it confirmed our humanity. Sometimes you can feel indomitable by just holding on or acting like humans, even when almost all aspects of your life are out of your control. Every such evening was a victory over the forces of darkness and evil which had overtaken us.

Yet another tangible indication of the German losses was the disappearance of almost all able-bodied men from among our guards. Increasingly, our guards came to include war cripples, old men, and finally, women. With some exceptions, this was a development for the better. The tired old men, in particular, tended to be less demanding and less interested in meticulous inspections and counts which would have kept them, as well as us, outdoors in inclement weather.

Several of the women guards were assigned to our compound. They were rough and loud, but each one soon came to adopt a child, usually a little girl, as her particular favorite. Thus, several times a day, some female guard would come to visit her favorite child, often bringing extra food or an item of clothing, and sometimes even a doll. These guards would hug the children and play with them, in the process becoming friendlier with the girls' mothers. I had seen and remarked upon such anomalies before. The softer side of these female guards seemed to be able to coexist with and not mitigate the harsh and inhumane treatment they extended to other inmates.

I had a part-time occupation each day. I accompanied my father on his rounds and learned to perform some simple nursing functions. There was an older girl, Ruth, who truly wanted to become a nurse, and my father taught both of us. Ruth went on to become a nurse in Israel. I, however, discovered I didn't care for the profession. The changes of dressings and the sights and smells of sickness did not repel me, but they did not interest me either, although I derived some satisfaction out of being able to help my friends. I learned to administer intramuscular injections— no mean feat since the skin of near-starving people tends to become thick and leathery. I even acquired a certain reputation for a light hand in this task. The injections, by the way, consisted of vitamin or liver extracts and were very effective against the vitamin deficiency affecting many inmates. The extracts were hard to get out of the German doctors and medics, even with bribes, so they were doled out parsimoniously to the worst cases among young people. I guess my father practiced an informal triage procedure without formal knowledge of the term.

The interminable afternoons were spent studying and socializing. After my mother's death, I became more friendly with Sonia, who despite the loss of her little girl in the Mila Street Kettle, remained, most of the time, an upbeat, cheerful person. There were many young people in our group, but I grew closest to Nina and Alek. In fact sometime in the spring of 1944 I fell in love with Alek. Alek and Nina were both older than I and involved with each other in a complex relationship. I was a close friend with each of them individually, and the three of us became inseparable as well. Had things played out otherwise, I believe Nina and I would have become friends for life, for I never felt more in tune with any other friend as I did with her.

Alek came from Lwow. His father had been a wealthy man (a physician, I believe), but since he was never mentioned, I don't know whether he had died or separated from his wife before the war. Alek's mother was another one of those helpless Victorian women, but whereas my mother was sweet and loving, she was spoiled and insensitive.

At the beginning of the war, like most of us, Alek's family had to subsist by selling foreign currency and personal belongings, and this job fell to Alek, who was 15 or 16 at the time. He developed a taste for the illicit trading, an appetite for adventure, and a craving for danger which was to stay with him for the rest of his life. We once spent an afternoon going through the list of items he had traded in. Absent from that list were wild animals and real estate, but the list included clothing, jewelry, pharmaceuticals, cigarettes, guns, pianos and many other things. By the time the Germans occupied Lwow in 1941, Alek was a seasoned black market operator, fearless and risk-loving. He had a Jewish girlfriend who shared his love of danger and who was alone in the world. Without any restraints on either of them, they pulled such stunts as dressing up in Italian uniforms acquired on the black market, parading through the town with bravura and, at first, with impunity. Alek and his mother had foreign passports sent to them by his older brother who lived in Switzerland. The little Jewish community in Lwow was furious at Alek's shenanigans, feeling he was endangering them all with his penchant for dramatic adventurism.

One day, the Gestapo came to the apartment where Alek's girlfriend lived somewhere on the Aryan side. She killed the two officers who came for her. After that, Alek hid her in an abandoned building that was soon to be renovated by members of this privileged Jewish group. Now the story gets murky. Someone reported the presence of the young girl on the grounds of the project and the Germans came in force to get her. She managed to shoot one or two and killed herself with the last bullet. I never found out who knew where she was hidden, and several people secretly accused Alek of denouncing her, since she had become a great burden and danger to him. I did not hear these stories until much later, but I don't think I believe them even now. Alek was reckless, romantic, not always loyal, but never vicious; denouncing his lover just wasn't in his nature.

My father was not too happy about my friendship with Alek judging, correctly, that I had picked the most unsuitable young man in the camp, but at 16, how could I resist all that romantic bravura? I see now that I was lucky it was a case of unrequited love. Although I suffered at the time, I would have been much worse off if Alek returned my feelings, or even pretended to.

On the other hand, both Alek and Nina were very bright, mercurial even, and the three of us held many intellectual discussions, honing our analytical skills. Nina in particular was very well informed. She was a tall, thin young woman with a face that had once been round, with protuberant hazel eyes and a generous mouth. Although neither one was especially attractive, they shared some very seductive attributes. Both were very good at selling themselves. They created an aura of vague mystery by hinting at past histories, loves, and adventures. When talking with others, they gave all their attention and concentration. That skill is the secret of success of many a seducer or seductress, and it works even when sex is not the object. The recipient of such attention is so flattered and happy that he or she will be willing to oblige in any way required.

Alek and Nina exercised their wiles quite unconsciously, and I felt privileged to be admitted to their circle, even as a friend and somewhat of a *mitschlepper* (fifth wheel). The effect they exercised on each other was quite explosive. They were always quarreling and making up, while I remained on good terms with both.

It was at that time that I began keeping a diary, a practice I continued for several months. I wish I could quote some pearls of wisdom from my journal, or at least some descriptive details about life in the camp. But the truth is I was so preoccupied with my complicated feelings that my diary could have been written anywhere. It contains only the barest references to the fact I was in a concentration camp and focuses on the emotional turmoil I was going through. Well, I was 16 going on 17 at the time, and my adolescence had caught up to me!

The most interesting aspect of this journal is its physical appearance. It was fashioned from toilet paper, the only source of paper in camp. This paper came in small, individual sheets, 5" x 4.5" in size. My little journal consists of about eight such sheets, folded in half, and sown together along the crease, creating a little booklet. I wrote mostly in ink and so small I now need a magnifying glass to decipher the text

A second interesting aspect is that it is multilingual. Although the bulk is in Polish, there are long passages in French, Russian, and even some quotations from *Gone with the Wind* in English. My conversations with Nina, and the correspondence between us, were also conducted in several languages, partly for practice and partly to romanticize ourselves.

As for the content of the diary, it alternates between what I now call "cosmic crap" and my romantic and sensual longings, imaginings and suffering. Most of it is much too embarrassing to quote, but I present here three short, milder passages to give some flavor of it.

(In English:) "My Dear. We will read today, for that is what I feel like doing [reference to French I was teaching Alek]. I will not tell you a story. Never again will you see the sadness in my eyes, or hear the sentimental note in my voice. My soul will not escape through any chink in the impermeable and unbreakable shell I have grown around it."

This next passage was written entirely in French: "I always thought that the greatest suffering is caused by unrequited love. But now I realize that there exists a worse pain: to be loved against one's will and be incapable of defending oneself from a passion which importunes and harasses. One who loves without response can conquer his passion, since he is both the sufferer and the creator of his suffering. But the object of a passion is lost, since the measure and limits of the passion are beyond his control." I haven't the remotest idea if this passage refers to a concrete situation or is a figment of my overworked imagination.

And again, some weeks later: "I looked back at my entries today, and am horrified by my own limitations and obsession. This is all I think about and I look at the world through the prism of my emotions. The word 'emotion' is really insufficient, too weak to describe the suffering I feel. It is the state of my soul. If ever I enter into a friendship pact with either of them again, it must be based on exclusivity. We cannot exist as a unit, and must break up into a pair and a singleton. Until infinity, it must be so in the future. Unless, of course, we end up each of us alone. So long for today."

It is tough to be a teenager anywhere, but how much tougher in a camp, and without a mother. My little journal was the only place I could pour my heart out. I think, for once, my father was clueless on how to deal with me.

In the fall of 1944, an event occurred which terminated my three-way friendship. Alek conceived an idea for a trade with someone in an adjacent camp, an adventure which involved his smuggling himself to another part of the camp for an overnight trip. He enticed Nina and me into helping him. My job was to watch for an opportune moment for Nina to hold the wires apart so he could slip through. When he returned, she would hide contraband he brought back (I believe a shawl and some cigarettes). The whole thing was planned by the three of us and was executed without a hitch. But somehow we were found out and reported to our leadership. Most likely Alek himself bragged about it, for such a feat is much more fun if one talks about it.

The entire community was appalled at our behavior. Alek had endangered himself, and given the German tendency to assign collective responsibility, he might easily have endangered all of us. Here we were lying low, in the hopes the Germans would forget us and not send us to work, and he might have brought their attention and wrath on us. And for what? Not even for a trade that might benefit the community, but for a selfish and frivolous thrill.

A "court" session was held to decide what to do with us. My father acted as my lawyer, asking for clemency due to my young age and inexperience, claiming I had fallen into bad company. (Why is it that our children always fall into bad company, and never are the bad company?) I testified on my own behalf as well. I was contrite and regretted my thoughtlessness, and explained truthfully the entire scheme which, in retrospect, looked very foolish to me. Alek acted arrogant and unrepentant while Nina was totally incoherent on the stand, weeping wildly or staring stonily into space.

The next day the verdict came down. Alek was literally excommunicated. He was to be ostracized by everyone save his mother for an indefinite time. Nina and I were not to be spoken to for a short time (I seem to recall it was one week), after which we would be forgiven, provided we promised not to associate with Alek ever again. My father spoke up as well. He requested that my punishment include no further association with Nina either, since he felt she was a bad influence on me. This was a devastating punishment for me. I was deeply ashamed of my part in the affair, but to be torn away from my dearest friend would be extremely difficult for me. I was beginning to see the light about Alek, and realized he had taken advantage of both of us (my diary refers to our giving him some of our food) and had been doing so all along even though he liked my company very much.

I discovered how hard it is to become transparent to all eyes. The silence around me soon became unbearable and I caved in. Meanwhile Nina was smuggling notes to me, leaving them on my bunk when she passed it, or putting them in one of the few books we passed back and forth. In one note she wrote: "The day will come—I know it, I know it for sure—and I want you to know it also, I want you to feel certain of it—when you will raise your head and march forward to the rhythm of the words, the day will come. Klar, if it ever proves useful—even for a moment—anything you gained from the time we spent together—if it gives you a second of happiness, then remember me for a moment, fleetingly, for so it must be, fleetingly, and then on, on—for the world is calling. August 25, Nina."

And again, sometime later, a long letter, starting as follows:

"Imagine, my dear child, that my father spoke with yours, and the latter declared that after the talk concerning our case dies down, he will give you a carte blanche and you may resume our 'socializing', provided I break up with Alek. I agreed and decided to wait a week or two. You can imagine how disappointed I was when I saw you visiting with Gina [a mutual friend, very vocal and hostile about our transgression]."

The letter goes on to say that she could live without me as well as I without her, and it reminisces about our friendship and extols its value. It asks me to "reflect upon it, and if there is anything you want to share with me, send a child with the French dictionary, and I will slip a response and send it back the same way. I want to understand you clearly, and not to cross you out of my budget prematurely."

I see now that this is a rambling, partly incoherent letter, alternating between moods, and clearly showing emotional instability. But at the time, I was too young and too mixed up myself to notice it.

This was the last communication I had with Nina. I really could not answer her, as I had not yet discussed the matter with my father. I wanted to act honorably and did not want to be caught passing notes secretly. Several days passed and ultimately the decision was made for me. Nina attempted suicide by taking the entire stock of Veronal (a sleeping powder) in her father's possession. Her father was a pharmacist, and had arrived in the camp with a large suitcase full of pharmaceutical supplies. She was taken to the hospital, her stomach was pumped, and after some time, she recovered fully.

When Nina's attempted suicide was reported to the German doctor, he moved her to the camp hospital for treatment. While there, she met the chief kapo, a brilliant and brutal man of about 40. He was a political prisoner who sold his soul to the Germans and now practically ran the camp. Nina became his mistress, had a private room in the hospital, and soon moved her parents there as well. I never saw her again. In the camp, she was considered a traitor who never made any attempt to help her former friends or even contact any of us.

This event tore the blinders from my eyes. When Nina first took the sleeping powder, we all understood how much she was affected by the ostracism. Had she come back, she would have been forgiven, for she had demonstrated the depth of her feelings, and because we held life to be sacred. But her affair with the kapo showed yet another side of her nature. People were much more complex than I had believed, capable of bizarre actions, and generally untrustworthy. In the process, whatever lingering feelings I still had for Alek evaporated. I was beginning to grow up. I resumed my friendships with other young people in the camp, but not with the intensity of my relationship with Alek and Nina.

In the summer of 1944, an odd event took place. A member of our group, a butcher from Krakow with a common Jewish name, Greenbaum or Greenberg, I don't recall exactly, was summoned to Commandant Kramer's office, where he was interrogated and told he was being sent to Switzerland. Although an ordinary, simple and uneducated man himself, apparently he shared his name with an illustrious Jewish scholar who could not be found and hence was presumed dead. The Swiss government requested that the scholar be released and sent to Switzerland, and the Germans were obliging with this little joke, which they were admitting freely to the butcher. Since his departure was to take place two days later, we frantically prepared lists of all the names of our group and sewed them into his clothes. If this miracle really happened, we begged him to get the list to some influential people and see if they could help us. It was a shot in the dark, and after he left we knew we couldn't bank on salvation from that quarter. After all, he might never get to Switzerland in the first place. Even if he made it, how would this simple man manage to get the lists to the right people, and what could they do if he did?

In the fall of 1944, it was announced we would be moved to a different camp, but that due to the shortage of transport, 150 people or so would go each week, so the transfer of all 600 people would take four weeks. The groups would be chosen alphabetically, except that the younger Dr.

Schwieger and his family were to go with the first group. Within a couple of days, the first group left, a week later the second group, then nothing. There were no further announcements, the whole matter was simply dropped. We had no idea whether the rest of us had missed something wonderful or terrible. It was not till after the war that some light was shed on the situation.

The butcher had indeed made it to Switzerland and had managed to get our story and the name roster to Jewish organizations and to Swiss authorities. In the fall, the German embassy was informed that all the papers of our group were authentic. The embassy was requested to inform the camp authorities that this group was to be protected. The orders arrived in Bergen-Belsen just before the removal of the third section of the group, and the action was stopped. It was too late for the people whose last names started with the letters A through L, and for the family of Dr. Schwieger, who apparently had angered some German administrator at one time or another. Those people were transferred to Auschwitz and went straight to the gas chamber.

Of course we did not know any of this at the time, so we could hope for them. With half the people gone, our three barracks felt suddenly very empty, even spacious. This, however, did not last very long. When it became clear to the Germans that the rest of us were staying at our "hotel," our accommodations were changed yet again, thus starting the third phase of our incarceration.

❊　　❊　　❊

This time we were crammed into a single, large wooden barrack located at the end of the camp. We were now separated from the road by a large group of Hungarian and Dutch Jews and isolated more than ever from knowledge of outside events. It became much harder to get reliable news of the progress of the war or to buy extra food. Nevertheless, we suffered no deaths that winter, while in the neighboring part of camp the inmates were dying in large numbers. Anne Frank was one of the victims of typhus that winter, most likely in the enclosure next to us.

We, the Polish Jews, had experienced the hardships and horrors of the war longer than anyone else. It is my theory that those of us still alive had been gradually tempered all along until we became hardened survivors, while the Jews recently subjected to Nazi persecution just were not immune to the hunger, cold and disease, and were totally unprepared psychologically for what they were enduring. But, in spite of our strengths, we were sorely tried that winter. The prolonged hunger was sapping our bodies' strength and our spirits were low as well.

Even so, enough news filtered to us to make us realize the end of the war was near. But how would it end? Would the Germans let us live to tell the tale? Did they have the wherewithal to kill us all? Did they have the stomach for it, knowing that retribution was near? We engaged in endless speculations on this subject. We now know that elsewhere the Nazis made supreme efforts to annihilate camp populations by subjecting them to death marches and starvation. All through March 1945 there were rumors that the Allies were approaching.

On April 4 or 5, with the Allies about two weeks away, we were informed we would be evacuated to Theresienstadt, a large camp for Jews in Czechoslovakia. The following day, our group, and the surviving inmates of the adjacent camp, about 4,000 Jews in all, were marched to the little railroad station, retracing the trek we made almost two years before. This time there were no trucks, no luggage, but just a mass of bedraggled, tired, sick people, helping each other to hobble along. At the station, wonder of wonders, another passenger train was waiting. We were loaded aboard, orders were shouted, the whistle blew, and we were off. Liberation would have to wait a little longer for us.

Bergen-Belsen was liberated by the British on April 15. They were confronted by thousands of bodies rotting in the sun and filling vast, uncovered pits. The condition of the living was so bad that 14,000 died within days of liberation, despite all the valiant efforts to save them. Josef Kramer attempted to whitewash himself and offered full cooperation. No doubt his wife destroyed the lamp shades made from human skin she was reputed to boast of. The typhus epidemic was uncontrollable, and the British had to burn down the camp, moving the survivors to a nearby Panzer tank corps school. The British marched local German civilians through the camp, and the colonel in charge spoke to them as follows:

"What you will see here is the final and utter condemnation of the Nazi Party ... such a disgrace to the German people that their names must be erased from the list of civilized nations ... this camp was in some respects one of the better ones. Chiefly because in this camp it was possible, in most cases, though not all, to die fairly quietly from hunger or typhus."

In September 1945, 48 members of the Bergen-Belsen staff were tried. Eleven, including Commandant Kramer, were executed in December.

CHAPTER 12

THE END AND THE BEGINNING

Traveling in the war-torn Germany of April 1945 was virtually impossible. All over the country bombed-out rail sections lay in ruin, as lines of authority broke down along with the stock and the equipment. It took our train three or four days to get from Bergen to the vicinity of Magdeburg on the Elbe River, a distance of only about 100 miles. Most of the time was spent idling at little stations or in the countryside, waiting to be routed to some patched-up length of rails. Our train was equipped with an anti-aircraft cannon. We were bombed by the Allies several times. The cannon, mounted on a car at the front of our train, responded each time, but luckily no damage was done by either side.

We lived in this train for a total of eight days. At no time were we freely given food by the Germans. When our removal had been announced, my father was able to exchange my mother's engagement ring for a large loaf of bread, so the two of us had some sustenance. It was wrenching to give up the ring, not because of its value but because of the memories. We now had one $100 bill left, sewn into the peak of my father's cap, and my grandmother's brooch hidden in the heel of my father's shoe. They represented the sum total of our possessions, pitiful, but more than most survivors had.

Fortunately, at all the German stations there were piles of vegetables lying loose waiting to be transported. Usually, we found piles of the despised turnips, but there were also beets, potatoes, and even carrots. To get to these goodies we had to run under sporadic fire. I was still young and agile enough to forage successfully. The half-hearted fire came from the guards accompanying our train, but they were more and more demoralized with each passing day. We disobeyed the orders to stay on the train with ever increasing boldness and impunity. And no, we were not locked in.

The next problem was how to cook this bounty. We commandeered some large cans and managed to construct little stands for them. Someone in our compartment had a knife, so we were able to peel the vegetables and cook them in a little water. We cooked outside whenever possible, but sometimes we were forced to cook in the train corridor, doubtless creating a serious fire hazard. We all had rather delicate stomachs at that point; eating raw turnips and beets would have been disastrous. For fuel we gathered twigs and small pieces of wood, also piled up on the stations or gathered in the countryside. Doing this, we survived for the four days of travel.

Then we came to a total standstill. We were within several miles of the Elbe, but there were no bridges left to cross the river. We spent four days there. Since most of us were still in reasonable condition, we fanned out into the surrounding country in search of food. Nowadays, I don't like to collect money for any causes if it involves going from door to door, but then such niceties were forgotten. With no sense of shame, I went to the nearby villages, knocked on the doors and begged for food. Even in the worst of times, when people in the cities are starving, there is always food left in the country. I must admit, the local farmers, confronted with the weird phantoms showing up on their doorsteps, proved quite generous. But they gave us the food and closed the doors promptly, as if they were trying to deny the reality of our existence.

We ate better than at any time in the camp. We did not stockpile food. Our existence at this point was so precarious, our future so uncertain, that there seemed no good reason to plan for it. Even so, the weather was balmy, our bellies relatively full, and we could see grass and flowers, and lie down and bask in the sun. Four days ensued that were suspended between the harsh realities of the past and the unknown future.

On the morning of April 13 there was finally an announcement. At 3 o'clock we were to form up, march on foot to the river and then swim across it. Even those of us who were swimmers were in no condition to swim across a big river. Did this mean that we would be pushed into the river at bayonet point and drowned like a litter of unwanted kittens? What to do? All morning people were melting away from the train, looking for hiding places in the surrounding woods. My father and I planned to do likewise, but only as a last recourse, should the orders be reversed or ignored. Hiding in what we viewed as hostile countryside did not strike us as a particularly good option, but it beat trying to swim the Elbe.

As it happened, we did not have to make this decision. At 2 p.m. the first American soldier came out of the forest. It was over!

Pandemonium broke out. The very first American who found us was a Jewish boy from Brooklyn. He was immediately engulfed in a sea of bedraggled refugees, and gave away everything he carried on his person. I'll bet he never forgot that day! To come unexpectedly across a train full of Jews in the middle of Germany, what an experience! There were tears of joy and relief in all our eyes. We hugged and kissed in joy and disbelief. After all those interminable years could it really be over?

The Americans who liberated us belonged to the forward elements of the army, and they had to move on. But they did not abandon us. Soon medics and officers arrived and began to assess the situation. The sickest among us were attended to right on the train, and the German women in the nearest little town were ordered to prepare large cauldrons of soup. By evening the soup, supplemented by K-rations, had arrived. We bedded down on the train, our stomachs full of food and our hearts full of hope and gratitude for the wonderful human beings who, far from being repelled by us, had rescued us and cared for us in a most practical and effective way.

The next day arrangements were made for our removal from the train. Basically, each household in the little town was ordered to take in refugees, house and feed us. We were instructed to knock on the doors and demand admission. By afternoon, the move had been made. I took my first bath in two years and changed into an ill-fitting but clean dress, supplied by my new landlady. It was interesting to note the sudden sympathy we received from the local population, all of whom claimed to know nothing about the horrors which had occurred in their country. There was only one woman who freely admitted that she belonged to the

Nazi Party, that she hated Jews and that she regretted Hitler's defeat. I felt more respect for her than the rest of the sniveling, lying Germans trying to save their skins by distancing themselves from their leaders.

I went out into the town square to meet my friends and exchange stories of the miracles which were happening. Here we encountered American soldiers, eager to communicate with us and, yes, by this time I could speak English quite well. Moreover, it turned out that the Americans understood what I said (I had not been sure of it before), and I in turn was able to understand them, provided they spoke slowly. Here I smoked my first cigarette, and started a slow descent into an addiction which was to last 20 years.

Soon a tall, somewhat corpulent officer came to the square. He was looking for English-speaking refugees in order to get some needed information. I came forward and was introduced to a captain, Dr. John Hollander from Milwaukee, Wisconsin. Captain Hollander had been put in charge of medical services in the area, had already commandeered a building for a makeshift hospital, and was looking for people to staff it. We had two doctors in our group, one of them my father, I informed him. I, as well as another girl, had some knowledge of nursing as well.

By evening the little hospital was functioning. Supplied generously by the Medical Corps, and with several German women assigned to do cleaning, cooking and nursing, we performed damage control as best we could. It was a sad experience for me because we lost most of our patients. One case in particular is engraved in my memory. We admitted a family of four. I don't know where they came from, since they were never well enough to explain themselves. They were brought in by the Americans, and we tried to feed them gruel and watered-down milk, but they could not retain any food. Their stomachs had shrunk beyond reprieve. One by one, they died peacefully within the next few days. Had we had intravenous feeding they might have survived. How tragic to make it to the end, and then die. I don't even know if they were conscious enough to know that it was happening to them.

Dr. Hollander visited our little hospital every day. When he came, he would take me by the hand and not let go until it was time for him to leave. He told me about his wife and children and life in the United States. After a few days he told us our whole group was going to be moved to a nearby town, I believe it was called Haldensleben. The Germans had built it especially for SS officers and their families and it now stood empty, since the German residents either fled or were ordered to vacate their apartments by the Americans. A new hospital in the town was already operating. It was staffed with German nurses and American army doctors. Dr. Hollander needed interpreters to make the rounds with the doctors who could not communicate with their refugee patients. He asked my father's permission to let me become an interpreter. Dr. Schwieger's daughter, Rita, who also spoke English well, came along.

The two of us were given a room in the hospital and began three weeks of delightful existence. The work continued to be sad and frustrating, but now with better facilities more victims were being saved. In the evenings our room became the gathering place for the various medics, both on and off duty. Of course some Americans were already "fraternizing" with the German nurses, but they did this secretly, whereas they could be openly friendly with us and speak English to "nice" young women. They brought a phonograph and records, taught us current songs, spoke about a star called Frank Sinatra, and showered us with food, candy and ciga-rettes. Our room became the social center of the hospital. Those were halcyon days. No one worried about the future; we just lived each day as it came. Being treated as normal human beings, we began to relax gradu-ally.

The rest of our group came to Haldensleben a few days later and moved into the empty apartments offered to them, so they too began to live with a degree of normality denied to most refugees from concentration camps. I saw my father every day and shared with him some of my boun-ty. By the beginning of May the war was coming to an end, but my father told me of rumors concerning the area we were in. It seems that accord-ing to the agreement between the Soviets and the Western Allies, the immediate area we were in was to be occupied by the Soviets. The Americans had progressed too far east and were about to cede the area to the Russians. My father said, "Let's go west. Let's take no chances of falling into Soviet hands."

On May 8, the day the war officially ended in Germany, we were informed of a French transport leaving to repatriate French prisoners of war the next day. I asked Dr. Hollander for help, and he gave me a note for a Lieutenant Smith, which is still in my possession. It says, "Will you take care of this girl and her family? She has worked faithfully in the hospital."

On the basis of this note my father and I were issued a pass to France. On May 9 we boarded a cattle train along with a bunch of French people. In the end I had in tow 13 friends who asked to come with us, none of whom spoke a word of French. No matter! Our passes were never checked, and for the next day and a half we traveled west, through Germany, Belgium and France, ignoring the frontiers as no check points were set up as yet in the chaos that was Europe. The sun was shining as the train crawled through the countryside with the doors open wide. Some of us sat in the doorway, our feet dangling, drinking in the sun. The French were excited about going home and we were in sheer delight to be leaving Germany.

We arrived in Paris late at night on May 10. There were representatives of many organizations to help the French and three which vied for the right to take us into their care. One of them represented the Polish government in exile, which had formed in London during the war. Another represented the Lublin government, as the communist Polish government was then known, and the third came from the JOINT Committee, a Jewish relief organization operating in Europe funded by American Jews. Needless to say, we went with this last one, ignoring the blandishments of the other two. We were among the first refugees to come out of Germany, hence the competition for our attention.

The relief organization placed our group of 14 in a private school. Suddenly, after having had some privacy, we were back in a dormitory situation. But our rescuers assured us it was not for long; those of us who wished to go to Palestine could do so almost at once. To go to America would take much longer, probably years, so other quarters and jobs would have to be found for such individuals.

Dr. Hollander had already forwarded a letter from us to 79 Jehuda Halevy Street, Tel Aviv, the magic words we had memorized years ago which represented to us life and freedom. The letter informed Aunt Sonia and the rest of our family that we had survived and my mother had not. Uncle Abrasha and his family also lived in Tel Aviv, while Uncle Solomon lived in New York.

My father and I had to make an important decision almost right away. Since he had always been a Zionist, and neither of us was materialistically inclined, we made a decision in favor of Palestine, in favor of idealism, and also in favor of a quick getaway from Europe and a return to normal life. I know now that, for us, it proved a wrong decision, because it led to our separation and adversely affected my father's quality of life.

We stayed in Paris for about four weeks while our papers were arranged. We were taking advantage of a window of opportunity which remained open for a very short time. The British rigorously controlled the quota of Jews allowed into Palestine each year, but in May 1945 the quota was empty because of the war, and everyone was eager to help the first refugees, so we received permission to enter Palestine legally within days. What took more time was to arrange for a ship to take us there.

Meanwhile we were being fed at the school, receiving double rations of food, wine and cigarettes that the French were giving to their own repatriates. We also had free passes for all public transportation and pocket money courtesy of the relief committee. But we were not in the mood for sightseeing. All around us people were literally dancing in the streets while we felt isolated from the general merriment in our barrack-like dormitory. The euphoria of the liberation had evaporated. My friend Sonia and I often walked in the streets at night. Streets and houses were lit up, and we could see people sitting down to dinner, whole families with children, tables covered with tablecloths and wine gleaming in the matched goblets. Would we ever achieve anything like that? The step from refugee to citizen seemed enormous both economically and psychologically. We felt like the outcasts we still were, and first began to realize how hard was the road ahead of us. In addition, for Sonia, the sight of every child brought back memories of her dead daughter.

I used my money and clothing coupons to buy a new dress and shoes and went to a beauty parlor, where I had my hair cut and styled for a couple of packs of cigarettes. I was not addicted to cigarettes as yet, only smoking "yenems" (somebody else's), and only when one was offered, so I could use my ration as additional money. Cigarettes were a common currency in Europe at that time and remained so for several years.

We were all eating too much. Our bodies told us enough, but our minds said there can never be enough food. I, for one, was getting "pleasantly plump." When my relatives in Palestine saw me for the first time, they were amazed to see a plump girl in a plaid dress and on high platform shoes (the current fashion in Europe) in place of the starving, ragged waif they expected, but they were tactful enough to say nothing. It is only much later that Nina confided their reaction to me, and both of us had a good laugh over it.

On the trip to Paris, I had met a young French war prisoner and the two of us arranged to meet on a square near his home. We made the date for

10 days after our arrival. I had very little to do in Paris so I went to the rendezvous. I was curious whether my friend would keep the date or be too caught up in his homecoming to remember it. He came late and we exchanged news. I knew already that I was going to Palestine. He had a job waiting for him after a period of rest and recuperation. I could see that he had come out of the sense of obligation and was raring to go back. He did not invite me to meet his family and we parted without planning to keep in touch. It was another little indication of my alienation from what I perceived as the normal life.

The most memorable event in Paris was my father's encounter with my childhood friend, Chris. He was walking along the street when suddenly an unknown woman rushed to him and started to hug and kiss him. He had not seen Chris for three years. During that time she had grown up and changed a lot so, at first, he did not recognize her, but of course she recognized him. He rushed back to our room all excited. Chris and her mother Marysia had survived! We met the very next day and heard their story. They had escaped to the Aryan side, Mary working in a lab, and were deported to Germany in 1944 as Poles, after the Warsaw uprising. They were liberated by the Russians, a dubious pleasure. At one point Marysia (now going by Mary), who was working in a hospital, put Chris on the typhus ward to protect her from rape by Soviet soldiers. After the war, they too had gone back to France, where Mary's relatives had survived. My father and I were about to leave Paris, but we exchanged addresses, with me providing Sonia's address in Tel Aviv. We have never lost touch since. Mary and Chris were thinking of going to America, so our paths were parting again, but we were to meet again in a few years time.

The day of our departure came. Our group, which had swollen to over 100 Jewish refugees, boarded a train to Marseille. We traveled through unspoiled French countryside. It was June and the flowers were in bloom and the trees full of leaves, hiding the scars of war. In Marseille, we were housed in hot, tin-roofed, military barracks, while we waited for the ship which was to take us to Palestine.

Meanwhile, we roamed the city. It was my first encounter with a port city and Mediterranean culture. The city was crowded, dirty and sleazy. It was dotted with bars and taverns, accessed through the ubiquitous curtains of beads. Sailors and street women lounged in the streets. Yet it was also vibrant and full of life. Through someone in our group we were invited for dinner with a local Jewish family related to her. Since my father and the refugee relatives did not speak French, the conversation was in Yiddish. The Yiddish of our hosts was interlaced with French words, sounding alien to our ears, but testifying to the adaptation powers of this *lingua franca* of the Jews. I marveled once again at the comfort and elegance of the house. So even Jews could live so well, but would I ever? It seemed totally unattainable.

The ship proved to be an old Portuguese tub. The sailors, dark, unkempt, and in ragged clothes, looked like men you would not want to meet in a dark alley. But this tub was amazingly sea-worthy, the weather balmy, the sailors rough but kind, and our few days at sea a joyous experience. Some of the passengers, all war survivors, were going to relatives, others to kibbutzim. Most of us were young and resilient, with hopes for the future.

The Zionist leaders traveling with us were *sabras* (native Israelis). They taught us Hebrew songs, as well as some emergency Hebrew. They told us about life in Palestine, where a struggle for independence was already in progress. We also heard about the Haganah and the Irgun, which were secret Jewish paramilitary organizations. In short, we were being deliberately focused on our upcoming life and away from our past. It seemed strange at the time, but was in fact very wise of them, as it occupied our time and minimized our grief and self-absorption. I made friends with the ship's cook, who spoke some French, and received fresh oranges and bananas every day, foods I had not seen for years and which were still rare in northern France.

We docked in Acre, a small port in northern Palestine, apparently the official reception place for legal immigrants at the time. Here again there was a concentration-camp-like facility awaiting us, but we were allowed an hour with our relatives before entering it. Uncle Abrasha drove his sister Sonia and his daughter Nina to meet us. It was a bittersweet meeting. I was their only blood relative to survive the war. They were all friendly with my father, but it was not the same. My mother was not there, and the encounter brought the grief back in full force for all of us. Nina told me I would be living with her for the time being, and my father would stay in Sonia's apartment. The two apartments were next to each other in the same building and on the same floor, so there would be no separation. Nina was making enthusiastic plans to introduce me to her friends and otherwise absorb me into her life. She had grown up and was now a handsome young woman although still attending high school, full of herself but at the same time generous and giving. We were talking, crying, hugging, all at once, trying to catch up in this brief time allotted us, on the six years of separation and our widely diverging lives during those years. Finally, they had to leave, promising to come every day until we were released.

The camp was depressing, but we spent only one and a half days there. Our papers were all in order, we had a place to go to, and the British clerks processed our case efficiently and sympathetically. Alas, the kindness afforded us was not to last very long. Soon few Jews were to be admitted legally and the battle to bring the surviving remnant of European Jewry to Palestine was to commence.

True to their promise, Abrasha and Nina were there to pick us up, and we drove away from the camp, through Haifa, and down the coast to Tel Aviv. Now the long nightmare of war was really over.

CHAPTER 13

AFTERMATH: PALESTINE

In June 1945, after tearful greetings from the rest of the family and a festive lunch in our honor, we settled the details of our immediate existence. I was to share the living/dining room with Nina in Abrasha's and Cyla's one-bedroom apartment, while my father slept on the couch in Aunt Sonia's two-bedroom apartment (Sonia and Maniek had two small children occupying one of the bedrooms). That same afternoon I was whisked to Sonia's dressmaker and was fitted for several flower-patterned cotton dresses, the standard uniform of Tel Aviv women. My sartorial rehabilitation had begun.

During the next few weeks we were the local curiosity. Since we were among the first refugees to reach Palestine, everyone wanted to hear our story. Even traveling by bus, Nina and I would be admonished for speaking Polish instead of Hebrew, which I was learning as fast as I could, and when she explained, I would end up answering questions about the Holocaust.

Everyone had relatives presumably lost in the maelstrom, and every retelling was accompanied by emotional outbursts from the listener. We could not refuse to talk, and it meant we were constantly forced to relive the horrors and could not get on with our new lives. I was anxious for other survivors to arrive so that the burden on me to talk would lessen. We survivors were given no psychological support after the war. It was expected that we would just pick ourselves up and carry on. Today, the "working through" might be handled much differently.

Meanwhile, letters to and from America flew at a furious rate, and soon an invitation came from Solomon and Sonia for me to attend college in New York and live in their apartment. They also confirmed that they were in possession of our $8,000 which would be made available to us at any time. My father and I made plans for both our futures. The money was to be used to open a laboratory, but my father initially did not feel up to it. He needed a year to familiarize himself with the language, the culture and the tropical diseases he would be dealing with in the new country, and just to catch his breath. He inquired about a job and found one in the Jerusalem lab of Kupat Cholim, a sort of national HMO serving a significant part of the population. Testimony from former colleagues in Warsaw was sufficient to get him the licenses necessary for him to practice medicine in Palestine. He was uncomfortable staying with Sonia, as the circumstances of both families were always strained, and he was not overly fond of my mother's family in the first place.

Soon he departed for Jerusalem, rented a room and immersed himself in work, easily picking up old friendships and seemingly content with his life. His pay was sufficient to cover his modest needs, my schooling and incidentals, as well as for a contribution to my room and board expenses. It was my job to prepare for admission to an American university.

The decision concerning my education was based, in part, on the difficulties involved in attending a university in Palestine. I spoke very little Hebrew, and to be admitted I would have had to get a high school diploma. Granted, I was bright and industrious, but schools in Tel Aviv were very tough. My cousin Nina was struggling after five years despite her by now fluent Hebrew; in fact I am not sure she ever got her diploma. For me, the process might have taken four years, and I was nearing 18 already. Furthermore, my father planned to settle in Tel Aviv while the Technion, which I would have attended to study chemical engineering had I stayed, was located in Haifa, so we would not be together anyway. We were even unsure whether my father could afford such expensive schooling so soon after establishing a brand new laboratory.

Thus the offer from New York was a godsend and we accepted it gratefully, since it took major financial pressure off our backs. The option of not going to college was not even contemplated, a logical continuation of the struggle to get me educated all during the war.

I still needed a high school diploma, preferably from an English-language institution, and this proved much easier to achieve. The British encouraged English-language education in all their colonies and dominions. (Before becoming Israel in 1948, Palestine was a British protectorate.) The British facilitated the process by offering a type of equivalency diploma called the London Matriculation, so named because the tests were administered and processed by the University of London. To prepare for the exams, I joined a private tutoring group, and did much more studying on my own than I might have in a regular high school.

At the end of one year I sat for the exams and passed—actually, scores were not revealed, but one could simply pass or achieve the First Division grade, which I did. It was on the basis of this diploma that I was accepted by both Columbia University and New York University. After obtaining a map of New York City and determining that my uncle's apartment on the Upper West Side was closer to Columbia, I chose to attend that school. Inquiring into the relative merits of the two schools never even entered my head.

These decisions set the pattern of my life for the first year in Tel Aviv. My father was busy working and studying, while I was busy preparing for the exams. Nina made every effort to integrate me into her circle of friends, but with less than stellar results. In the first place, her friends were chronologically one or two years younger than I, but years younger in some ways, while much more socially adept in others. They were wrapped up in their lives, relationships, friendships, studies and the political situation. A short, plump girl who did not attend their school and already had one foot in America did not interest them. Since I was Nina's roommate and frequent companion, they had to tolerate me, but after I moved out of Nina's apartment I saw little of them.

Nina herself was very supportive of me and put up with all my criticisms and bitterness, unfailingly consoling me and offering me her unconditional love. She sat with me in the bathroom, as I was unused to being alone even in that most private of places, and talked with me when I could not sleep at night, fought with her mother to let us sleep on the terrace during the hot, breathless nights and was generally a tower of strength. But I also viewed her as a bit flighty, very social and overly concerned with her appearance. Because of my skewed perspective, I was not in a position to see her as a normal teenager who, in fact, was exhibiting a great deal of maturity and sensitivity in her interactions with me. This testifies to how wrapped up I was at the time in my own misery, my disappointment in not experiencing more happiness and exhilaration in the aftermath of the war.

Other than being occasionally cranky, I did not show these feelings of disappointment or speak of them to anyone. Friends and relatives seemed to feel that now that the war was over, I should just pick up my life as if nothing had happened. This at a time when I was still startled by every loud noise such as a car backfiring, and fought the impulse to look for the nearest shelter. It must be said in fairness to the people I came in contact with that little was known at the time about the effects of prolonged trauma on civilians, although shell-shocked soldiers were better understood.

Consequently, no one offered me help with my feelings of exclusion and sadness and I learned to cope with them alone, keeping my feelings to myself and pushing them deep down every time they intruded into my thoughts. In time, I got very good at it. Much later, with evidence of solid successes under my belt, new relationships forged and new concerns to occupy my thoughts, the bad feelings almost went away—in this case repeated denial produced positive results. But the lesson I learned is that, in the end, each of us stands alone.

I made one close woman friend during my stay in Palestine. Ruth was a quiet, rather intellectual girl, part of Nina's crowd although she didn't fit in very well. It was the shared feeling that originally attracted us to each other, but later we found we read the same books and held many discussions, feeling free to express our unorthodox and controversial opinions on many matters including the increasingly tense state of Palestinian politics. We felt superior because the rest of Nina's crowd would have been uninterested in or intolerant of our positions.

Ruth was a very wealthy girl. She was the only person I knew who lived in a private home in Tel Aviv, and a very spacious and luxurious one at that. Her widowed mother and older sister ran the family business—a cosmetics and pharmaceuticals company—and were both sophisticated, elegant and self-assured women. Ruth's mother always had a male escort for her outings and her sister was engaged to a handsome, suave gentleman. They seemed like creatures from another planet, not only to me but to Ruth as well. Not that Ruth was ugly, far from it. But somehow she did not acquire the all-absorbing fascination with her own looks and appearance which seemed to consume her mother and sister. She wore her long, blonde hair in braids wrapped around her head, no make-up, and simple cotton dresses or khakis. Perhaps it was her form of rebellion against her family—nothing but a normal teenage phase. At any rate we were a great comfort to each other, but the valve of deepest confidences was open only one way. I did not share my feelings of inadequacy, rejection or alienation with anyone.

On the surface, my life moved serenely and according to plan. I spent the first year living in Nina's apartment. I loved Uncle Abrasha, who was a generous, loving, uncomplicated man. He had a little leather finishing business staffed by several Arabs with whom he was on the best of terms. He worked long hours, since they needed constant supervision. He came home for dinner and a short siesta in the afternoon, returned to work and finally ended the day about 8 p.m., too tired to do anything but fall into bed and listen to the latest news in the tense political situation in Palestine.

Aunt Cyla was the complete antithesis of her husband. Although a very intelligent woman, she was confined to cleaning house and cooking, both of which she did well and efficiently, maybe too well. I learned to cook several Israeli dishes from her; she was a most competent house-wife. She was crazy clean—today we would call her anal-retentive. When company came we sat around a glass-topped dining room table. Cyla would come out while the company was still there and wipe off finger-prints from the glass using a rag and a little alcohol.

A one-bedroom apartment is not enough to fill anyone's life, so Cyla sought escape in fiction, which she read in several languages. Cyla also had a great deal of trouble relating to people. She was so reserved and formal it was hard to know her even living in her house, but I now think she was groping towards me as a kindred soul. Separated by a generation and other invisible barriers, we never connected, which is a shame.

Aunt Sonia had a totally different personality—open, brash, loving and very much down-to-earth. Somebody once persuaded her to read a book, a current best-seller. For two months, she would end every conversation by saying, "I must get back to my book." Finally, the ordeal was over, never to be repeated, at least while I lived in Tel Aviv.

She was the one who equipped me with clothes and shoes, and who came closest to mothering me. Her son Eitan, who was seven at the time, paid me little attention, and the feeling was mutual. Her daughter Etti, however, was about two and a half and an adorable imp who took full advantage of her status as the family darling. She expressed her domination by refusing to eat. Meal times became circus times with adult members of the family clowning around in an effort to distract her and let her mother shovel some food into her. Etti certainly did not look as if she were starving and the methodology used to get her to eat was the worst one possible.

I refused to be drawn into this family drama. So soon after my own period of deprivation if not starvation, the whole concern struck me as ludicrous and almost obscene. I thought Etti would profit from some benevolent neglect and the sensation of genuine hunger. Finally, Sonia became totally frustrated and hired a child specialist to teach Etti to eat. The family was banished from the kitchen, and listened to the child's pitiful cries while her nose was held and she was forced to swallow. After Etti hysterically vomited the meal, she was fed the regurgitated food and within two weeks learned her lesson, but at what cost? At any rate, she became very heavy as an adult.

All during that year I visited my father in Jerusalem and he came to Tel Aviv occasionally for the weekends. We roamed the old city soaking in the history, while socializing with his friends. My father read Hebrew newspapers aloud to improve our fluency in the language.

I remember one of his friends in particular, a doctor from Warsaw who moved to Palestine just before the war. He and his wife lived in an old Arab house with all the windows opening on the inner courtyard and none to the outside of the house. They had the sense to keep the Oriental spirit of the house, except for introducing some needed European furniture.

In private, my father chortled over his friends' story. Back in Warsaw, the couple had been unable to conceive a child. Adoptions were not unheard of but did not appeal to him or his wife, so they decided the wife would have an affair and terminate it as soon as she became pregnant. They must have known that the problem lay with him.

This plan was carried out and eventually a little girl was born, but the wife came to like her lover and refused to give him up. The husband, having found out the location of their trysts, went there one day, found them in a restaurant, accosted the lover in public and beat him up. Such goings on were unheard of in the sedate, middle-class Jewish milieu at that time.

That was the end of the affair, and it gained our friend a well-deserved reputation for eccentricity. Although by this time the daughter was fully grown, according to my father she never found out how she had been conceived, which was hard to believe with all the gossiping going on.

The couple held an open house on Friday nights and we went there often. Fifteen or 20 people would gather for tea, dessert and conversation. Topics would range from politics to the latest book, gossip, and back to politics. But at 10 p.m. sharp, the host invariably got up, bade his guests good night and retired to bed. The guests, however, were free to stay and visit with his wife. Without television, the art of conversation flourished and I, although young, was encouraged to participate and managed to hold my own.

In the course of such gatherings my father was often introduced to single ladies who gently hinted at their matrimonial availability. He turned them away with good humor but quite decisively, making a joke of it as we were walking home from such parties. Some of the women tried to ingratiate themselves with me, hoping to get to my father that way. I was a bit surprised. My father was elderly in my eyes, not very good-looking and overall did not seem to me a great matrimonial prize. But because of his profession and earning potential, he would have represented a safe home for these lonely ladies.

Once a would-be nuptial candidate held a long discussion with me about books. My father said later he didn't see why he should support anyone's reading habit. We both laughed about it, but on that occasion, I pointed out to him he would be lonely once I left for America. "Don't worry about it," he said. "It is only for a few years. Your job is to get a good profession so you can stand on your own two feet. I will manage." In the nearly three decades between my mother's death and his own, I don't believe my father ever looked at another woman.

By this time, I was beginning to meet some of my old friends and acquaintances from Warsaw. In meeting people I knew before and during the war in Palestine, the strangest of coincidences occurred. Early in 1947, I was preparing to make the move to New York for college. At that time in Palestine it took two years to become a citizen, and since I had arrived in the summer of 1945 my two years were not up and I could not get a Palestinian passport. However, I needed a passport for the necessary student visa to the United States. A typical bureaucratic absurdity, but a serious matter at the time.

It occurred to me to try my luck at the Polish consulate. Perhaps they would take pity on me and issue me a Polish passport. Nina came with me for moral support. We explained my problem to the receptionist and were instructed to wait in the hall. Suddenly, I saw a familiar woman walk past me. Could it be? "Panna Janka?" I yelled. She turned and looked at me without any sign of recognition. It is hard to recognize people in unexpected settings. Besides, I had changed a lot in the intervening years. She walked over to me. "Don't you know me? I am Klara Salamon," I said. "I was in your gym class." Indeed, she was my gym teacher from the Teachers' Union School in Warsaw and, at one time, my very special friend.

"Of course!" she said, finally recognizing me. "Now I see it!" We were both overjoyed to find each other alive and well. In the manner of all survivors, we exchanged our stories. She had survived in a Communist partisan group, living in hiding in a forest and sabotaging the German war machine. She married a fellow Jewish partisan. After the war the Polish government rewarded them for their dangerous and brave service, appointing her husband as consul in Tel Aviv. "You must both meet him," she pronounced enthusiastically, leading us urgently towards his office.

She knocked, we entered, and behold: there was the Polish consul, none other than my former gym teacher in Slonim! Panna Janka was as flabbergasted as I was. My name had never come up in her conversations with him.

In view of what had happened to all of us, the consul's past offenses were trivial (though not forgotten) and we were truly glad to see each other alive. I got my Polish passport with no questions asked, although it rather absurdly allowed me to go to every country except Poland.

I did realize that once again I was living a charmed existence, taken in by loving relatives, guided by a caring father, and building a future without compromising my educational and professional goals. Still, I felt different, an outsider looking in on life. Part of it was simply due to being a teenager and part to the fact that, as I was planning to leave Palestine soon, I did not get personally involved in the fight for the independence which consumed much of the population, though not yet my relatives and friends. Good reasons, but insufficient to explain my feelings, which must be attributed to the war. The war engendered feelings of rootlessness, a disconnectedness with normal society. I was coping, but such feelings do not disappear overnight.

Nina and I often went to a cafe near the sea where we met her friends and where, over a cup of tea and a piece of cake, we could spend an afternoon chatting, table-hopping, gossiping, all very frivolous and reminiscent of my mother's life before the war. Nina's best friend was learning bridge from her mother, who ran a social game in her house and offered to teach both of us, but it turned out we were disinclined to be serious about it. However, I made a mental note of it as an interesting possibility for the future. Now I am an avid duplicate player.

By the spring of 1946, I was nearing the end of my studies and my father felt ready for a move. We requested our money from Uncle Solomon. It took two months for him to come up with it; clearly it had been tied up in his business. When it came it was exactly $8,000, worth much less than its value in 1941 when Solomon took possession of it. Whatever profits had been made on this money—this money which had kept us in Europe through the war and cost my mother's life—my uncle had kept. My father, true to his nature, held it against my uncle for many years and wouldn't even see him when he eventually came to the United States.

Only my intervention convinced him to get in touch with his only relative in New York, after which they became friends. My father even rented an apartment in the same building where Solomon and Sonia lived, obtained inside information from Solomon that the building was about to go co-op and eventually made a $25,000 profit in the process.

We found an apartment at 100 Allenby Road, an excellent, central location on Tel Aviv's main commercial thoroughfare.

I had a two-week window between taking my exams and moving in with my father. During the previous year, I had become familiar with Tel Aviv and Jerusalem, so I decided to sample the kibbutz life. I went to a small kibbutz where I was assigned a bunk in a four-bed dormitory for single girls and put to work digging potatoes. Neither the accommodations nor the work was much to my taste. I was unaccustomed to physical labor. By the end of the day I was ready to fall into bed, while the kibbutzniks were ready for an evening of eating, business meetings, political discussions, singing and dancing. Singing and dancing the *hora* seemed to be their main idea of fun. Back in Tel Aviv most young people's parties culminated with rolling the rug away and dancing to the music of Benny Goodman, Frank Sinatra and Bing Crosby, so I had developed some skill and love of ballroom dancing.

I was ashamed to admit it, but I was ready to pack it up after a few days. My hands were blistered and every muscle in my body rebelled against the unfamiliar regime, but nonetheless I was determined to stick it out for my two weeks. The kibbutzniks were quite friendly, but very self-centered and uninterested in "culture" or events outside their little world. (I was becoming something of an intellectual snob.) They worked hard, exulted in physical labor and were preparing to defend their country against a much more numerous enemy. Their plate was full enough without cultural exploration.

As it turns out I didn't leave voluntarily. After the first week, there was a terrorist attack on a nearby British military unit and the few guest workers in the kibbutz were asked to leave. Kibbutzim members refused to give any information during searches conducted by the British, not even divulging their names, since every kibbutz housed illegal immigrants and members of blacklisted defense organizations. Since this search was expected, they felt it best not to involve outsiders. One week in a kibbutz was enough to assure me I liked neither communal life nor physical labor. I did not feel sufficient patriotism to overcome my aversion.

After this experience, my second year in Palestine began, and was very different from the preceding one. I acted as my father's assistant, bookkeeper, housekeeper, hostess and chief "bottle washer." Business picked up little by little as we were advertised by word of mouth, with many patients referred by sympathetic doctors from Poland. My father taught me how to make reagent solutions and the simpler tests, "the chemistry" as it was called in the trade, while he concentrated on the microscope work. He never achieved the volume of his lab in Warsaw, so I had enough time to shop about three times a week and cook simple meals, as well as attend to the cleaning and laundry. In spite of all these responsibilities, I was usually done by three o'clock and free to go swimming, to a cafe or to my classes.

The process of planning for my move to America was time-consuming. My London Matriculation diploma came two months after the test. I applied to college, sent them my meager academic credentials and waited again. I was admitted to Columbia in the winter of 1946-47, too late for the spring semester. The plan was then to begin classes there in September 1947. Traveling documents also proved cumbersome, a contrast with the unexpected ease I had had getting my Polish passport.

Meanwhile, to perfect my English I attended another little group, and took the Cambridge Proficiency Exam, another British invention to anglicize the natives. After passing that exam, I was licensed to teach English in all the British colonies and dominions (but not in Great Britain itself). I found the study interesting and pleasant, and immersed myself in Shakespeare and the great English poets and novelists. I continued to read voraciously, concentrating on British and American authors. That was the year I discovered Upton Sinclair's Lanny Budd series, as good a way to learn 20th Century history as any; Theodore Dreiser's *An American Tragedy*; and John Galsworthy's *The Forsyte Saga* as well as many other novels which evinced good writing, great characterizations and interesting plots while remaining "good reads." I shared a passion for reading with Aunt Cyla. We always recommended books to each other and discussed them afterwards.

My father dealt with his teenager by refusing to acknowledge anything reprehensible I may have done. When Aunt Sonia reported I was smoking, he said I wasn't, since he had never seen it. One time I went to a party and inadvertently got drunk. I came home sick and dizzy. Every time I put my head down the world spun sickeningly. My father accepted the fiction that it had been "something I ate," gave me some aspirin, and acted sympathetic but low-key. He tolerated the dance music I played, complaining mildly that I always played the same two songs: one fast and one slow. Of course he was exaggerating, but I understand him much better now that I am occasionally subjected to rock and roll.

At the same time, the political situation in Palestine was heating up, and there was a great deal of hostility between the British and the Jews. Even before, when my father lived in Jerusalem, no Jewish theater would show *Henry V* because the movie was dedicated to the red berets—the paratroopers who were enforcing the British "occupation" of Palestine. My father and I went to see it in an Arab theater with Arabic subtitles, shown on a minuscule screen, allowing him a good, long nap.

In the year we lived together in Tel Aviv, there were numerous terrorist incidents, usually associated with the Irgun. These were frequently followed by all-day curfews, searches and other activities harassing the population. Once we all had to vacate our apartments and leave them open for inspection while we spent the day in a field on the outskirts of town. It reminded me of a similar action soon after the Germans occupied eastern Poland in 1941 but, of course, this time we were not afraid for our lives. A push or a shove maybe, some rough language and yelling, but there was no fear of a British soldier killing an innocent civilian or not responding to the needs of the sick, the old or the children.

During the all-day curfews we got to know our neighbors. There was a Yemenite family living in our building. The father was a building contractor and all his adult sons worked with him. One of them became interested in me and we had several trysts on the roof of the building. He was dark and handsome, and had the sweetest and sunniest personality imaginable. He seemed honest, hard-working, and uncomplicated. He seemed to have no need for soul-searching. To him life was good, his goals clear, his family dear. On the basis of our few encounters he proposed to me, assuring me that he was already doing well enough financially to support a wife and that once Israel was independent he and his family would flourish. No doubt they did.

I was flattered, amazed and shocked, all at the same time. My suitor was certain his family would love me. At the time we knew each other slightly but they liked me already. It was a little bit tempting to lose myself in the warmth of such a clan, but not tempting enough. I was not willing to abandon my career hopes on such short acquaintance. Besides, I must admit I had a slight prejudice against Yemenites: the only other Yemenite I knew was Aunt Sonia's maid. Intermarriage between the "white" and Yemenite Jews was practically unheard of. Just thinking about my attitude now, I cringe, but it was the prevalent one at the time, just as racism was prevalent in the United States when I first came here. It took a lot of growing to learn to accept and respect different people, even for someone like myself who had suffered so much from just such attitudes expressed by the Germans.

My other relationship was with Arnold, a friend from Bergen-Belsen who was about 15 years older than I. He rented a room in an apartment and worked for a jeweler. Arnold was a gifted jewelry designer and craftsman. He had no material worries, but his life seemed to be very lonely. He spent his leisure time writing letters and anxiously waiting for replies, corresponding with old friends in Poland or those who had landed in America after the war.

Since Arnold was contemplating a move to America, he wanted to learn English, and proposed I become his paid tutor. My father approved. He liked Arnold, whom he considered a contemporary. He also respected Arnold's craft. One time Arnold converted my grandmother's brooch (which spent the war in the heel of my father's shoe) into a diamond ring and a pin for me. I wonder whether my father understood that the English lessons, while legitimate, were also an excuse for spending time together and becoming good friends and more. I am sure my father would have considered Arnold too old for me, not educated enough and, in general, a possible distraction from my career goals. Arnold himself told me the same things many times and I blew hot and cold, all of which made our relationship rather tentative.

I must say, however, that until I met my husband Bert, I was never as comfortable with any man as I was with Arnold. We shared a common history in Bergen-Belsen, similar cultural background, language, friends and a similar way of looking at life. We laughed at the same things and the same things made us sad. We even shared some political convictions which would not have made us popular in Palestine at the time. But we held back because of the age and education differences which divided us. Arnold treated me as a mixture of a woman and a child, another attitude which might have hampered our closeness over time. However, a relationship with an older man is a nice thing for a young girl. It can be very reassuring, provided the man is wise and honorable.

We continued to correspond after I moved to New York. In the beginning while I was still relatively lonely, his letters were a source of comfort to me, but after I made new friends they came to mean less. Arnold came to New York about three years later. We met several times, but I had moved on. We both acknowledged it and parted on good terms but with poignant regrets. Some years later Arnold married a woman closer to his age. I believe the marriage was a happy one.

In spite of all the good things that were happening to me, I felt a lot of discontent during my second year in Tel Aviv. At one point I thought I needed a vacation. My father could spare neither the time nor the money to accompany me, but he suggested a weekend in Bat Yam, a seaside resort nearby. I went and stayed alone in a hotel. Since it was out of season there were very few guests. Bat Yam had a beautiful beach, but it was too cold to swim and the weather was dreary like my mood. I ended up writing some very bad poetry and boring myself out of my skull. In fact, I was so bored I cut my little fling short, even though doing so was an open admission of the failure of my adventure.

During that time I also suffered from a physical ailment, a rare occurrence for me. I had a series of abscesses, some of them in most inconvenient places, and all very painful. My father treated them with penicillin so that none of them lasted long, but the problem persisted for several months. Apparently this was a common reaction to life in a subtropical country with germs Europeans weren't used to. I think now my low spirits at the time may have adversely affected my resistance to sickness, for otherwise I am a very healthy person, rarely catching even a cold.

Finally the time came for my departure. This was to be my first solo venture into the world and I was both excited and apprehensive. For the first time in years, I was to be truly separated from my father and I knew I would miss him sorely.

The first leg of the trip was a short flight to Cairo, on an Egyptian plane of all things. (Relations between Jews and Egyptians were precarious at the time.) It was a small plane with no stewardesses, only a pilot and a co-pilot. Among the passengers there were three other young women going to New York and we made friends even before boarding. The two pilots flirted with all of us, letting us sit in the co-pilot's seat and "fly the plane" one at a time, so that between all the chatting and flirting I had no time to be afraid, even though this was my first flight. I have become much more cowardly since.

In Cairo, we all stayed in the same hotel, a place of great elegance and antiquity with doormen springing out to open the great double doors, and several waiters attending to us in the grand dining room. The hotel manager took us under his wing and arranged for a taxi to take us to the Pyramids and the Sphinx, making all the financial arrangements to prevent our being cheated. One of the young women had a friend in Cairo who was working for MGM, managing movie distribution for the area. He took the two of us on a private tour of Cairo, showing us the markets, a museum and a nightclub with the obligatory belly dancers.

We then took a train to Alexandria, our embarkation point for the United States We had an interesting experience in that city. We all went out to a highly recommended restaurant. Unfortunately the place was so popular there were no free tables. While the maitre d' was trying to resolve the problem, he was called to a table and came back with an invitation for us to join the party sitting there. He assured us he knew the lady and her daughter, and we would be perfectly safe there. We accepted the invitation.

Our hostess introduced herself by claiming she was not Egyptian but of Italian extraction. (Nobody we met in Egypt admitted to being Egyptian.) She brought her 17-year-old daughter to the restaurant two or three times a week. Here, her daughter had a chance to dance under her mother's watchful eye. The daughter was still in school. She was taken to and from school every day in a chauffeur-driven family limousine and had never walked in the street alone. Yet she was allowed to dance with any stranger who passed her mother's inspection. Of course, after each dance the gentleman escorted her back to the table and that was the end of the acquaintance.

Soon, men came and invited all of us to dance. "Go! go!" encouraged our hostess. "You're safe. I am watching out for you." We compared our backgrounds with that of her daughter. I never met anyone who lived such a sheltered life; even her husband was to be picked out for her. But meanwhile, she was permitted to have some fun. At the end of the evening our hostess insisted on paying our bill, advising us to save our money for the trip.

The next day we boarded the ship on which we all traveled third class. I shared the cabin with three other women and, as usual, drew the upper bunk. On the way we made a few stops. Because of my Polish, communist passport I was not allowed to disembark in Greece, which was experiencing a communist rebellion just then, but I was allowed to visit Naples. The cost of seeing Naples was several packs of cigarettes. These cigarettes were available and very cheap on our ship. Along with all the other unmarried women, I was not permitted to go to Pompeii, since some sights there might shock our tender sensibilities. How times change! I finally saw Pompeii several years ago, as well as the Pompeii exhibit at the Metropolitan Museum, with no damage to my sensibilities.

As soon as we passed Gibraltar and left the smooth Mediterranean Sea, everyone got sick. Being seasick is no joke—I thought I was going to die. Our steward was very kind and advised us to eat, bringing tempting dishes to the cabin. After a couple of days I got over it, and was fine for the rest of the voyage, which lasted for about 10 days.

At last we saw the skyline of New York City, passed the Statue of Liberty and docked at a pier on the West Side of Manhattan. I passed the immigration check with no problems, in spite of my trepidation. At that time I was still terrified of any encounter with an official or a policeman, all of whom I viewed as natural enemies. I found my luggage and Aunt Sonia, who came to meet me, in that order. I recognized her immediately. My cousin Adzia, her son, was waiting in the car outside, and we went straight to the hospital to see Cousin Helen, who had given birth to her first baby the day before.

I was truly on my own! The next day I went to register, and introduced myself to Professor Drew, the head of the chemical engineering department at Columbia. At that time, Columbia University engineering students attended Columbia College, an all-male school, for the first two years, so I was sent to Barnard College. Professor Drew seemed rather skeptical of my proposed brilliant career. I don't think he had much faith in my staying the course, but he worked out my schedule with me. I would be at Barnard only for one year, and begin taking engineering courses at Columbia my sophomore year. At the age of 20, I was all set to begin my career.

CHAPTER 14

NEW YORK CITY

The home I came to in September 1947 was neither as happy nor as welcoming as the family homes had been in Palestine. My uncle Solomon ruled absolutely, alternating between benevolence and hard cruelty. For example, I assumed my invitation included payment for college. I came to the United States with $100 in my pocket, all my father could spare at the time. College tuition at Columbia University amounted to $350 per semester. Solomon did not raise the issue, making me ask him for the money he knew very well I didn't have. He made me squirm, saying he would think it over. The next day he came up with the money, but only reluctantly. During the first semester I applied for a scholarship. After that my education never cost my uncle a penny.

He continued, however, to feed and house me for four years. When he and his wife Sonia were in Andrews, North Carolina, a small town in the far western part of the state where they had a large chicken farm, my cousin Adzia was instructed to give me $15 a week for my expenses which, together with my baby sitting money and an occasional $100 from Israel, was adequate provided I lived economically.

Many times I walked from 87th Street and West End Avenue, where we lived, to my classes on 116th Street to save the dime for the subway. I am not complaining. It didn't hurt me any. The experience was even good exercise, and since most of my friends were equally poor, no shame was attached to this condition. Often, we would spend an evening at Lion's Den, a coffee shop on the campus dispensing coffee for 8 cents a cup and jukebox music for 10 cents a song. We usually went Dutch.

About a year after I moved to New York, a distant cousin asked me to be a bridesmaid at her wedding. I accepted, not knowing this committed me to buying a gown for the occasion. Solomon was furious at the expense, and I got chewed out for it, ignorance of costs not being an acceptable excuse. I could never repay the $40 cost of the gown, an enormous amount of money for me at the time.

I knew Solomon was well-to-do, maybe even wealthy. He drove an expensive car. We often ate out in local but very good restaurants, and he dressed well and expensively. He had a generous side; he just wasn't gracious about it. At one point he bought his daughter Helen a house in Larchmont, but since he put it in his own name so her husband couldn't get his hands on it, his generosity was not fully appreciated. He also continuously subsidized his brother Abrasha and sister Sonia in what a year later was to become Israel. Like the ancient gods, he liked to be propitiated and made to feel superior and important. When you're forced to be on the receiving end of charity from a rich relative, being made aware of it at every opportunity is not pleasant.

I was not the only target of Solomon's parsimony. He kept his wife on an even smaller budget. Many a time, when Solomon was away or out and we wanted to go to a movie, we had to scrounge around for the 70 cents for two tickets to a local cinema.

Sonia truly had no sense of money; it just melted away in her hands. One time she went to the Klein Department store, a cross between Wal-Mart and a flea market, and came back with four evening bags, each beaded in a different color. At the time no one in the family even had an evening gown, not counting the lavender one from my notorious bridesmaid stint, which definitely did not become me. Poor Sonia, she just couldn't resist a bargain!

Sonia was a lovely woman: romantic, sweet, innocent and generous. I treated her like a younger sister. I loved her, but would never confide in her or ask for advice. She bore Solomon's temper tantrums with great equanimity, and kept house both in New York and at the chicken farm in North Carolina, shuttling back and forth without complaint. She lavished her love on her little Pekinese dog, her children, and later her grandchildren, while gently and with great dignity mediating between Solomon and the world.

The family was very self-absorbed and anything but thoughtful. On the first day I started school, which was three days after my arrival in New York, I took the subway. No one bothered to tell me there were two possible trains, and I took the wrong one. Thus, when I exited on 116th Street I found myself in the middle of Harlem. I had never seen so many black people in one place, and I found it a little frightening. I approached an elderly gentleman inquiring about the way to Columbia University. He showed me the direction and told me to walk, which I did, arriving all perspired and late for my first class, which happened to be in American history.

I was truly mortified: what an inauspicious beginning to school! After class I apologized to the teacher, a gorgeous young woman, who explained the subway system to me. In time she and I became good friends, though only in the context of school. As I have said, my knowledge of American history (a required subject) was limited to what I had gleaned from Upton Sinclair and Margaret Mitchell. Terms bandied around in class like "Boston Tea Party" or "Monroe Doctrine" were meaningless to me, while the rest of the class, which had been taught American history since childhood, understood them very well.

I approached our instructor, explaining my difficulties in following the history presented thematically, rather than chronologically. "What would you suggest?" she asked. I proposed one period a week open to all foreign students, most of whom, surely, were sharing my problem. My complaint was relayed to the department head and was acted upon. The extra period was assigned to our instructor and, together, we worked out the best way to overcome our deficiencies. I ended up with an A+ in the course. Several years later, I heard the same instructor was bringing my name up in class as a role model for other students. I truly admired her competence, her self-confidence, her good looks and elegance, some of it God-given and the rest coming from a smooth life path.

My academic career was very successful on all fronts. Barnard College required all freshmen to take a year of English, but anyone receiving an A for the first semester was excused from taking the second one. Out of a class of 300 freshmen three were so excused, and I was one of them. I was also doing very well in math and physics as well as in chemistry, a class which had a well-deserved reputation for high quality and great demands placed on the students. When I eventually transferred to engineering school, my success continued, though not on the same scale, as the subject matter became more difficult. I think chemical engineering was one of the most difficult majors at Columbia since it required about 25 percent more credits than other fields. A minimum of four years of chemistry (sufficient in itself to get a degree in the subject) were augmented by courses in thermodynamics (the hardest subject I ever studied), unit operations, organic and inorganic technologies, and basic courses in electrical, mechanical, civil, and industrial engineering. Quite a program! I just managed to finish in the top quarter of my class, and considered it an achievement to be proud of.

I studied long hours, alone or with a study partner, pacing the floor of my room, reciting to myself the facts I had to remember, or poring over complex engineering problems. I found all the subjects I took interesting. Years later, when I was working on my master's degree at Montclair University, I took a course titled "Intellectual History of Europe," and the teacher paid me a compliment by saying I was wasted on science and should have been a historian. Although my choice of chemical engineering had been made for practical reasons, I lived with it happily through my whole working life.

My social life was also quite satisfactory. At the beginning of the first year I met the other female Barnard student who planned to study engineering, in her case industrial. Elna Loscher—my only American friend at the time—became a life-long friend. Her parents welcomed me to their home. In fact their home became one of my two homes away from home, a refuge for holidays during many of which my own family was away in North Carolina. I was a frequent visitor for Friday dinners, and went along to Temple Emanu-El where the Loschers were members.

During my second summer the Loschers went to Europe and asked me to stay with Elna and keep her company in their apartment. I was taking a course in nuclear physics at the time and stayed with Elna for a month. Some nights we never went to sleep; we just sat up talking non-stop on every imaginable topic. I don't know how I got through the course, but somehow I made it by getting hold of past exams and memorizing them. The professor was old and rarely changed final exams.

The course covered many topics, among them units on cosmology, relativity and quantum mechanics. Einstein's work figured largely in the curriculum and I learned that he could not accept a random, statistical view of particle behavior (the essence of quantum mechanics). "God does not play dice with the universe," he said. That statement gave me much to think about. In the first place Einstein, in spite of his pioneering work in physics, was essentially a man of the 19th Century. Clearly he believed in a loving, caring, hands-on God intimately involved in human affairs. However, I could not reconcile this God with what had happened to me and my people. Why was I so consistently lucky, while others who were just as quick-witted and ingenious were not? A dozen times or more I was on the brink of death, and each time we either made the right decision or fate intervened. Was it really just statistics? On the other hand what else could it be? Would God really pick me out of the multitude and say: "This one shall live?" I went on to live a good, productive life but accomplished no great deeds to warrant such distinction.

It certainly seemed to me that the heavenly throne was not currently occupied. Yet as a scientist thinking about the origin of the universe, I could not believe that the universe had just happened. Perhaps the fierce intelligence which created it destroyed itself in the process, or perhaps, having created us, it abandoned our universe for some parallel one, leaving us to our own devices. I guess my views make me an agnostic. I keep an open mind on the existence of God, and treat the subject intellectually except in times of extreme stress. When needing comfort, I am suddenly transformed into a fervent believer.

All my other friends were from Europe, usually from Poland and all Holocaust survivors. It is not that we talked a lot about the past, but all of us felt largely excluded from the "mainstream of American life," and flocked together to have our own sense of belonging. Of course, by doing this we also reinforced our alienation and made it harder for ourselves to integrate into the mainstream.

On the first day of my first engineering class, I was chatting with a Russian student sitting next to me when a young man sitting right behind me tapped me on the shoulder and inquired whether I had come from Poland. We introduced ourselves; he had guessed my origin from my accent and we went out for coffee after class. That young man's name was Henry Crane, and he soon proposed that we pull forces and do our homework together. Thus was born a very successful study partnership of two complementary personalities. I often understood concepts more quickly, but Henry was more dogged and thorough. He uncovered aspects I thought I understood but didn't, and wouldn't let go of a problem until we were both sure we knew it inside out. Henry was living at the time in an apartment belonging to a Mr. Rindner, and since the apartment was located on 114th Street, right next to the university, we often studied in Henry's room.

Mr. Rindner had come to New York from Poland in 1939 on vacation but his son, Richard, stayed in Poland and survived the war. Coincidentally, he was one year behind us and also studying chemical engineering at Columbia. The three of us became inseparable friends. The apartment was very large and there were usually three or four subtenants at a time, all of them students, and all of them becoming, at least to some extent, part of our circle. Mr. Rindner stood *in loco parentis* to all of us, a wise and compassionate father figure. His apartment served as an informal meeting place for our whole group.

There was one other home where I was welcome, that of the Gruss family. Mrs. Gruss was the aunt of Lila, another friend from Bergen-Belsen. Since the end of the war, Lila and I had met already in Palestine while she was visiting her boyfriend who had also been in Bergen-Belsen.

Lila's boyfriend was killed during Israel's war of independence. She mourned him for several years but eventually began to go out with another man, Tolek Schwieger, the son of Dr. Schwieger from Bergen-Belsen. He was also a chemical engineering student at Columbia, but one year ahead of Henry and me. He lived with his parents. His father had a practice on Park Avenue and later moved to the Midwest. Tolek also became a friend. The two later married and moved to Switzerland. Tolek died around 1994.

All of us had parties together, brought girlfriends or boyfriends to them, shared our successes and failures, confided in each other, and provided an excellent support group giving us all a sense of belonging as well as a sure place to go on Saturday nights. But there was never even a hint of romantic interest between me and any of these men friends. In fact I was "one of the boys," and got to hear many stories of sexual adventures and misadventures.

I carried this non-involvement policy into my school situation. My chemical engineering class had about 30 students, of which I was the only woman. We were together in most of our classes and during long labs. It was important that the men feel comfortable having me around, so I became one of the boys there as well, breaking the ice at beer parties— even though I hate beer—by telling the first dirty joke, out-smoking and out-drinking most of the men. We knew nothing of feminism in those days, so I made my own rules. In one way I was hiding and surrendering my femininity, something I would not do today, but in another I was successfully invading male territory. All through my professional life, I was a role model to young women where it really counts: in one's life's work.

I had one other friend from Bergen-Belsen. Adam lived by himself in the basement apartment of a brownstone house not far from me. He studied psychology at Columbia and supported himself by working there part-time. He too became part of our circle, but he and I had a special relationship. All along I felt he was not doing well emotionally. His only sister had gone to Australia after the war and married there, and he was obviously very lonely. He had come to New York at the invitation of a former teacher, to whom he was very attached. She was a married woman, naturally much older than he, but I felt he had persuaded himself there was a mutual romantic element in their relationship.

Adam was very moody. A handsome and charming man, sometimes he could be chivvied out of his black moods. I would bring him home and feed him, buy food and cook for him in his place, or talk him into accompanying me to a party, or to the Lion's Den, or to a movie. But at other times he would not answer the phone or his doorbell, or would let me in and then just go back to bed. He tried buying himself a dog for companionship, but the dog seemed to share his owner's personality—skittish and unpredictable. The only difference between them was that Adam didn't piddle on the carpet. I think it helped temporarily to have someone else to care for, but it didn't last.

Adam had every chance of success. He was very bright and well-liked by his professors, who, knowing his financial condition, got him a hefty scholarship to supplement his earnings. But nothing could overcome his black moods permanently. One time when I came over I found him in despair. A paper was due the next day on Margaret Mead's *Growing up in Samoa* and Adam felt incapable of concentrating that day. I made him tell me something of the book and wrote the paper for him. We got a "B," not bad for a collaboration between a totally depressed man and a partner who had never read the book or taken the course.

For a couple of years I was Adam's closest friend, but by my senior year he began to distance himself from me and my friends. I was very busy with my schoolwork that year and anxious about what the future would bring once school was over, so I did not pay as much attention to Adam as I had in the past. One day he came to the Rindners' apartment sporting a wedding ring. He had just gotten married, he said, but would not divulge his wife's name. I wasn't there at the time, but having heard, hurried to his apartment to hear the story. He was there, I know, for the light was on and extinguished as soon as I rang the bell, but he would not let me in. A few days later, he took his books and went to a meadow in the Bronx, his favorite place to study. There he committed suicide by taking poison.

Adam may have had personality or mental problems even without the war, but I consider him a victim of the Holocaust just as much as people gassed by the Nazis or the family whose death I watched right after we were liberated in Germany. Their bodies could not adjust to the plenty now available; in Adam's case it was his spirit.

My closest friend during those years remained Chris. She and her mother Marysia (who changed her name to Mary, and later softened it to Mickey) had spent a couple of years in Paris, and now lived in Passaic, New Jersey. There, they rented a room with kitchen privileges. Mickey worked in a medical lab. Chris attended the Pratt Institute in Brooklyn, majoring in textile design. We visited each other often, went to parties at Columbia, and hunted for boys, only to find most of them far too immature, not a surprising judgment in light of our exceptionally hard previous life experiences.

Sometimes I visited Chris and Mickey in Passaic. I considered Mickey my friend as well and continued to admire her. She had gone through so much, yet remained cheerful and level-headed. She was always realistic and practical. She had the good luck to meet and marry Dr. Tylbor (another Holocaust survivor), who was her husband for a number of happy years. Chris also found a very nice young man, Herman Ranes. I became good friends with Herman, met his family and remained Chris's confidante and she mine all through those years.

After Chris graduated, she and Herman married and lived in Greenwich Village. Chris worked for a textile firm and did very well financially, but Herman, who was an urban planner, found his professional life more difficult. They decided to move to California and both prospered there, with Chris eventually becoming a full-time artist, thus fulfilling her life-long dream. But our friendship suffered through the move. For many years neither one could afford the long trip or even regular telephone contact. As time went on, letters, our main means of communication, became less and less frequent, until contact dwindled to just Christmas cards. By the time we had the means to travel, the bond had loosened, so to call us friends now is an exaggeration. We exchange vital family news, have met several times and have met each other's children, but that's about all. Yet I know in the back of my mind that if and when we meet again, the common past will revive our friendship.

For the most part, my school years were placid and uneventful. Hard work and good friends with not much going on romantically—that was my life. My home environment was rather lonely and cold. Helen and her family soon moved out to their own place. We remained friends until she died in 1996. My cousin Adzia, Solomon's son, was a taciturn man, both of us coming and going in the large apartment without much contact with each other. We had corresponded when I lived in Tel Aviv. Adzia had written me beautiful letters describing his past life in the army and his current life in New York. I expected us to become close friends. It was a disappointment to me when this did not materialize, but his wife later told me that unbeknownst to me, he did keep an eye on me. He was just much more reserved in person than on paper, perhaps really shy.

One day Chris was visiting me and, for some reason, we went into Adzia's room. There was a picture of a young woman displayed prominently on his night table, but the family did not know who she was, as Adzia was very secretive about his social and romantic life. However, Chris knew who she was, exclaiming, "What is Iza's picture doing here?" It turned out that Iza's mother and Mickey were best friends and the two families visited often. Iza's father was a doctor, so of course he and my father knew each other. Iza herself had attended the same school as Chris and I in Poland, and even though she was three years ahead of us, she and I had met because of our mutual interest in drama. Chris was the first to let the cat out of the bag. Soon Iza became a frequent visitor, and we became friends. She and Adzia married a couple of years later after she finished medical school. She's a widow now and lives in New York City. We see each other and speak on the phone regularly.

In my junior year, I had a rather unlikely romance. I met Joe through Adam. Both studied psychology, but Joe was in graduate school. He was the only non-Jewish boyfriend I ever had, but was not religious. Nevertheless, we went to church together once. He had promised his parents to attend the church they had married in on Easter, and wouldn't go without me. He was a free spirit and had a wild streak, somewhat inconsistent with his small-town, Midwest upbringing. He got his degree that May and had a job waiting for him down south. He suggested I go with him—I don't believe marriage was even mentioned—but I would not give up my life's design for a relationship which, while close and ardent, seemed to me ephemeral and impermanent. "Could we not correspond for a while, and reconsider in a year when I graduate?" I asked. With Joe it was all or nothing. I never saw him or heard from him again.

Around the time of my graduation from Columbia University I entered into a brief and unsuccessful marriage. I was in love with the concepts of love and marriage. Many of my friends were getting married, including Chris and Henry. It was the thing to do when one graduated, and I very much wanted to conform to "the thing to do." Undoubtedly, my desire to stay in the United States and avoid yet another upheaval and adjustment to an almost new country (which the return to Israel would have been) subconsciously played a part in my actions.

I was drawn to my first husband by our shared history of survival, but that proved an insufficient cement for two otherwise incompatible personalities. Like myself, Sidney came from Warsaw. His father died when he was a child and his mother was too poor to bring up both him and his younger brother. He was placed in Dr. Korczak's orphanage, where his mother and his beloved little brother visited him every week. Like all the children there, Sidney revered Dr. Korczak, considering him a veritable saint. The beginning of the war found Sidney in a summer camp in eastern Poland, and in 1941 he was evacuated deep into the Soviet Union, where he spent the rest of the war studying and plying the shoemaking trade. After the war he came back to Poland in search of his family, only to find them gone.

Lonely and depressed, he continued west to Germany, where he entered a university and studied civil engineering. It was here that he met Richard Rindner and the two became close friends. When Sidney emigrated to the U.S. in 1950, it was natural that Richard's home was his first port of call, and since I was a frequent visitor as well, we were bound to meet almost immediately. Richard and I became his mentors on how to proceed in New York and, in my case, the relationship soon progressed beyond this. We were married in June 1951. The marriage caused me to give up graduate school after a year and take a job at the research and development department of a small detergent company. The marriage failed soon after.

The work on my first full-time job proved rather tedious. No basic research was done. The company attempted to arrive at the best formulations of various cleaning agents. I thought that both the research and testing were conducted in a haphazard and rather unscientific manner.

I was involved in organic chemistry research, synthesizing and testing a number of organic additives to detergents. I was in charge of testing the detergents, which involved distributing white towels to the plant workers, then laundering them with our detergents and testing them for whiteness. The company also made tallow out of slaughterhouse and restaurant refuse and the carcasses of discarded animals. Understandably, the workers' hands were very dirty and so were the towels they used. It is easy to see what a crude test that was. I really begrudged the time spent on it, even with an assistant who collected and laundered the towels.

One day during lunch, the plant manager found out I had worked as a nurse of sorts in the concentration camp. He immediately put me in charge of the first-aid program. Thereafter, almost every day some burly, inarticulate worker would arrive at the lab politely seeking my help. These were men who would have their lunch seated right on the whale carcasses they rendered!

The complaints ranged from splinters and cuts to headaches, bellyaches, fever and flu. I removed splinters from giant, callused hands, apologizing for the pain I was causing, cleaned and bandaged cuts, dispensed aspirin and referred all other cases to doctors. The recipients of my care were invariably extremely grateful, gazing in awe at the tiny ministering angel and vowing to follow my advice religiously. I worked there for a year and a half. During that time my marriage broke up and I fell in love with one of my co-workers. We have stayed together and in love for 43 years.

This co-worker was named Bert Samuels. Our relationship started as a friendship and not even an exclusive one. Bert, I and Mel—a young chemist in my research lab—all lived in Manhattan, but only Bert owned a car. Soon, Mel and I became paying passengers in Bert's car. In the daily, two- to three-hour trip to and from New Jersey and the enforced intimacy of a car, the three of us became close friends, so much so that when Bert's parents first met me they were mystified as to the precise dynamics within the trio.

Gradually however, an additional, separate friendship grew between Bert and me. We began to spend evenings together, taking in a movie or having a drink. This finally progressed to full-blown dates. As is often the case between men and women, my feelings crystallized before Bert's and I had to wait for him to catch up.

Once the budding romance almost foundered on an innocent mistake I made. Bert was laid up with a heavy cold and I offered to come and feed him. He was living in a brownstone apartment, which I had not yet seen. I reasoned that a bachelor establishment would not have complete kitchen equipment. Keeping this likelihood in mind, as well as the patient's probable lack of appetite, I decided to keep the meal simple to make but light and nutritious to consume. I stuck to spinach and eggs, a childhood delicacy, but while in the market, I succumbed to the lure of smoked oysters. I had never had them before, but they sounded most sophisticated. Poor Bert tried valiantly, but blaming his illness finally excused himself from eating. After we were married, I discovered spinach was one of the few foods he hated. We also both agreed that smoked oysters were vile and were never to grace our table again.

The two of us went through a longish, ambiguous period—somewhere between friends and lovers—both of us still free to date other people, but taking advantage of that privilege less and less. Meanwhile, I had acquired an apartment mate, Renata, a young Italian woman who was half-Jewish. Young men were always buzzing around our apartment, some my old college friends, some Renata's boyfriends. One time I went with Renata and two young men to Atlantic City. On that occasion, Renata and I were supposed to share one room, and the two men another. Instead, Renata spent the night with her date while the other young man, whom I barely knew, felt that this entitled him to a like privilege. He had to be convinced rather forcefully that this was not the case. I was not a one-night stand, nor was I interested in embarking on a new relationship while my romance with Bert was developing slowly but steadily. I have no idea where the over-eager lover spent the night, but the next morning he appeared, grumpy and unshaved, in stark contrast to the other radiant couple in the car.

Bert's parents finally figured out the relationship between us, particularly once we began to visit them without Mel—the latter having acquired a Hungarian Jewish girlfriend who did not like Polish Jews, or possibly did not relish any competition for Mel's affection, male or female. Bert's family on his mother's side was extremely close. His parents lived together with two of his mother's sisters and one brother. Although they were not religious they lived in a totally Jewish environment, socializing exclusively with other Jews. Thus, Bert's marriage to a Jewish girl was of a paramount importance. They just would not have felt comfortable otherwise, having to be careful all the time what to say, what jokes to avoid, or what food to serve. Since Bert had once been engaged to a gentile girl, my being Jewish immediately scored points for me, and my Lomza origins which they shared did so even more, overshadowing my low status as a recent immigrant "from the other side" as my future mother-in-law used to say.

Once it became clear that Bert was serious about me, I was subjected to a merciless and tactless grilling on my ancestry—both a plus and a minus—my education, my professional prospects and the absence of family support (read: money) in my life. Their curiosity did not offend me. I felt, or rather I was hoping, they had a right to know. Bert, who had recently moved away from home and family entanglements, was somewhat alienated from them, particularly from his rather domineering and intrusive mother. I believe he was offended by the interrogation, but seeing my cheerful compliance, did not interfere. I helped him to mend fences with his family. I am not sure he appreciated it, but I believe his mother did.

Back at Theobald Industries, at the end of 1953, the management decided to dispense with the research program and fired the entire research staff. Finding myself out of work did not faze me. I was young, healthy and bright and had full confidence in my ability. Indeed, within a month I was working for Foster Wheeler, a large engineering design company in Manhattan. My new job couldn't have been more different from the old one. I was now working in the company's "think tank." Instead of routine lab work, I performed highly technical and complex engineering calculations, dealing with both theoretical and practical problems.

By that time Bert had become production manager at Theobald Industries and was working extremely long hours. At one point, he even contemplated a move to New Jersey to eliminate the long, and now lonely, commute. He invited me to come along on an apartment search. We looked in the Newark/Harrison area, but found nothing suitable. We were hungry and tired and, to our dismay, discovered we had about one dollar between us, aside from the tunnel toll. In the mid 1950s, a dollar could buy much more than it can today, but still not a good meal for two.

We stopped at a nice-looking, rather fancy restaurant where we explained our predicament. Could any meal be obtained for a dollar? The maitre d', amused by the situation, offered us a chef salad. We were seated at a table covered with a white damask cloth, gleaming silverware and china in front of us. Hot rolls and coffee and water in crystal goblets appeared on the table. A very professional waiter, flanked by two assistants, built the salad from artfully arranged ingredients on a separate table, wheeled it up to us and inquired solicitously if anything else was desired. Informed that nothing was, he left us alone to enjoy the exquisite food and the elegant surroundings. We never did find out how much this meal really cost; we couldn't even tip the waiter, who waived our apologies aside. "It is my pleasure," he maintained.

In the end Bert's work load proved unbearable. He was working literally day and night, supervising three shifts and camping out at the plant for brief naps, which were all he could spare. By the fall of 1954, he decided to quit and look for a job outside New York, receiving strong encouragement from me. Leaving the New York area was a major decision for both of us, especially if it involved heading for the hinterlands. Both of us shared the New Yorkers' view of America, in which anything west of the Hudson, except California, was a wilderness. After a thorough search which confirmed the fact that New York City offered unpromising horizons for a chemical engineer, Bert landed a job with Allied Chemical (now Allied Signal) in Buffalo, where he would work until he retired in the late 1980s.

One big change in a person's life often accelerates other decisions. Moving to Buffalo was a big step and we decided to do it together. We were married in Jamestown, New York, where Bert's brother Stan lived, on January 16, 1955, one week after Bert started his new job. The wedding party was a gift from Stan and his wife Roz. Bert's whole family came in from New York, but disappointedly, none of mine came.

Two of Bert's aunts who owned a boutique gave me my wedding gown. Other aunts and uncles gave us generous gifts to help us get started. Bert's mother turned over to us a $1,000 savings account which she had accumulated over the years in Bert's name, saving a little here and there from her table money and her "girdle money," a euphemism she and her husband had developed for any small sums he gave her which did not have to be accounted for.

I rejoiced in becoming a member of a large, close-knit family, including Bert's brother and his wife and son, his parents and innumerable aunts, uncles and cousins. Bert's brother and his wife came to be like a brother and sister to me. Both are gone now, but Harvey, their son, is very dear to us. Many young people try to distance themselves from extended families. I, however, relished becoming part of one. I participated eagerly in family gatherings and festive occasions. Alas, in recent years those have been supplanted by funerals.

In those days our resources were rather meager. Furthermore, I had to give a month's notice to quit my job. Consequently, Bert found our first apartment in Buffalo by himself, and I did not see it until I arrived there for the wedding. The move itself was chaotic, as such things usually are, involving synchronization and reconciliation of disparate events and depending on an uncaring moving company and the help of relatives and friends. But the wedding itself was lovely and joyous—largely a tribute to my new sister-in-law Roz, a very efficient lady. Finally, we moved to our new apartment, the furniture had arrived, a new bedroom suite had been purchased for the princely sum of $300, and the curtains were hung.

All during the years of working in New York City, I heard about other survivors and former friends. Some were slowly adjusting and making a place for themselves, but they were in a minority at that time. Frankly, the lives of all my friends appeared to me to be a mess and it was hard to envisage how we would all overcome the instabilities and settle down, but eventually most of us did.

The saddest story of failure to make a happy life after the war was that of my father. He was too old and too emotionally shattered to adapt well to post-war conditions. It was not obvious while I lived with him in Palestine, but when I moved away he must have felt his responsibilities moved with me. The first two years I was in New York he never wrote to me at all. I started by writing him weekly letters, which gradually stretched to monthly, bi-monthly and tri-monthly. I found it hard to communicate with a wall. At first I wrote all the details, but gradually they became irrelevant and I confined myself to major events and the letters became stilted and formal. How much could I discuss my health or report on the subjects I studied and the grades I was receiving, without receiving some feedback? He didn't know any of my new friends, and attempts to describe my life often misfired.

For example, I wrote him about spending my first summer in Long Beach, Long Island, as an au pair. My father interpreted this as my being a servant and held it against my uncle. When the story got back to Solomon, guess who got scolded? My direct contact with my father was limited to infrequent and expensive phone calls, during which we shouted at each other that we were well, and that it was good to hear each others' voice. The phone calls would end with my entreaties for him to write and his promises to do so.

This was the time when the bonds between us loosened irrevocably. I believe the distancing was far larger than it had to be, even with the large physical distance separating us, although mutual love survived to the end.

I was in constant contact with Aunt Sonia, who reported that my father was not taking care of himself, was becoming more slovenly, more eccentric, and that his behavior was beginning to hurt his practice. I think now he was suffering bouts of depression accentuated by his loneliness. After two years he began to write to me. He wanted to leave Israel. But he never said that his motives were positive or that he wanted to join me. No, his letters were bitter and full of invectives against the "socialism" in Israel and the difficulties in making a living because of the social system. Sonia's interest was interpreted as prying, Cyla's reserve as coldness. My cousin Nina wrote that my father was often invited to dinner by both families but usually refused. My father had always been very stubborn; we had clashed over it many times. But now he was simply becoming unreasonable.

The story of his favorite tie offers an example. This piece of apparel had become so worn and offensive that Sonia, after many unsuccessful trials to persuade him to dispose of it, came one day, stole it, and threw it in the garbage bin downstairs. When my father realized it, he rushed to the bin and retrieved it. After that he wore it all the time, I guess, to safeguard it and establish his authority. From his own accounts and those of the family, he did not sound like the man I had known.

My father finally came to United States in 1959 and settled in New York City. He worked as a lab technician and lived in a rented room. He had no trouble supporting himself, his needs being modest and jobs in his field plentiful. But he also had an incredible stroke of luck. His lawyer uncovered an obscure law dealing with medical licensing. The United States had a reciprocity treaty with imperial Russia which had lapsed in 1914, allowing each country's doctors to practice in the other one. My father had received his medical diploma in Kharkov in 1912, and was thus eligible for an American license under a grandfather clause in the treaty. All he needed to do was to take an exam in English. He did that by writing an essay and memorizing it. During the exam, he wrote his essay with an introduction which segued his topic into the essay's actual title. He prepared a sort of all-purpose composition on his history and experiences both during and after the war, impressions of New York, and adaptation to life in America. It proved good enough to pass the test.

After that he held several jobs. The best one was a position of resident physician in a small hospital for wealthy alcoholics located on Central Park West. He had a room on the premises, cleaned by the hospital staff, and ate all his meals in the hospital dining room. It was an ideal arrangement, even though the work was not challenging. The patients included many professionals and even celebrities. He enjoyed these interactions, telling me many stories about the interesting characters residing in the facility. Collecting and telling stories had always been his specialty.

By this time I was living in Buffalo, but he came to see us several times a year and I came to New York to see him. Unfortunately the hospital closed, and after several other jobs my father settled on a small group practice which specialized in treating Medicaid patients. This worked out well for him. He got a percentage of the fee, and the office took care of all the paperwork connected with collecting the money from the government. Here too he was well liked by the patients, because they sensed his genuine interest in them. He just could not resist caring for individuals, although he was bigoted against most minority groups.

He had to function as a general practitioner as his license did not include specialization. He was always taking refresher courses for physicians at Brooklyn College to update himself in the different branches of medicine. The one interest which did not desert him almost until the end was his love of learning.

After the hospital closed, he took an apartment in a brownstone on the Upper West Side, and quickly reduced it to shambles by refusing to employ any cleaning service as he did not trust anyone's honesty. He rarely cleaned it himself—he really had no energy for it—and never threw anything out. A couple of years later I presided over his moving out (by that time Bert and I had moved to New Jersey). I must have thrown out a ton of newspapers occupying every available space, including part of his bed. There were bags of paper napkins brought home from restaurants, sugar packets, and a variety of ill-assorted crockery and silverware, all chipped and bent.

Every time I visited my father in those days, I ended up crying. My heart was breaking over what had become of this wonderful, bright man. He had become suspicious and miserly. When he first came to the United States, he used to send me and our children lavish and extravagant presents. Hanukkah and Passover became red banner days for our whole block, as I shared the bounty I could not consume with my family alone.

Now, he begrudged the money to take a taxi to and from his job, and money to keep himself looking neat and well-dressed, in spite of my assurances that I would help him anytime he needed it.

Finally, the day came when he had to call on my help. His eyes were failing. The diagnosis was irreversible retinal deterioration combined with severe cataracts. He was terrified of being incapable of taking care of himself, and turned to me. We already had Bert's mother living with us, as she moved in with us in 1966 and lived with us for 14 years until her death. And in 1969 we added a room for my father. As soon as he moved in, I persuaded him to go for a second medical opinion. The advice was to remove the cataract from the eye which was completely blind. This surgery produced unexpectedly positive results. The second eye was operated on as well, and within half a year my father went back to work in New York City while continuing to live with us in New Jersey.

He was very inconsiderate. I guess over the years he had gotten used to pleasing only himself. Every day I took him to a bus stop to go to New York in the morning on my way to work, and picked him up at night at about 7 or 8 p.m. I fed him separately, the children and Bert and I having already eaten, whereupon he would doze at the kitchen table with a newspaper. Late at night, he would wake us all up by clumping noisily around and putting on the radio, while he performed his evening chores. He took a bath once a week only under duress, after which I had a major job of cleaning up the bathroom. The bathroom often had to be cleaned even if he just shaved or used the toilet.

He did not connect with my mother-in-law or my children. He criticized the way we were bringing the boys up: they did not read enough, they did not know enough Hebrew, how could I let them play with dolls (GI Joe's), our synagogue was like a church, and so on and so on. I was always trying to mediate between him and my family. Luckily they did not understand most of his criticism, since he tended to speak to me in Polish. That period was a great trial for me and Bert, though we tried valiantly to shield the children from all the problems. But the stress he put on our family was almost unbearable.

I felt that daily travel to New York was too much for my father, and his day too long. I suggested he work only three days a week, with a day in between to rest, but he wouldn't have any of it. What would he do with himself? He could no longer travel to Brooklyn College to take his refresher courses. Reading was an effort, but his mind remained as sharp as ever. He and I still enjoyed long intellectual discussions, and sometimes Bert would join in.

In 1970 he participated in my son Mark's bar mitzvah, saying the *broches* (blessings) over the wine and the challah. In 1971 I suggested he rent a room in the city, stay there during the week, work four days and come back to us for long weekends. In retrospect, I believe it was not a good idea because I took better care of him than he did himself, watching his diet and nagging him to rest and relax. At the time he thought it was a good idea, but once he moved the effort of the travel became too much and he would come back only every two or three weeks.

In 1972 he began to complain of leg pains and fatigue. He resisted seeing a doctor for several weeks. Perhaps he had a premonition of the end. When he finally went to a doctor and was hospitalized for testing, he never came out. His health wasn't good enough for the prostate surgery he needed, and the hospital transferred him to a nursing home near our house. He refused to eat and pulled out all the tubes inserted in his body. Finally, his doctor and I realized he did not wish to prolong his life and sadly agreed to let him pass on, keeping him as comfortable as we could. He was largely uncommunicative at this point, except with me. He recognized me until the last day, and when he could no longer speak would squeeze my hand and hold it. He died peacefully in his sleep early in 1972. When I went to his vault, I found he had amassed $100,000. Between that and his social security, he certainly would have had no need to work had he continued to live with me and found some interest in life.

My father lived 30 years after my mother's death, but they were not happy years. He managed to alienate most of the people who cared for him, or could have come to care for him. He could not even bring himself to enjoy his grandchildren. In the end he had only me. This seems to me a perfect example of a survivor who did not truly survive, but merely lingered on—another soul ruined by Hitler's atrocities.

CHAPTER 15

THE GOOD YEARS

Most people associate Buffalo with snow, wind, and cold. It's all true, but nevertheless that is where I spent some of the happiest years of my life. In January 1955, the move to Buffalo brought with it several felicitous changes. First, I married the man I loved and became a member of his close-knit family. Second, the move from metropolitan New York separated me from my Holocaust survivor friends and threw me in among the Americans, both Jewish and gentile, who treated me like one of their own—just another upwardly mobile, middle-class, educated woman. I could finally integrate myself into American society and almost, though not quite, lose my status as an outsider. Finally, I moved from an urban to a suburban setting and discovered the pleasure of friendly and helpful neighbors. These friendships were as serendipitous as they were fleeting. They relied on proximity and good will rather than on shared interests, but they were pleasant and useful while they lasted. These were the contours of my life in the Fifties.

After we settled in our apartment, I began to look for a job. I was collecting unemployment insurance, which reduced the sense of financial urgency. For the first time in many years, I was enjoying the absence of pressure and a new-found leisure. However, the unemployment office and my conscience soon intensified my half-hearted attempts to find work. After a while, a little boredom began to poison all that leisure.

Finding a position in Buffalo proved unexpectedly difficult. I just could not get a job in industry; the prejudice against professional women was still very strong there. One after another, managers rejected me, informing me that men would refuse to work for a woman engineer. At a brewery, I was even told the presence of menstruating women adversely affected the fermentation process.

By the end of six months, I was getting more than a little anxious. My unemployment checks had run out and I had no prospects, but providence once again stepped in to save me. During my last appointment at the unemployment office, I was sent for an interview at Erie County Technical Institute, a two-year technical college.

Rex Billings was the supervisor, and we hit it off right from the first meeting. My views on education were acquired by reflecting on my own experiences at Columbia University. Prior to my interview with Rex, I didn't even know I held many such opinions, so I had to think fast on my feet. Luckily my ideas dovetailed with his, and I was offered a one-year faculty appointment right then and there. I was to fill in for an instructor who was taking a leave of absence. He never came back, and after the year passed, my appointment became permanent.

My job offer came about three weeks before the start of term. I was handed all the necessary books and instructed to show up on the opening day of school. My load that first semester was rather staggering. I was to teach general chemistry, physical chemistry, chemical engineering calculations, and math. At first I was unfazed by the challenge. After all, these were the very subjects I had studied and done well in. As I was only three years out of school, the material was still quite fresh in my memory. I reasoned that a bit of a review and dividing the courses into manageable chunks ought to be sufficient preparation, but as the fateful day approached I became more and more nervous. It was a pure case of stage fright.

The first day passed in a blur of activity, leaving me limp with fatigue. Later, when I became friendly with my students and looked back on that day, I discovered that we had frightened each other out of our collective wits. I was so afraid of "empty time" that I overcompensated by preparing enough material to last a week or more. I lectured fast and furiously, and terrified the class with my expectations. By the time we discussed that original experience, we had settled down and were able to have a good laugh about it.

I knew almost immediately that I had found my calling and life's work: teaching. My previous jobs were just jobs; teaching proved to be my vocation and avocation. I discovered how much I had missed working closely with people as an integral part of my day, and how much I loved playing an important role in younger people's lives. I enjoyed the challenge of breaking down complex ideas into logically sequenced small chunks that could be absorbed and related to previous knowledge. My forte was in understanding the material thoroughly and being able to explain it in a very organized way. I always walked out from a successful lesson with a "high," particularly if, in the course of the lesson, I had seen imaginary light bulbs switch on over my students' heads. With experience came a better ability to pace myself, to sense when the class was saturated and I was about to lose my audience.

In one way I was truly lucky in my first teaching job. The Korean War had ended not long before and half of my students were veterans studying under the G.I. Bill, that wonderful invention that educated a whole generation of bright young men and contributed mightily to American prosperity in the second half of the 20th Century. These veteran students were mature. Many were married and had young families, and were eager to acquire the knowledge needed to succeed in business and industry. They were completely focused on class activities and eager to do sufficient homework to make sure they absorbed the new concepts. Naturally, they were never a behavior problem, and their admirable presence influenced the younger students as well. I just had to make sure that my younger students were not overshadowed and intimidated to the point of not participating themselves, by keeping them involved and on their toes.

Unlike my later work at the high school level, I confronted a vast array of abilities and backgrounds. Some of my students were very bright and sophisticated. I was always directing them to additional readings and providing extra hard problems to challenge them. Others struggled with the basics with varying degrees of success. One youngster in my math class could not deal with the decimal system or fractions. I had him come in to my office and helped him by using simple money problems.

Some of the students were extremely poor writers. The English department emphasized literature over writing. I felt it was more important for these young people to be able to read and write about science. I suggested that we require a joint paper on a scientific subject, to be graded by me on the subject matter and by an English teacher on the writing quality.

Once a student handed me a paper which was obviously too excellent to be of his own hand. It was totally inconsistent with his previous writing style and the level of his knowledge. I gave him an "F" and wrote that I appreciated his typing skill but since, unfortunately, mine was not a secretarial course I was unable to reward him adequately. The incident was never verbally mentioned by either of us.

In addition to the joy in the classroom, Erie County Institute provided me with good friends. Our department was rather small; there were only six faculty members among us. We all got along very well; the spirit of camaraderie was wonderful. I never encountered its equal anywhere else.

We had an ongoing bridge game in the departmental office. In the late afternoon people dropped in to play a few hands. Arden Pratt, one of the instructors, kept scores which eventually numbered in millions of points. The subject of bridge had come up in my initial interview. Rex used to kid me that I would never have gotten the job if I had had no interest in the game. I was not a good player then, but the interest which had been spurred in Palestine came to fruition in Buffalo, and I have remained an avid player.

Our social life revolved mainly around people we met at our respective jobs and friends we made at the Jewish Community Center, where we participated in theatrical activities and made friends with Gretchen and Jules Gordon, an aspiring actress and a lawyer respectively. Gretchen, who was much more worldly than I, became somewhat of a role model for me and a confidante whenever marital problems arose and, of course, I reciprocated. Gilda and David Waldman were former New York friends who had moved to Hamilton, Ontario. We visited each other and traveled together to Stratford and Toronto for the theater. Bert and I also visited Montreal and Quebec City. In short, we were living like other young professionals—working hard and enjoying our freedom.

However, this lifestyle was soon to change. During my second year at Erie County, we were expecting our first child. Erie County, which was operated on both county and state funds and thus burdened with two sets of arbitrary rules, forbade women teachers to work past the fourth month of pregnancy. We found a way to get around that, though. One day, the school president called me in and informed me that being the "ignorant male" he was, he was incapable of estimating the stage of a woman's pregnancy. So, unless I formally apprised him of any pregnancy, he knew nothing about it. Accordingly I worked until the end of the summer term, just two weeks short of Mark's birth.

I was not planning to go back to work anytime soon. I was simply following the pattern of my generation, believing that a woman's foremost job was to bring up her children. I not only accepted this dictum but embraced it!

My pregnancy was very easy and did not interfere with any of our activities. Since neither of us was particularly knowledgeable about the process, we attended a series of lectures given by a matter-of-fact, outspoken nun. My mother-in-law Rose, who was visiting at the time, came along to one lecture. At first the nun was extolling the joys and benefits of breast-feeding, and my mother-in-law was in her glory relating her own experiences. But soon the nun changed the topic to actual birth, showing us a film which included the frontal view of the event in all its gory details. My poor mother-in-law, an excessively modest and prudish lady (she never understood a dirty joke), was mortified and didn't know where to look. To be exposed to such frank talk and graphic details in the presence of several strange young men and women was utter torture for her. Naturally, she declined to accompany us to the next lecture.

Since I had come to the United States when I was 20, I had a distinctly foreign accent. I have often been told that my accent is attractive and I should do nothing to get rid of it, as if such a feat were in my power anyway. Towards the end of my pregnancy, the Pratts' son, who was about five, finally noticed it and asked whether my baby would be born with an accent.

During that summer we decided to buy a house. My job had paid for a new car and provided enough savings for a down payment on a three-bedroom house which, with appliances and carpeting, cost us under $16,000. We moved just days before Mark's arrival.

Everybody was so nice and helpful. Naturally we decided to buy a layette from Stan and Roz who, at the time, operated a children's clothing store in Jamestown, New York. We went there one weekend and selected everything we needed, relying heavily on Roz's advice. When we realized we had bought far more than we had intended, we were informed that the layette was a gift from Stan and Roz. How thoughtful of them not to tell us in advance and inhibit our selection! My students gave me a baby stroller, and the staff a bassinet with a dressing table. Students, colleagues and neighbors were endlessly solicitous, helping me carry books and packages and asking after my health. Bert's parents, who were by then retired, came to help and stayed for two months. Every woman should feel important and admired during her pregnancy.

But labor lasted all day and the pain was aggravated by the unsympathetic attitude of the nurses, who informed me that I was a big girl and should behave like one. The baby was more my idea than Bert's, and all through my pregnancy he acted emotionally aloof to the upcoming event. In fact I felt somewhat aggrieved and abandoned, not realizing that I was paying the price for forcing the issue. But all it took was for him to catch one glimpse of Mark to fall in love with his son. When I arrived in my room after several hours in recovery, he came in with tears in his eyes, professing deep love for Mark and me. Clearly he had experienced an epiphany, and equally clearly lost his sense of judgment when he extolled Mark's beauty. We have pictures of Mark and Sam (our younger son) as one-day-olds, and as far as I can see they are indistinguishable not only from each other, but from most such pictures of other babies. I think hospitals keep pictures of a generic baby which they dispense to all their patients.

It was a great feeling to hold my own baby. He was so helpless and so totally dependent on me. It called forth a great outpouring of love from me, another of nature's insurance policies. I am basically not a baby person. I much prefer children when they are old enough to express themselves verbally. No one had alerted me to how much learning goes on in that first, non-verbal year, and I think I missed many little cues.

Having a baby is a much more pleasant reason for being in a hospital than illness, obviously. This was a happy atmosphere, and a busy time, with babies being brought in several times a day for feedings and cuddling. Nevertheless, I must note that the Catholic patients were visited daily by a priest, the Protestants by a minister, whereas I was visited by an insurance salesman. We did not belong to a synagogue at the time, so I had no reason to complain. Still, it left me with a bitter taste.

My neighbors were a mixed lot, but we all had certain fundamentals in common: we were all solidly middle-class with a strong work ethic, house pride, solid marriages and devotion to our children. The street we had moved to was the friendliest neighborhood I ever lived in. On our block alone there were six other children Mark's age. The women were in and out of each other homes, as none of us worked, sharing not only coffee and lunches, but helping each other in times of need. For example, when one of my neighbors had a miscarriage, she asked me to come along to the hospital and hold her husband's hand. At that time there was only one car in each family. Most husbands car-pooled to give their wives access to daytime transportation, and the women shared the cars with each other to shop, drive kids to and from school, temple, or doctor's appointments.

Most of us were far from our birth families. Friends provided the children and us with the feeling of an extended family. There were block parties, babysitting exchanges and informal get-togethers. The men were also friendly, but did not form a support group for each other as the women did. Men seem to find forming relationships with other men much more difficult. They tend to stay away from intimacy and fall back on the safe topics of sports and cars. My husband, who is bored by both topics, has always admitted to a preference for the company of women.

I had gone to school with men, and had always worked almost exclusively with men, so I was very used to male company. This was my first experience in the world of women. I enjoyed it immensely, and have never been without such a group since.

My next-door neighbor Ruth was a socially active, money-conscious Jewish woman with no intellectual interest. Her husband once confided to me that he envied us because we had professions we loved. They later moved to a custom-built house in a more upscale suburb.

Next to my friend Ruth were Sandy and Ron, the only other Jewish couple on our block. He was a pharmacist whose dream was to own his own drugstore, a dream he achieved soon after we moved there. Sandy, a former school teacher, was one of my best friends on the street, and the only one with whom I maintain some contact to this day. She had taught in an inner-city Buffalo school, and could not get over the fact that at the age of three Mark could distinguish a triangle from a rectangle, knew all the colors, and could correctly name every dinosaur that ever lived on Earth. Suburban children enjoyed many cultural and intellectual advantages thanks to their constant exposure to books and parents always eager to explain and teach.

Across the street lived Annette and Bill, who had two adopted children, Patrick and Moira. Patrick was Mark's best friend, and I participated in the anxiety and happiness when Moira came to them. Annette lived in constant fear of the adoption agency inspector who came periodically to check on the children's well-being, sternly prowling around the house and quizzing the children about their domestic life and progress in school. Annette and Bill were both highly religious. Bill's day was not complete without attending mass; he went every day before work. Most everything I know about Catholicism I learned from Annette, who came from a family full of nuns, priests and monks. I learned about conservative and liberal Catholics. Annette herself believed priests should be allowed to marry, as did one of her priest uncles, who anticipated such a change within a generation. I think it might have happened had John XXIII lived longer or if John Paul II hadn't stayed Pope so long.

Bill and Maureen were old friends. Bill had been a coworker at Erie County Technical Institute. In fact, when we had been looking at houses, we spotted Maureen, whom we also knew, while visiting the house on Fancher Street; she invited us in and encouraged us to buy it, extolling the pleasant neighborhood (she was absolutely right). At that time, Bill and Maureen had two children, Jeb who was two and Howard, who was four months old. As a young child, Howard suffered fevers and convulsions. When he entered school it was discovered he was severely learning-disabled. He was unable to master such skills as reading, writing or telling time.

Back when we were buying the house, Maureen and I had agreed to exchange babysitting duties. This worked for a year or two, but her house was ultimately just too chaotic for me to be comfortable in. She was not the world's best housekeeper. Bill and Maureen were both highly intelligent people, and very good, interesting company; they were the most intellectual people on our block. What they were missing was any interest in the mechanics of running a house with two, three and eventually four children.

On my other side lived an Irish family. The father could usually be seen sitting on the doorstep with a can of beer in his hand, his big belly proof of the frequency of such imbibing. Their oldest son, Joe, baby-sat when my in-laws were away and cheerfully and inexpensively performed heavy cleaning chores in many houses on the block.

On Halloween, there were three little girls, daughters of the baker who lived on our block, who always dressed as angels. Indeed they looked and sounded completely angelic when they came to the door in their white dresses, with little halos over their heads, and rosy make-up on their cheeks and lips. Bert's aunts used to make sure they visited Buffalo during Halloween just for the pleasure of seeing and hearing the adorable little people. In those days, the streets were safe and so was the candy. All our children participated in this beloved holiday.

Milk was delivered daily, and if you left a note in the milk box, cheese, eggs, buttermilk and other dairy products would be left as well. Our bread man also carried cake and other bakery products, and the produce van arrived several times a week with a good selection of fruit and vegetables. Since there was also a little grocery store within walking distance, and a library nearby as well, we were not too discommoded by the absence of the family car on days when the family breadwinners were using them.

After getting over his colic at about three months, Mark became an easy baby to raise. He was a serious little boy, playing with whatever toys were offered him, trying hard to respond to every challenge. He would spend long hours fitting colored rings onto a peg and looking to me for approval on whether he had gotten them right. Blocks, puzzles, books, trucks, all provided him with hours of busy enjoyment. Both he and later Sam loved tiny stuffed animals, referred to as "buddies," and matchbox cars. Mark in particular always walked with as many tiny cars and buddies as could fit in his little hands.

Food was a different matter altogether. One day, when Mark was eight months old, we were visiting our in-laws in New York. Up to that time he ate whatever I shoveled into his mouth, but on that day, I put a spoonful of spinach in his mouth, he rolled it around for a moment and then cheerfully spat it out. He had discovered power! That was the last time he ate a vegetable for a number of years. In fact, for several years he subsisted on bacon, hot dogs, milk, cookies and vitamins. I didn't know brains could be fashioned out of bacon and frankfurters! Moreover, the hot dogs had to be peeled. Today Mark can't believe I did this, but I had nightmares of being forced to eat food I disliked intensely as a child and would not subject my own children to the ordeal. Cooking bacon became a major chore in our house, with Bert transformed into our main chef for that specialty; he became real expert at this chore. The only other acceptable food was spaghetti (or "pisghetti" as Mark called it) in tomato sauce. When I expressed my anxiety over this state of affairs to our pediatrician, he assured me that by the time he was 30 Mark would be eating normally and I need not worry!

We threw Mark a birthday party when he turned one. In the interest of protecting the house, the party took place in the garage, which was new and in pristine condition—a recent gift from my in-laws. The birthday boy and his five little guests all sat in their strollers, with paper crowns on their heads, staring at each other uncomprehendingly. Chocolate cake was served, duly pounded, after which it was partly consumed and partly worn, with generous amounts festooning the walls and floor of the garage. (I am convinced small children think their food is not quite dead yet and must be slaughtered prior to eating.) I wish I had preserved it for posterity, but I was not a camera bug in those days. Anyhow, the party was pronounced a great success by all, the guests were carried off straight to their bathtubs and the garage was hosed off, leaving no trace of the delightful event.

Mark learned to walk and talk at the appropriate times, though because of his short stature he appeared precocious to other people. Since he was our first child, we took him everywhere and he was always comfortable with adults. One time, when he was about three, we were having dinner in Niagara Falls, Ontario, in an elegant English restaurant. The food was typically English: bland and rather flat. At the end of the meal, Mark called over the waiter and with great aplomb "sent his compliments to the chef." He had enjoyed the dinner, "because it was not too tasty," by which he meant not too spicy.

During the first year of Mark's life my in-laws spent over six months visiting us. They had one older grandson, Stan and Roz's son Harvey, but he had come when they were both still working and they could not spare the time to travel to Jamestown very often. But now that they were at leisure, they watched Mark's development with love and fascination and were unable to tear themselves away. No sooner did they go back home to Great Neck, New York, than they were planning another prolonged visit with us. My mother-in-law was always a help to me around the house and a fountain of knowledge for me and my neighbors on baby problems. Although she tended to be bossy and domineering, I always listened to her advice respectfully and often took it—she was a sharp lady. But when I disagreed with her, I just went my way without any compunctions.

My father-in-law was the sweetest man I ever met. He was all goodness and love. He had one leg shorter than the other and walked with the aid of a built-up, heavy boot, but he never complained. He was content to sit in the corner and watch Mark play, patiently read him the same story over and over, and perform any task for Mark, including the diaper detail. An ideal father-in-law, always full of praise for me and the children, he was just the kind of grandfather children adore: all love, indulgence and no criticism.

By the time Mark was a year old, my in-laws had moved to Buffalo, renting a little apartment about eight minutes' walk from our house. We now entered into a symbiotic relationship. I provided the transportation as I had learned to drive by then, and they responded with babysitting and general help with the children, except during the winter, when they went to Florida. This arrangement worked very smoothly during the Buffalo years, particularly since Bert traveled a lot. My biggest problem during those years was my nervousness over being alone with the children in the house at night. Somehow the total responsibility for the small children, combined with my fear of intruders (which remained with me from my own childhood) made me very uneasy whenever Bert was away. I compensated by staying up late and catching naps during the day whenever the children were napping or away from home. I never confided my problem to anyone, not even Bert.

The habit of internalizing my problems and dealing with them by myself had become very strong. In retrospect I realize how silly and unnecessary my suffering was. If I had shared it with Bert, some solution would have been found to alleviate my distress. On the other hand, dealing with problems on my own had become a point of pride with me. I needed to be in control and project an image of a strong, self-sufficient person.

Sammy was born in 1960. In every respect, our two children enacted the typical child-ranking pattern. Mark was the older—always ambitious, anxious to please, and overachieving; Sam, the second child, was born to be more self-assured and laid-back. When he was little, Sam was the easiest imaginable baby to raise: always smiling, satisfied, serene and rarely crying. Presented with a new toy, he would look it over carefully and decide whether it was suitable for his ability. If he decided against it, he just refused to touch it. Weeks later, when he felt ready, he would master it with no sweat. Thus it appeared that he learned new skills and tricks totally effortlessly, with no struggle.

I saw Sammy really angry only once. He was about a year old at the time, and Bert and I were invited by Bert's company to spend an extended weekend at a lodge in the Adirondacks. We went, taking Mark with us and leaving Sam with a trusted nurse under my in-laws' supervision. When we came back, Sammy greeted Mark and Bert joyfully, but wouldn't look at me for two days. I had betrayed him by leaving him at home. It is amazing that such a little person could both feel so deeply hurt and cause me so much pain by laying so much guilt on me. I remembered a similar episode when Mark was a baby and I was laid low with pneumonia. My friend Gretchen came to care for Mark, who was not allowed near me. Mark too had been angry when I returned to care for him.

Sammy said his first word at nine months, and first walked at the same time. However, his first tooth did not show up until he was 14 months old. By that time he was already forming simple sentences and phrases, and they seemed ludicrous coming out of his toothless mouth.

Later on, his unwillingness to exert himself extended to letter recognition. Mark had begun to distinguish letters at three and would call them out at the slightest provocation, when exposed to signs, book covers or newspaper headlines. In fact, after a while, it got a bit tiresome. But Sammy would have nothing to do with such activities. We had a Dr. Seuss dictionary, and both Mark and I would try to teach Sam the letters, but he remained cheerfully confused. How could he not distinguish a G from an H? They looked so different. Then one evening, Mark, who was then about seven and a half and enjoyed reading aloud to me and Sam, was doing just that, the three of us lying on my double bed, one child cuddled up to me on each side. When the book was finished, Sammy piped up. "It is my turn to read to you now," he said, and proceeded to do so. At first I thought he had memorized the book as children are wont to do, but further examination disclosed he was able to read even the *New York Times*, stumbling only over long words. I had been taught by an older cousin, but Sam had taught himself to read all on his own.

One time Bert took Sam with him on some errands. When he got back, Sam wasn't with him. "Where is Sammy?" I asked. "My God, I forgot him at the gas station!" exclaimed Bert. He got back in the car and went off. When he got there, Sam, who was then about three, was being fed and entertained by the men there. He had lost none of his composure, and wasn't one bit worried. In fact, he was having such a good time he was unwilling to leave his new friends.

Aside from leaving our children with their grandparents, or our next door neighbor Joe when we went visiting or out to see a movie, we never left our children to go away longer than overnight. We took few vacations. Small children do not travel well and usually require much more parental attention away from home. Whenever we attempted it, the trip ended in unmitigated misery and disaster for everyone involved. This, however, didn't mean the boys never got out. When Mark was about five he had his first sleep-over at grandma's and grandpa's. This proved very successful and was repeated from time to time, giving him a sense of independence and maturity. Sammy waited impatiently for his turn to come, and enjoyed it immensely when his time came. Both boys were very close to Bert's parents and remained so to the end. I recall Mark as a teenager solicitously leading his grandmother into a restaurant, pulling out her chair and taking charge of her coat, all courtesies he did not perform for me, as he considered me fully capable of fending for myself.

As time went by, our financial situation steadily improved. After Sammy's birth I hired a cleaning lady and haven't been without one since. My generation certainly lacks the obsessive devotion to cleanliness our mothers had. Soon we were able to afford a second car, albeit a secondhand one, and suddenly both Bert and I had several more degrees of freedom, and my in-laws had a much superior transportation service. During the last couple of years we were in Buffalo we even joined a pool club for the summer. Mark was placed in a day camp which operated at the pool club, I swam, chatted and played bridge, while Sam trailed after me some of the time. The club was absolutely safe and I did not worry when Sam wandered off, but when it was time to go home and I went in search of him I would invariably find him perched on some pretty young woman's lap, flirting outrageously and chatting without stop. He was so cute, cuddly, and friendly, so articulate for his age that everyone adored him. But he tended to gravitate to young women. I thought he would surely grow up to be a ladies' man, but he didn't. He grew up to be a family man.

School became the chief activity in Mark's life. He completed three grades before we moved away. Actually, he started pre-school, an activity he loved, at four. He didn't need lessons in socialization, having grown up among a large group of peers, but he learned to participate in more organized activities, gradually adapting to the regimentation which is part of the educational system. At the graduation, all the children wore little black graduation caps and gowns and showed off their various new skills. One of them was skipping, which the girls performed flawlessly while the boys looked and sounded like a herd of elephants—a very graphic demonstration of the developmental differences between genders at that age.

The adjustment to kindergarten was easy after a year of preschool. When Mark was in second grade, I began to wonder about American schools. He never did any homework and always came home with As. My memories of my own early schooling were quite different. One day I arranged for an appointment at the school and was referred to the school psychologist. She looked up Mark's I.Q. test and read me the result: 108. It appeared that Mark was a very average child, who applied himself and was achieving exactly as expected. She made no comment on the correlation-or rather lack of it—between his As and the absence of homework assignments.

This did not square with my observations, nor certainly those of my father-in-law, who had declared Mark to be a genius on the day of his birth, but I was reluctant to contradict the expert lest I appear a pushy Jewish mother and perhaps even make things awkward for Mark. However, I retained private reservations on the validity of the I.Q. tests and the observational skills of teachers who continued to rate Mark as average. Later, after we moved to New Jersey, Mark's fourth grade teacher praised his intellectual potential and performance at our first parent-teacher conference of the year, and provided him with outlets for his very superior abilities.

Meanwhile, Bert's progress up the corporate ladder was steady, although he claimed that with each raise and promotion he was earning less per hour, as his work load kept growing. The company was building new plants all over the eastern seaboard, and Bert spent increasingly longer periods supervising the design, the building and the start-ups of plants, particularly in Moundsville, West Virginia, a dreary town which, given a choice by the state of having a college or a prison built there, chose the prison since it would provide more jobs suitable for the locals. Going there was no picnic for him, as it meant long hours of travel usually on his own time in uncertain weather, even longer hours of work and tedium during his free time. But he loved the sense of creating something from scratch and following it through to completion, a reward increasingly missing from people's professional lives— the psychological importance of which is not generally recognized.

Bert's prowess and success at work were even more remarkable to anyone who knew of his serious disability. He had congenital keratoconus, a malformation of the cornea similar to extreme astigmatism, resulting in his seeing multiple images. The condition had been discovered when he was young and he was warned his eyes would deteriorate with age. Now this was beginning to happen; reading blueprints and other small print documents became a laborious, time-consuming process. Bert compensated for it by working extra-long hours. He felt that his condition should remain a secret from his employers, as it might hinder further promotions, raises and bonuses. Thus, we both suffered anxiety whenever some new health test requirements were announced by the company. Although we didn't talk about it, I am sure that the specter of partial blindness was always on Bert's mind. Many years later, after corneal transplants became a reality, Bert's condition was corrected by surgery and we both breathed a sigh of relief.

One night during the dead of winter, as snow storms raged all over the area, Bert was in transit, coming back from Moundsville. Meanwhile, Mark, who was at the time under two, developed a severe earache. As is often the case in such situations, our own pediatrician was unavailable, and his substitute promised to come as soon as possible. In Buffalo at that time, doctors still made house calls. When he arrived, he prescribed a barbiturate for Mark.

Barbiturates occasionally have an opposite effect on very young children. Mark proved to be such a case. Instead of being sedated, the poor thing was climbing the walls. I was walking with him in my arms trying to soothe him while he was screaming at the top of his lungs, when the phone rang. The snow storm was so bad that the plane bringing Bert home was forced to land in Jamestown. Bert was planning to stay there overnight with his brother. Meanwhile the pilot was planning to continue on to Buffalo, minus his passengers. But when Bert heard what was going on at home, he got right back on the plane and continued the harrowing journey home, ever the devoted husband and father. Two hours later, when my arms felt like lead and my heart was wrung out with pity and anxiety for my baby, Mark finally fell into an exhausted sleep. Soon after, Bert and the doctor arrived, practically bumping into each other, just to look at the angelic, tear-stained little face.

That was the most serious illness we experienced with either of our children. Apart from the usual colds, they grew up healthy, and, when the time came, did well in school as well. Of course, when Mark went to kindergarten and the teacher put him next to his best friend Patrick Garrity at nap time, the two pals continued to talk. Instead of separating them, the teacher failed them both in the "subject." The idea of their failing nap time was a source of general merriment for the adults, but I think Mark and Patrick were offended at our laughter. They continued to be best friends as long as we stayed in Buffalo, although Patrick later went to a Catholic school.

There was also the time when Mark was in first grade and walking to school by himself. For some reason one day he was late for school. About two hours later, a neighbor reported seeing him loitering in the street and attempting to hide from her. This was most unlike my well-mannered, rules-following little boy. I jumped in the car, with Sam at my side, and went in search of him. It turned out that the school door was closed after the bell and he didn't have the strength to open it by himself. Failing to attract anyone's attention and afraid I would be angry, he decided to play hooky. When anything happens for the first time, children don't know what the adult reaction will be to their actions.

When Mark was five we had to make an important decision: should we give him a religious education or not? Bert felt it would be hypocritical for us to teach him religion when we felt no need for it ourselves, but I felt that depriving him of such background would, in essence, deny him the choice later on. How can you choose something you know nothing about? Furthermore, I reasoned that we were living in a heavily Catholic area—there were only three Jewish families on the block, with Protestants also in the minority. All the other children were going to church and were already or were about to be subjected to some form of religious education. I did not want Mark to feel left out when the subject came up among the children. Our two Jewish neighbors were already annoyed at us for having a Christmas tree, causing their children to ask for one too. Both Bert and I had had them as children and did not consider them a religious symbol.

In the end we joined a nearby Conservative temple. In his first year there, Mark came home just before Hanukkah with a little homemade *dreidel* (a spinning top decorated with religious symbols). Bert's reaction to this accomplishment was a comment that the dreidel had cost us $400— the cost of membership dues. But the die was cast in favor of formal religious training.

In general, the children on the block were getting good, hands-on experience with religious tolerance. They saw the different religious practices being followed, and they saw their parents all being good friends and respecting each others' beliefs. Once, when Mark was little, he asked me, "Why can't I cross myself like Patrick?" I went into a thorough explanation on respecting but not imitating other people's practices, and elucidated that crossing oneself meant invoking God, Christ and the Holy Ghost, two of them entities we, as Jews, did not worship. But it turned out Mark wanted my permission to cross the street by himself.

The greatest trauma during my life in Buffalo was also a public one: President Kennedy's assassination. Like everyone else who lived through it, I remember exactly where I was when I first heard the dreadful, unbelievable news. My neighbor Annette ran into the house where I was sitting on the floor playing with Sammy, tears running down her face and screaming, "The President's been shot!" For the next week we were all glued to our television sets.

Kennedy had been the first president from our generation. He articulated and embodied a new way of thinking and new social ideas. With him we all looked to a better future. With his passing, we all experienced a curious loss of innocence. What could you trust in if the President, and later his assassin, could be killed before our very eyes? We cried while he lied in state, through the funeral, when John-John saluted his father's coffin, and as Jacqueline's dignified grief elevated us all.

I have retained a fondness and a great reservoir of goodwill for John Kennedy. I was sorry to learn in recent years that this idol had feet of clay. I really would have preferred not to know about it. This knowledge does not serve any purpose, and shatters comfortable illusions I held for many years.

Thus those years passed, filled with the dramas of births and the wonder of children growing up before my eyes, acquiring new skills and maturity at a very noticeable pace. When Mark went to third grade, Sammy started kindergarten (a half-day activity in those days), giving me some regularly scheduled time to myself for the first time in years. By the spring of 1966, I was getting tired of intellectual stagnation. Before the children were born, we did some traveling and attended plays in Canada, but afterwards cultural excitement was restricted to attending a Captain Kangaroo concert or a play like "Winnie the Pooh." We also attended a few classical music concerts and a few plays before the only dramatic theater in Buffalo closed down. The only art museum in town was heavy on contemporary art, something which I did not, at the time, appreciate. In fact, I rather agreed with Sammy who, when exposed to the collection at age two, pronounced the pictures to be jigsaw puzzles. Reflecting upon those years, I marvel that I was content in spite of the intellectual and cultural aridity of my life.

My life was a slice of genuine Americana. I am not so sure things are all that different for young families today, particularly if they live in the hinterlands. Today I require much more intellectual stimulation. On the other hand, my life is no longer filled with either the demands or the joys of a young family. My life was right for me then. By 1966 I seemed to be over my experiences during the war—a young woman successfully integrated into American society. If this success demanded a deep repression of my feelings, I didn't know it at the time and didn't think about it. With all due respect to psychoanalysis, a little repression is sometimes good for you.

Boredom finally goaded me into planning changes in my life. We now needed and were able to afford a bigger house. In spite of having added on a playroom several years before, we were bursting at the seams. Sammy's bedroom was particularly tiny. At the same time, Bert's parents were not faring too well financially, inflation and ill health having eroded some of their income. They had helped us for many years; it was now time to reciprocate. We consulted them on the advisability of building a house big enough for us all, with a downstairs bedroom and sitting room for them equipped with a private bath. We identified a suitable plot and entered into negotiations with a builder. This was an exciting time, planning our dream house with the wherewithal to implement the dream.

At the same time I was looking into going back to work. Nine years had passed since I left Erie County Institute, and I had done nothing professionally in the interim. One year after I left, I was offered my job back. It was tempting, but I couldn't leave Mark then. I doubted I could get my job back now. Nine years of inactivity was a long stretch. Meanwhile, science had moved on; a Ph.D. or at least a master's degree was now required for a college appointment. Perhaps it was more practical for me to consider high school teaching.

I was inquiring into that option when Bert came home one day with a rumor from work—the entire development department was about to be moved to Morristown, New Jersey. We put all our plans on hold until the rumors were verified. The official announcement followed soon after. We had two months to relocate to New Jersey. Needless to say, my in-laws were coming with us; their life in Buffalo was predicated on our presence.

We lived in Buffalo for 11 happy years. We made good friends there. It was wrenching to part from them, both for us and the children. The easygoing, healing years were over but I was ready for the challenges ahead.

CHAPTER 16

THE EVEN BETTER YEARS

In July 1966, we moved to West Orange, New Jersey, to a spacious bi-level house where we still live. The move was traumatic for several reasons. During our house-hunting we stayed in a local motel. Both of us were heavy smokers at the time, Bert averaging two and a half packs a day, and I about half that. One evening, in our motel room, we both suffered simultaneous fits of coughing. "This is ridiculous," said Bert. "We just have to quit." Then and there we made a pact to quit cold turkey. While I succeeded, Bert failed almost immediately. He continued to smoke, periodically trying to quit, but always failing. He kept smoking for many years, even after his only brother, Stan, died of lung cancer. Bert finally stopped several years ago after suffering a mild stroke.

Quitting smoking was one of the most difficult things I ever did. The strong, specific craving for tobacco subsided after a week or two, but the irritability lingered for a couple of months. Perhaps my timing, with all the stress of moving, was not perfect. On the other hand it was a busy time, when the many decisions and changes grabbed my attention distracting me from my craving for nicotine. Anyhow, there is never a good time for doing anything difficult you really are unwilling to face.

The day before the packers came, my father-in-law, still in Buffalo, had a heart attack and was rushed to the hospital, where he lingered for a week

241

before dying. What was to be a joyous, forward-moving occasion became a nightmare. He never saw the new quarters, and we spent the next few days first hopeful, then anxious, and finally grieving for this wonderful man. My mother-in-law camped out at the hospital, indifferent to her own fate, much less the fate of her belongings.

To make matters worse, we were experiencing the worst heat wave in memory. The thermometer hit 108 degrees. Going outside became practically impossible. The blast of hot, stagnant, humid air made it hard to breathe. Although the motel room was air-conditioned, the conditions began to take their toll.

After the sad and emotional funeral, we left my mother-in-law with her family for a couple of weeks to spare her the confusion and let her grieve in peace while we went back to our new house to put it in order. Most of that load fell on me, since Bert, having missed work for a number of days, had to go back to the office, where he too would be adjusting to a new situation. That was a summer out of hell. It remained unbearably hot most of the time—we did not get central air conditioning until many years later. Mark and Sam did not know any children in the area, did not go to camp, and the town had no pool, leaving them at loose ends. They remained difficult all that summer, while I was trying to organize the house, get them registered for school, and make arrangements for Rose when she arrived to occupy the room which had been intended for her and her husband.

By September we were finally settled in. The kids were in school, but I was at loose ends myself. Living with my mother-in-law proved to be a mixed blessing—two strong willed women, each determined to rule the roost, in the same house, with Bert caught in the middle. My home was no longer a perfect refuge. Rose and I didn't fight, but there was an undercurrent of tension. In her mind she could not accept the change in her status from mother of the house to grandmother-in-residence.

My old New York friends, with whom we were again socializing, and Uncle Adek in Chicago all chided me for sitting at home and letting my brain go to waste. My home life was not conducive to spending too much time in the house anyway, and the street we moved to was not nearly as friendly as our block in Buffalo. Although there were some children nearby, their mothers seemed to have an established social life away from the area. We were getting by financially, but not saving much, and large expenses involving bar mitzvahs and college were looming in the near future. It was time to think about going back to work.

By this time, I had been away from my profession for over 10 years. There was no doubt in my mind that I wanted to go back to teaching, but I had to decide on which level to teach. To join a college faculty, I needed to upgrade my engineering knowledge, most likely by getting a master's degree. If I settled on high school teaching, I needed to become certified in New Jersey, which, although a lengthy procedure, allowed me to begin substituting as soon as I had accumulated six credits in education. There were many more high schools than colleges in the immediate area, and working in the public school system would also provide better synchronicity with my children's schedule. So I decided to teach high school.

By January 1966, I was taking two education courses at Montclair University and enrolled in their Master in the Art of Teaching program. I was almost 40 at the time, and a bit apprehensive about going back to school after so many years. Did I still have the brains to absorb new knowledge, the discipline to study, the nerve to take tests?

I do not have a high opinion of the education departments in many American colleges, although I am not sure how they should be changed. Teaching, in my opinion, is still an art. Yes, one can improve with experience, at least to some extent. But I have met too many old teachers who never become good at the craft, and many new ones who were very good from day one, and improved even more with time. The love of the subject one teaches, a deep interest in young people, enthusiasm for teaching in general, and a high energy level are all very important. Many teachers get into the profession as a sort of last resort and never warm up to it. They really should get out as soon as they can, both for their own and their students' benefit. Finally, there is this mysterious thing known as chemistry between teachers and students, so essential in the classroom.

From my observation, students rarely perform in high school out of pure love of knowledge; you really cannot expect such a sophisticated concept from teenagers who are dealing with hormones, complex social environments, their families and the growing awareness of the future. Getting good grades to please their parents and their teachers (particularly if they like the teachers) and getting into a prestigious college is about the best you can expect. Teachers must use that and the spirit of competition to lure them in. A good teacher's job is to transform this motivation into a love for the subject.

These are the things they should have told us in Montclair, using case studies as is done in medical and law schools. Instead, we studied old philosophies of education, some psychology, some descriptions of new approaches, all taught by people who had never spent a single day teaching in a high school. They were constantly challenged by veteran teachers in our classes.

In addition to education courses, I was required to take several science classes. One of them, advanced inorganic chemistry, was taught by an elderly German Jewish professor. He and I became friends, and both of us were appalled by the ignorance of basic chemical principles exhibited by some students in the class, many of whom were already certified science teachers. My own education at Columbia, although a bit outdated, had been so systematic and thorough that I was able to keep ahead of most of my colleagues in the class. I also took a course on intellectual history of Europe, the only course at Montclair whose rigor and academic requirements were reminiscent of Columbia. I enjoyed that course immensely.

It was at that time I discovered my own love of learning in spite of the inferior nature of some of the courses I was attending. I was drawn in, almost against my will, my active mind and aggressive nature forcing me to participate, and getting more out of my experience than the credits I needed.

Meanwhile, in the spring of 1967, I did some work on the side translating technical material from French, Polish and Russian into English. My knowledge of those three languages was quite fluent at the time although, having learned them as a child, I had to look up many technical terms. I continued doing translation for many years.

By that fall I had my substitute certificate and signed up with several area school districts, restricting my work to math and science. By doing this, I earned some money, maintained the flexibility I needed with my young children at home, and made myself known to the science departments in the area, which facilitated the coming job hunt.

I was now juggling two part-time jobs, running the house, chauffeuring the children to Hebrew school, Little League and other obligatory suburban activities, taking Rose to various doctors, going to college part time, doing homework, and any other chores which needed doing. Bert was working very hard at his new location and was required to travel extensively. Luckily, I experienced a burst of physical and psychic energy such as I had never known up to that time. Energy which, though somewhat attenuated, is still one of my main attributes.

This alone should have told me I was largely over the trauma of my earlier life, at least to the extent of becoming fully functional, although the memories, the horror and the sorrow would stay with me forever.

A teacher's preparation culminates in an internship. I had already taught in Buffalo, though my students had been older. However, the rigid New Jersey state system would not accept my experience and forced me to teach essentially without pay for 12 weeks.

I was hoping to find a position close to home, and had applied, among others, to West Orange High School, the secondary school nearest my home. At the time I anticipated teaching chemistry, the subject I was most expert in, but the chemistry teacher there rejected me. Many teachers don't want to be bothered with dealing with neophytes, spending time to train a beginner while unsettling their own classes in the process.

A few days later, Bert and I went to a party on Long Island at a home of a previous colleague of his. One of his guests, Magda, was a sort of godmother to Bert's co-worker. She turned out to be the chemistry teacher in West Orange who had just rejected my candidacy. "I couldn't stand another prospective teacher who can't even write the element symbols correctly," she confided. "The quality of current student teachers is dreadful. But please re-apply, and I will be glad to take you." Of course I did and I was accepted. Was God playing dice again?

So, in September 1968 I went to Mountain High School in West Orange, New Jersey, to do my student teaching, starting on the first day of school. Normally, I would have been observing for a couple of weeks, and then been asked to take over one or two classes under the close supervision of my mentoring teacher. But, as it happened, Magda had to take two days off immediately to take her son to college. Since I already had a substitute certificate, the school saved money by leaving me in charge.

When Magda came back, she suggested I continue with four of the five classes. Her knowledge of chemistry, acquired in Vienna, was truly encyclopedic, but she was an old-time school teacher—very rigid and old fashioned. She would assign reading of new material and then ask for questions, although most of her students did not understand enough of the subject to ask meaningful questions at that point. She was impatient and unable to adjust to changing conditions in the classroom. In fact, she was convinced the students were the ones at fault and should be doing the adjusting. True, but largely beside the point. In teaching as in other professions, one has to deal with realities, not fantasies.

By the spring of 1969 I was ready for a permanent, full-time job. I was now certified to teach all sciences at junior and senior high school level. No amount of requests to the state that my certificate should be limited to physical sciences produced any reaction. I had never taken a biology course in my life. Bureaucracies don't readily respond to special situations. Knowing it was not uncommon for school administrators to require teachers to cover multiple disciplines in the interest of scheduling ease, although often to the detriment of students, I did not want to be put in a position in which I was forced to teach a subject I knew nothing about, simply because the state said I was certified in it.

Looking for a position turned out to be quite simple. Livingston High School had an opening. The head of the science department there, Ed Fabrizio, knew me because of my frequent substituting stints in the school, and liked me. The rest went quickly. He and the principal interviewed me on a Thursday. The district superintendent interviewed me on Friday, and by Monday the job offer arrived at my house.

I was originally hired to teach chemistry, but even before I started working, a physics teacher left and proved so difficult to replace (physics teachers are always in short supply) that my qualifications for teaching physics exceeded those of other candidates. Accordingly, I was asked to teach both chemistry and physics, which I did for many years.

In 1969, when I started working at Livingston High School, my life changed again. At first, my responsibilities were enormous: a full-time job teaching, a house to run, children to ferry to various activities, and catering to my mother-in-law who was living with us, all with a husband who worked long hours and was away much of the time on business. Somehow, my energy matched the demands.

Since I had never gone to high school and my own teen years had been so different, it was lucky that my own children were becoming teenagers during my first years of teaching. They taught me a great deal about adolescents and helped me to relate better to my students.

Right from my first day at LHS, I knew I would love my work, and did so for 26 years. Although taxing at times, it was a delight which lasted until my retirement. The first few years I relied on my instincts, which were mostly good, and slogged through, mainly by reacting to situations as they occurred. Gradually, however, the fog of the overwhelming demands on my time and attention cleared. The administrative details of keeping attendance, preparing lesson plans and filling out innumerable forms dreamed up by the educational bureaucracy eventually became a routine I could do with my eyes closed.

Ed Fabrizio was an excellent boss in this respect. He shared with me a desire for streamlining paperwork so that his teachers could concentrate on what went on in the classroom. His motto was, "If it's not broke, don't fix it!" When Ed saw my success in the classroom, his guiding hand became very light, allowing me to try out new methods and tinker with my teaching techniques. I learned to respond quickly and decisively to the many different problems and agendas my students brought to my attention. There is always room for improvement—I think that is my life's motto.

After some years of teaching physics and chemistry, Ed gave me the opportunity to concentrate only on physics. In fact, although I taught two levels of physics, over the years I made my reputation as the Honors Physics specialist. Physics was an elective course at LHS. To get into the honors course a student had to demonstrate both ability and application. My students tended to be very ambitious and hard-working, a combination which usually ensured success. Physics has a reputation for being a very difficult subject, and I was known as a tough and demanding teacher. All of which could be quite intimidating to students, but at the same time secretly challenging and exciting. The trick was to use those feelings and develop a sense of mystique surrounding them.

I conveyed an impression to my students that they were special, because they chose to test themselves, and I was an ally helping them to pass the test. I did, in fact, rejoice at all their successes and suffered their setbacks and failures with them. Correcting tests was always an emotional experience. I rooted for them all the time, and was disappointed in them and myself when they faltered. The climate of cooperation between my students and me, engaged as we were in a common and difficult endeavor, was the stepping stone in trying and make them see the beauty and elegance of physics, the sheer majesty of a few simple laws governing the behavior of the universe, to attempt to have them share the love I have for the subject.

I am a firm believer in an interdisciplinary approach to any subject. I love connections between seemingly disparate topics. I myself have many interests, and I tried to bring them into the classroom. Sometimes a student would coax me into a digression. I believe that was considered a triumph among the kids but, while letting them believe they had conned me, I was never diverted against my will. I wanted to bring economics, history, and the arts into my classroom and let the kids get a glimpse of the complex design of our society.

For example, I was always an ardent, albeit selective, environmentalist. Every year we talked about energy conservation regardless of whether the topic was fashionable just then or not. My goal was to show the students the need for making informed, rational decisions rather than impulsive and emotional ones on issues that were extremely complex and had grave, though often unpredictable consequences. I was alerting my classes to the dangers of acid rain, ozone layer damage and the greenhouse effect long before these threats entered the public arena.

I learned to deal with parents, both en masse and individually. Every year, teachers met with parents during an "open house" evening. During these brief presentations, I laid out for the parents the many goals I had in my course. The first, of course, was to prepare my students adequately for college physics; no one should have to take a serious physics course in college for the first time. But in addition, I strove to improve my students' problem-solving skills, and that necessitated their putting in some "frustration time" while doing their homework. Relying on me always to show them the way would not develop the self-confidence they needed to tackle new, never before encountered problems. My job was to develop techniques for approaching such problems without panicking, a way of thinking yourself into the situation and eventually translating it into the equations and mathematical solutions that are the language of physics. To succeed at a complex, difficult task, one must be prepared to struggle and allow time to become familiar with new concepts.

Physicists say we don't "learn" very abstract concepts; we just get used to them. I explained to the parents how I would improve their children's language skills as well as their ability to interpret charts and graphs, so important in our lives today, through lab reports and class activities. In short, while teaching a new discipline, I also attempted to help my students to grow and mature as responsible citizens.

Dealing with individual parents concerned about their children's progress also required interpersonal skills. I remember a case early in my career when a mother tearfully accused me of ruining her son's life by failing him. I responded: "Surely one failing grade never ruined anyone's life. Besides, I did not fail your son. He failed himself." I learned to be prepared by knowing a student's progress in other subjects, particularly math, so that I would know whether a student had a general problem or an isolated one, and to convince the parent that we were on the same side with the child's best interest at heart. Sometimes, the parents themselves were the problem, their expectations excessive and unrealistic. Many parents seemed to have relinquished their authority altogether, in fact towing the line drawn by their children and their children's peers.

I remember a rare exception. I had failed a student, and his parents came and thanked me. "It was a rude awakening, but one our son needed badly," they proclaimed. The following year, the same student took physics again; his parents insisted I be his teacher once more. I can't say the boy experienced a total transformation, but he learned enough to apply himself sufficiently to pass the course. Over the years, my reputation and experience allowed me to be a student's advocate, counselor, critic, or disciplinarian as circumstances demanded.

I recall a case of cheating, which has always been a serious problem in schools and one most administrators don't like to talk about. I always corrected tests the day they were taken and returned them the next day. I did this because instant feedback is pedagogically so valuable. Some students learn more from their tests than from lessons preceding them. This speed in marking tests produced occasional grading errors on my part, and I had to respond when these were pointed out to me. One student came to me to point out that I did not notice he had solved a problem correctly. I corrected what I thought was my error and changed his grade, but kept the case in my memory.

When this happened a second time, I became suspicious. Such an omission occurred very rarely, and chances of its happening twice in a row were very small. Next time, when the tests were handed in, I photocopied this student's test, thinking perhaps these "ungraded" problems were being added after the fact. Sure enough, after we went over the test in class (another very important teaching technique I never skipped), the same student approached me with yet another ungraded problem on his test. Was he ever embarrassed when confronted with the copy I made earlier! I gave him a zero for the test and barred him from the privilege of challenging me for the duration.

The use of humor is another successful teaching tool. I enjoyed shocking or surprising my students from time to time. Once, I was showing a film demonstrating a light property called "Total Internal Reflection." In the film several people were sitting on the edge of a swimming pool with their feet dangling in the water. The film was shot from the bottom of the pool with the water surface acting like a mirror positioned on a ceiling, so that the camera and my class saw the inverted feet floating upside down in space, dissociated from their owners. Predictably, the class burst out laughing. After the film was finished, I began to muse on the nature of humor. "Seeing something unexpected tickles our funny bone," I said. " After all, no one expects mirrors on the ceiling unless he or she goes in for kinky sex."

The students looked at each other in disbelief, as if checking with each other, "Did she really say that?" Suddenly, spontaneous applause broke out, the only time I was rewarded by this reaction. I believe that it was at that time I acquired the nickname of "Dr. Ruth" among my students. Through the very active student grapevine, knowledge of my nickname soon reached me.

Bert shares my inability to resist a joke. One year on the first day of school, he needed me for some reason since forgotten, and was in the hall waiting for my class to let out. The door was open and he overheard me teaching the first rudiments of vector concepts. I lectured, "Imagine I go riding in my car and get lost on some side road with no visible land-marks. Suddenly, the engine quits on me. I pick up my car phone and call my husband to come get me. What information would he need to find me?"

"He has to know how far you went," called one student. "And the direc-tion," called another. I proceeded to outline the detailed information I would give my husband. At that point Bert walked into the classroom. "You called?" he asked with mock innocence. The class found the inci-dent hilarious, particularly when they realized that far from being set up it was the result of an incredible coincidence and very quick thinking on my husband's part.

I was always on good terms with colleagues in my school. We shared our professional concerns, and many a lunch hour was spent bellyaching about a particular student or parent, an administrative decision, or a new state law dealing with education. Within our smaller group, more private concerns were shared: problems with children, relatives and even husbands, although truly private marital problems were excluded.

The importance of this group for all of us cannot be overemphasized. It was equivalent to having one's own private psychoanalyst available at all times to listen constructively and offer advice. The advice was useful and often sage and loving, since we knew each other so well and shared so many of the same problems. We truly helped each other through some of life's most difficult crises, enhanced each other's joys, and generally provided the much needed periodic respite from the company of teenagers—an escape into the realm of adulthood.

New Jersey proved much more interesting to live in than Buffalo, particularly because of the proximity to New York City. We took the children to the various museums. The Museum of Natural History was their favorite, but they enjoyed the Metropolitan Museum of Art as well. At about the same time, remembering how my parents had ensured my exposure to cultural activities as a child, we took the children to see *Fiddler on the Roof*. Years later, Sam confided that his love of the theater and desire to act were born that day. Sensing his obvious enjoyment, we enrolled him in a class of improvisational acting at the local YMHA (the Jewish equivalent of the YMCA). From time to time, parents and siblings were invited to see the young actors—ranging from 6 to 10 years of age—perform. They would be given instructions to be flowers, or specific animals, act out various emotions, or improvise skits given only the subject matter.

On one occasion, Sam (who was then 6 or 7) and a little girl were given such a topic: he was to be a recruiter for the crusades, and she a housewife to whose door he had come. In the course of the little scene, the "housewife" inquired: "What is a crusade?" "I don't know," responded our little son nonchalantly. "Well, maybe I will go anyway," said the little girl, thinking perhaps it was something like a cruise. Acting in front of a friendly audience helped the children gain poise and self-confidence.

Meanwhile Mark was acquiring the same skill in public speaking through the Boy Scouts, as well as in many school activities. While Sam was taking the acting course, Mark was taking one in creative science. Mark was very lucky in having two inspired science teachers, both in biology, who I am sure had a lot to do with his choice of molecular biology as his life's work. His biology teacher in junior high school taught the course around a theme of structure and function, making the curriculum much more imaginative and interesting than merely going through the various class-es of plants and animals. He would send the kids home with broad and challenging assignments such as "define life," causing many a spirited discussion at dinner tables such as ours.

In ninth grade and later in high school, Mark was taught by Dr. Mora, a teacher who, in spite of having a Ph.D. in biology, chose to work with young kids because he loved them. He and Mark soon developed a rap-port through lab reports. Mark would put a joke into each one: a report on trees would include "Polus Telefonus." A report on electrolysis of water was entitled "Divorce, Chemical Style," to which Dr. Mora replied, "Let's split and get out of here!" I think Mark spent as much time thinking up appropriate jokes as writing the report, but he certainly came to asso-ciate biology with fun and pleasure, so important in a student's mind.

We joined a Reform temple, Temple Emanu-El in Livingston, which remains our temple to this day. There the boys began their preparation for their bar mitzvahs.

At eight, Sammy started guitar lessons, and quickly progressed from strumming to a serious study of classical guitar, a study which continued until he graduated high school. Sam's guitar eventually became a source of family entertainment. At nine, Sam became a Cub Scout, and Bert became the Cub Master of Sam's pack. For about three years our family was immersed in Scouting activities. Bert took a day off from work every month to prepare the monthly pack meetings. He loved all the boys and was extremely creative, inventing demonstrations and activities for them. Once he perfected a demo of magical topology, removing a vest without taking off the jacket. Another time he built a table before the boys' very eyes in just a few minutes. There were races and competitions, such as crawling under an enormous canvas, retrieving some object and crawling back, while the audience of parents and siblings was convulsed with laughter. Nobody ever lost Bert's races. There was always a prize for par-ticipation for everybody.

Meanwhile Mark had become a Boy Scout, and gradually progressed through the different ranks, achieving the Eagle Scout rank at about 15. Camping with urban and suburban boys and their fathers was not always easy. Bert participated in most camp-outs happily, and told some funny stories about them. One father showed up for the weekend clad in a suit, a homburg, spats, and carrying a big, black umbrella, a perfect picture of an English gentleman. Another father, unnerved by the absence of bathrooms—in that location, only outhouses were available—drove a whole hour at five in the morning to his own house, in order to avail himself of civilized amenities, scaring his wife out of her wits in the process. Naturally, at that hour, she took him for a burglar.

Sam never continued scouting past the rank of First Class, about halfway through the Boy Scout program. I was very sorry about it. He was becoming more interested in other activities. With Mark's departure, Sam must have felt as if he would have to assume a leadership position, which he was not keen to do.

I have a great admiration for the Scouting movement, its philosophy, its involvement of male adults and the lessons it teaches the boys. However, my admiration is purely theoretical. My three men tried to interest me in camping, promising to take over all the chores. I went with them once, but I guess it was too late in my life. Sleeping on the ground, crawling into a little tent, and all the other accouterments of life in nature left me cold. Watching Bert's attempts at cooking on the little portable stove made me so impatient that I took over the cooking. Even with my total lack of experience in outdoor life, I did better than he, but I grumbled all the way anyway. My idea of a vacation is a hotel with all the amenities, meals served by waiters and interesting cultural or historical artifacts to visit. Our only family attempt at camping was never repeated. I must have made enough caustic remarks to discourage it.

I did, however, faithfully attend the Little League games when Mark played. I listened over and over to the explanations of kindly neighbors, but I never really grasped the concept of baseball. Mark was very small, but fast, and specialized in stealing bases successfully, although he rarely caught a ball. In high school he became a sprint racer.

Outside of sports and camping, whose value in the boys' lives I woefully underestimated, I was a very involved mother. We had a routine. After the boys came from school and I from work, we reviewed the upcoming activities, including the first priority of homework, upcoming meetings, music lessons, Hebrew school and so on, before embarking on the day's after-school activities. At dinner, we discussed the various events of the day. Since my job as a teacher was so understandable to my children, they were always interested in what happened in my classes and got a different point of view on education from the one they were undoubtedly hearing from their peers.

I thought it was all working so well, attributing the absence of rebellion during our boys' teenage years to the open lines of communication both Bert and I were maintaining with our kids. Later, I got an intimation from one of our boys that they had viewed my behavior, in particular, as too intrusive, too bossy, and too focused on the need to excel, giving them an idea that my love for them was conditional: that is it depended on their continuing to excel.

Bert and I created a home in which learning, personal responsibility and conscientiousness were valued and stressed. We didn't just talk about it, but acted as role models for our boys. I trust that now that they are grown men, and have our continuing love and support, even when we have reservations, they view the matter differently.

I have not read many Holocaust survivors' memoirs, nor books written by their grown children. This was part of my avoidance strategy. From the little I do know about the subject, my behavior was rather typical of survivors: one's children were to make up for all the lost ones—a heavy burden on them. I was unaware of any of this at the time, and Mark tells me he felt no such pressure specifically. Their achievements came as the result of their abilities, for which I claim no credit, and their applying themselves, for which I do.

When we were bringing up our children, parents were not as self-conscious as they are today of the effect they have on their offspring. Coached by Dr. Spock, who encouraged us to trust our instincts, we did what "came naturally," but that proved often to be repeating our parents' mistakes, or going all the way in the opposite direction. When our children were teenagers I, at least, did not appreciate the importance in their establishing their own identity; that is what teenage rebellion is all about.

In this respect my own life was so different, with my growing up and assumption of many responsibilities so sudden and at so young an age. As is the case with most parents, my intentions were good. I was filled with the age-old desire to spare my children pain and suffering. Of course, this doesn't work. Each generation must learn to become adult and independent on its own.

The outcome is that to this day my sons are leery of my influence. They tend to inform me of their life decisions after the fact, and do not involve me in their decision-making processes. I hear from friends that this is not uncommon, but will the time ever come when we can meet as equals? I just don't know. I sense that living as separate equals is what our kids want.

All too soon, Mark and Sam grew up. The senior year was an exciting time for each of them. We experienced with them the anxiety of college applications, even though both were doing so superlatively well in school there was no doubt of their acceptance by a first-rate college. The University of Pennsylvania and Cornell were their "safe" schools. Both boys boasted many extracurricular activities, including their summer programs, editorial positions at school publications and winning honors in statewide academic competitions. The drama club was particularly important in Sam's life with its camaraderie, hard work and cast parties following each successful production. (I think he played lead roles in all the plays produced during his high school tenure.)

Sam graduated three years after Mark, but there were many similarities between their last years of school. For example, each of them got their driver's license their senior year. Our boys didn't own cars, but had ready access to either Bert's or mine after school as we only needed them to get to and from work. I seem to remember four car accidents, none serious, but all costly and three of the four due largely to the inexperience of the drivers. The last one which involved Sam, however, was different in that respect.

He was driving with a friend, on a nasty, rainy night. Traffic was crawling, and a light turned red when he was already in the intersection. Rightly, under the circumstances, he continued, only to hit broadside a car moving on the green light. Because of extremely poor visibility, neither driver had seen the other. The damage to both cars was very slight, one might say insignificant, as neither had been moving very fast.

The owner of the other car, however, insisted on calling the police. Two strangers offered to present witness accounts in court against Sam, an unusual occurrence attesting to the great deal of hostility between the generations in the late seventies. Like most teenagers, Sam looked fairly unkempt and must have been considered a menace by the elderly, proper lady in the other car. She didn't live in our town, but came to West Orange just to lodge a complaint against Sam. On the advice of our lawyer, Sam pleaded not guilty.

When he was notified of the court date there was consternation in our house—it conflicted with Sam's invitation to Washington to receive his Presidential Scholar Award from President Carter. A copy of the invitation was sent to the judge, and the case was postponed. We hoped that such an illustrious postponement cause would go far to create a favorable mind set in the judge.

On the day of the trial, Bert and Sam appeared in court, both in suits and ties and Sam sporting a new haircut. Sam sat alone at one table and Bert sat in the back of the courtroom, while his opponent, at the other table, was flanked by two lawyers and supported by two angry witnesses. Sam presented written character testimonials from his school principal and our rabbi, and the whole thing suddenly looked like adults ganging up on a very nice yet hapless kid. The judge ruled both parties had used poor judgment and dismissed the case. Bert and Sam came home flushed with victory, and we all went out to celebrate.

Each of my boys won the Presidential Scholar Award, a distinction initiated by President Lyndon Johnson to honor one boy and girl from each state. The recipients spent a week in Washington D.C. attending a variety of cultural and festive events, seeing some behind-the-scenes operations at the Smithsonian, the Library of Congress and other government institutions. The week culminated in a VIP White House tour for the medallists and their families, a party at the State Department, and the award ceremony. This took place at the White House, where the President addressed us (Ford in Mark's case, and Carter in Sam's), and an official handed out the medals, immortalized individually for each student by a photograph to record the event. The large photographs arrived a few weeks later and were framed and proudly displayed everywhere. At the time, we were told we were the third family with two siblings so honored.

Finally, each senior year would draw to a close. All the award ceremonies were over, the prom tuxedos returned, the colleges decided on and the yearbooks signed copiously.

Both of my sons were class valedictorians. Mark spoke in his valedictorian's speech about the need for excellence, drawing rave reviews from parents and bringing much *kvelling* (joy in Yiddish) to Bert and me. Three years later, Sam spoke about keeping oneself open and receptive to new knowledge and experiences. His opening sentence went something like this, "In my high school years I learned to like three new things: Shakespeare, jazz and broccoli." Thereafter, the speech was to be known as the "broccoli speech."

Mark spent his pre-college summer in Israel and Paris, and Sam as an acting apprentice at Mount Holyoke College with Mom and Dad enthusiastically attending every new production performance. Each came home briefly at summer's end to pack and get ready for college. We ferried their belongings to their respective schools, met their new roommates, helped them to settle in and each time came home sadly to our diminished family.

I dreaded the empty nest in advance so much, that when the time finally came, I had already done all my pining and the actual experience proved easier than I had anticipated. Besides, my children were not too far away: Mark at Princeton, and then MIT for his Ph.D. in molecular biology, and Sam at Harvard and then to New York University for a master's degree in acting. Thus, we were weaned from each other gradually. The day your child calls someplace else "home" and his previous home becomes a place to visit represents an important change in the parent-child relationship.

After his first year of college, Mark took a summer job with Hoffman La Roche and lived with us, but he was somewhat lonely since all his friends were working away from home. After that, neither Mark nor Sam spent a summer living at home; the suburban setting is no place for young adults. This of course meant that they were home only for long holidays, and we did not see them otherwise unless we visited them. We made sure to attend all the public events in their school life. Still, as must happen, we were growing away from each other.

All through these years, there was another story weaving through our lives: the story of Rose. As the years went by, the situation in our house gradually changed. The boys became more independent while Rose became more needy. Finally, in 1972, a nurse's aide was hired for my mother-in-law. She remained with Rose until her death seven years later.

Like many old people, Rose measured her life from event to event. She was determined to see both boys graduate from high school and succeeded, but died shortly before Mark finished college. Her love for the boys and pride in their accomplishments was the final joy of her life. Both boys felt connected to her, particularly Mark, who being the older one remembered her better from her heyday. Whenever the family went to a restaurant together, he was at her side, guiding her solicitously and patiently repeating answers to her questions over and over as her short-term memory was gradually deteriorating at the time. While in college, one of Mark's activities was visiting lonely elderly people in a nursing home. He would go twice a week and spend an hour with each of them, just chatting and making them feel connected to the world outside.

As Rose's health deteriorated, the care she received from her nurse during the day and me at night became insufficient. The last two years of her life were a nightmare for us all. We were always looking for weekend and night nurses; few of them came up to the standards of Rose's regular nurse. All this while Rose was getting increasingly frail and confused. Her life became a continual shuttle between the house and St. Barnabas Hospital. Finally, she suffered a series a small strokes.

One day, when I came home from work, the nurse told me Rose had been sick all day and was sleeping. "Don't wake her for dinner," she said. When I finally decided to wake her, at about 8 p.m., I couldn't rouse her at all. By now she was beginning to breathe heavily, frightening me into calling the ambulance and accompanying her to the hospital. (Bert was not home that day.) She had slipped into a coma and never woke up.

Thereafter, Bert and I visited her every day and talked to her, hoping we were reaching her at some level, but her coma was deepening; soon she required life support systems. We were spared the need to make the decision to discontinue the support. After a week in the hospital, she slipped away quietly.

The death of Bert's mother in 1979 was another important watershed in our lives. It removed the stress her living with us created, but it also left a big void in our lives. With Rose gone and the boys in college, we were back to the beginning, just the two of us, no one else to be responsible for, to cater to or consider. A new phase was beginning.

CHAPTER 17

REAPING LIFE'S REWARDS

The dramas in our lives take place early on. Graduations, first jobs, weddings, and births—all of those now lay behind me, as did the caring for elderly parents and children still living at home. Suddenly, from being caretakers focused on the needs of others we could become more self-centered and more self-indulgent. Bert and I entered a relatively serene period in our lives. We were both at the zenith of our careers, with the peace of mind and self-confidence that come with this position. Our health was still good, the energy level permitting enjoyment of extracurricular hobbies, and finances allowing us to follow our desires. We had paid our dues, and our time had come to reap the benefits.

Having prudently provided for our children, our lifestyle was not hampered by their educational expenses. I say that with justifiable pride: Princeton, Harvard, and three years at NYU weren't cheap. Luckily, Mark's Ph.D. at MIT was essentially paid for by a fellowship. We were resolved, and succeeded in our goal of leaving our boys debt-free upon completing school. In fact, each of them had a nest egg for future contingencies. We might have cosseted our children too much. Even in high school, we advised them to concentrate on their studies, school and other extracurricular activities, leaving the task of earning money to us. In college, they supported themselves during summers, but did not have to save money to pay for college costs. Mark told me later that, in his opinion, we went overboard. He would have appreciated his education more if he had had to provide, at least partly, the cost of it himself. As they say, the road to hell is paved with good intentions.

Having the house to ourselves was a real luxury. I appropriated everyone's closets. Since my weight keeps going up and down (lately, mostly up, to my regret), I have accumulated wardrobes in several sizes, in the vain hope they will be of use someday. With all that space, there is a tendency to save everything. Sometimes we forget what we own or, if we do remember, we cannot find it. Bert has a study and a studio, I have my own study, there is a guest room housing our treadmill, and our bedroom has been enlarged into a combination bedroom/dressing room. In short, we now have organized space for everything and a full choice between togetherness and privacy.

The hobbies we developed together include traveling, cultural activities and ballroom dancing. We took vacations in either Europe, Canada, or the western reaches of the United States every summer, and became seasoned travelers with plenty of pictures and other mementos to remind us of these pleasures. We had season tickets to the opera, ballet, concert halls and repertory theater. When all this became a bit much for Bert—a cultural overkill—I pursued some of these activities with Lee, Irene and Ester, my friends from school. However, Bert and I never tired of going to art museums together; in time Bert became a member of the Metropolitan Museum and The Museum of Modern Art (MOMA). In 1979, when our horizons opened up, Bert was only five years from his *de facto* retirement, when his life would change radically yet again.

For some years, ballroom dancing became our principal hobby. It started as a conscious decision to combine physical fitness activities with pleasure. At the time, I walked every day on the oval in front of my school building, and in the halls inside when the weather was too inclement. A few years later I joined a health club and embarked on a program of regular exercises. Bert walked aerobically as well, though he found it a dead bore. But, in spite of this, both of us were concerned with the inexorable weight gains. Food in America is just too tempting, and life too sedentary.

Bert conceived of ballroom dancing as a means to counteract these tendencies. We had always been good, if untrained dancers, both of us endowed with a good sense of rhythm, flexibility, and grace, though Bert was better than I on all counts. He started taking dance lessons in a nearby dance studio. Soon, I was going with him to the weekly Saturday night dance parties, and watching enviously the intricate steps he and the other dancers could perform.

In the end, we both connected with a studio in Summit, New Jersey, and began to take lessons, at first in a group and then privately to improve styling and choreograph routines for competitions. At one time we had two teachers—a woman for Bert and a man for me—and became regular participants in local competitions, even going as far as Baltimore for dance events. While we were dancing, our weight came down and stayed down, and my closet filled up with swirling skirts and dresses designed to show off the dancer at her best. We became friends with several couples and sat together at the various events, creating an effortless social life for ourselves. My figure was so good that on my 60th birthday I wore a miniskirt to school, to the delight and amusement of my students, most of whom knew of my dancing activities.

Cha-cha, swing, rumba and tango were our favorites. They also better suited our physiques—you need to be tall and willowy to look right waltzing. By the standards of the dance studio we were average dancers, but at weddings and bar mitzvahs we clearly stood out and drew admiration from the audience which always formed around us whenever we got on the floor. Once, at Irene's daughter's wedding, people thought we were professionals doing a floor show. All very flattering, nice stroking for the ego, and a way to be special, motivating us to persevere in the truly hard work it takes to become reasonably adept dancers.

We have a whole shelf full of trophies from our various competitions and, deservedly, Bert has many more than I. Of course organizers of these events, hoping for return customers, are motivated to give out as many awards as possible. Winners tend to return more often than persistent losers. For that reason, there are competitions on two or three levels of bronze, silver and gold, available for different age ranges in both American and international dance styles. (An octogenarian cannot compete against a 20-year-old.) Separate medals are also given for dancing with a teacher (pro-am), or with another amateur (am-am). In view of all this our winnings are somewhat less impressive but still respectable, given how late we started.

All of this was a great deal of clean, healthy, and expensive fun, but eventually we tired of it. Age and arthritis contributed to the aches and pains following an evening of vigorous dancing. It got to the point where we had to overcome a lot of inertia to go to a party. One evening we looked at each other and decided we didn't have to do it anymore. And so this phase ended, leaving us with several videos, pictures, the aforementioned trophies, good memories, and one couple, Louise and Jeff, who remain our good friends to this day.

Like all relationships, marriage is never static. Ours changed gradually after the two of us were left alone. We grew closer together. As we grew older we came to understand how completely we can rely on each other both physically and emotionally, and what good friends and companions we are. We are never bored with each other's company and always find something interesting to discuss, disagreeing on many subjects, but respectful of each other's opinions. All this becomes much more important and better appreciated as one gets older.

Our boys made separate lives for themselves. Mark had a very successful academic career, going straight from Princeton to MIT where he pursued studies in molecular biology. I worried that he was becoming a real workaholic, but he assured me this was a normal condition for graduate students. He shared an apartment in Boston with his friend David, a medical student at Harvard, having had his fill of dormitory life. His recreation centered around folk dancing, a hobby he had picked up in Princeton and was getting extremely proficient in. In fact, in Boston he joined the Mandala Group, an almost professional dance ensemble, and traveled with them locally as well as to Sweden and Macedonia, participating in dance workshops and giving performances. Once the group came to New York and performed at Carnegie Hall. Needless to say, we attended that performance! Mark really was a terrific dancer, and an excellent dance teacher and group leader. Every one of those dances may look the same to the uninitiated, but each one has its own choreography, and Mark remembered them all. It was through dancing that he met Christine, his future wife.

It had always been his ambition to spend some time in France, a country which had intrigued him ever since he had visited it following his high school graduation. Accordingly, during his final year at MIT he made arrangements to spend a year in France, beginning his post-doctoral assignment at a research laboratory on the outskirts of Paris.

The impending move probably accelerated Mark's wedding plans. He and Christine were married and went to France together. Their wedding took place in a Quaker meeting house. We all sat around the large room meditating, and anyone moved to do so could get up at any time and speak.

Friends and relatives spoke on a variety of subjects, giving advice and cheering the young couple on. I myself spoke to them, encouraging them to go forth and multiply, though not in those words.

Some of the remarks were very moving. The most touching words were spoken by one of Mark's friend's retarded brother, to whom Mark had been kind over the years. His speech was almost incoherent, but the word "love" was repeated over and over. Clearly he felt honored to have been invited, and the sincerity and depth of his affection was quite evident through the clumsy sentence construction. At the end of the session, Mark and Christine married each other, and of course the requisite judge was present to make things official. Finally, all those present signed a giant wedding certificate witnessing the event. Most of the dancing at the party was of the folk variety, and so expert that hotel workers and guests kept popping in just to watch it.

At Christmas in 1985, we visited Mark and Christine in Antony, a suburb of Paris, where the two had a lovely apartment. By that time, they were both somewhat disenchanted with living in France, their idealism having encountered reality. In France, an unfurnished apartment is truly unfurnished, lacking even the basic appliances: they had to buy a stove and a refrigerator. Christine could not work, French laws being very rigid about foreigners. In addition, both of them encountered the monumental French bureaucracy which is alien to Americans.

We found the French very nice, contrary to their international reputation for surliness. The day after Christmas we went to the butcher who had sold them the holiday goose. This proved to be a mom-and-pop store and Madame, delighted that I spoke French, took me aside. "*Ils sont si gentils, vos enfants!*" ("Your children are so nice!") she said. We had brought Christine a dress she had admired back in the States (the conspiracy to get it included Christine's mother) as her Christmas present, and bought Mark a suit in Antony. The tailor altering it was exceptionally nice, assuring Mark he could come at any time for further alterations. "One does not always notice problems until one has worn the suit for awhile," he said.

A year later, Mark and Christine came back and settled in Princeton where Mark continued his post-doctoral work and Christine got a job. Unfortunately, the marriage broke up after a few years. I know the trauma of the divorce affected Mark deeply for some time. Eventually, however, he got over it and got on with his life. Afterwards, he started going out with Laura. In 1995, when Mark got a job in Salt Lake City, the two moved there together.

We have visited them several times since and are very fond of Laura. Laura is an English as a Second Language teacher, working in a college in Salt Lake City, and a linguist by profession, so she and I have a lot in common. She and Mark share an interest in folk dancing, which has now spread to Balkan and Middle Eastern music. Mark plays several instruments I never even heard of before, such as the oud, the saz, and the rebab—all string instruments. Laura has a very pleasant voice and sings in a choir, as well as solo. They've become very proficient and true purists in the field, rejecting any hint of commercialism. Like many young couples, they cook together but have their specialties. Laura, for example, is familiar with Turkish dishes, having lived in Turkey for several years. They have a number of friends, but complain of the paucity of cultural activities in Salt Lake City. Luckily, they both love skiing and hiking, activities eminently suited to the beautiful mountains surrounding the city.

Mark has moderated his work habits since his days at MIT. He still works hard and fairly long hours, but the weekends are devoted to recreation and travel. Bert and I both feel that he is doing well professionally and he and Laura seem close and content with each other.

❊   ❊   ❊

Sam's first love in school was writing. As a young boy he wrote short stories and poetry. His forte was a gentle humor, mostly poking fun at himself. In one story he bemoaned his inability to keep pets successfully, one goldfish character even committing suicide by jumping out of the aquarium. His stories showed sensitivity, unusual maturity, and a considerable writing talent.

Among his high school activities was running the school literary magazine. In the summer before his senior year, he went to Cornell for a writing course. The course culminated in a writing project— Sam's topic was "the Origins of Jazz." Here he demonstrated an ability to make a difficult and rather technical subject accessible to the general reader and make it eminently interesting to boot.

But his life's passion was acting. Back in high school, when *You're a Good Man, Charlie Brown* was presented, he was Snoopy. At one point in the play, he would come down into the audience and flirt with some little girl sitting conveniently near an aisle. One little girl he selected announced she was never going to wash the hand he had gallantly kissed. In his last year he played the lead role in *The Man Who Came to Dinner*, showing clearly his potential ability for comedy and character.

He began spending his summers as an apprentice in the summer theater run by Mount Holyoke College. There he played a variety of parts and helped with all other aspects of putting on plays as well. He learned some carpentry, practical electricity, even sewing so he could fix anything that broke. "Sewing," he told me once, "is not really a skill, just a matter of courage."

At Harvard Sam majored in English literature, since there was no drama major, but he took every opportunity to pursue acting. He even directed Shakespeare's *Twelfth Night*, all in black and white, with thirties-style setting and costumes. Every year, he took part in Harvard's public speaking competition, winning first prize in his senior year. He performed in the Hasty Pudding play, another Harvard tradition.

Sometime in college, Sam abandoned his goal of becoming a writer and switched his plan to acting. Bert and I were uneasy about his choice, knowing how difficult it was to succeed in that field, particularly with no previous connections in show business. But it was his life, and we supported him both financially and emotionally in his endeavors. After college, he spent a year working and acting, and then went to NYU's Tisch School of the Arts, where he worked towards a master's degree in performing arts. For three years we went to every show the students put on, and rejoiced at Sam's progress.

After Sam graduated, he got an acting part almost immediately in a regional theater not far from our home, connected with an agent, did some commercials and another play. He was progressing slowly in the field and supporting himself by doing office work in the meantime. Sam was offered a promotion in every job, but refused them all, not wanting the responsibility and commitment which might interfere with his acting career, which came first.

In the meantime, he met Adeline, and soon the romance blossomed. They were married in 1988. Like Mark's wedding, Sam's was also unique, taking place outdoors in the hills of Connecticut. A little flower "chuppah" was erected for the purpose. Under it they were married by a Unitarian minister to the strands of classical music. The ceremony was followed by a buffet luncheon eaten *al fresco* with more classical music wafting on the air. The guests wandered around on the manicured lawns, admiring the vistas all around them, the perfect blue sky and the balmy weather. It was truly an idyllic and pastoral setting marking the start of a very successful marriage.

A year later, Sam and Adeline moved to Los Angeles, where their daughter Miranda was born in 1991. Sam continued to have some success in his profession. He had a part in the movie *Broadcast News*, and did more commercials. But he was gradually becoming disenchanted with show business, particularly, he told me, with actors' personalities. My own observations of celebrities gleaned from books, magazines and television, indicate that many are extremely self-centered, even narcissistic, and driven by a destructive, single-minded competitiveness, which makes them rather unpleasant people to associate with.

Having responsibilities as a husband and father may very well have also contributed to Sam's decision to leave the financially and emotionally unreliable show business rollercoaster. A new career necessitated further education. The family moved to Iowa City, where Sam became a part-time teacher and student at the University of Iowa, working for dual degrees in writing and communications, a common arrangement in graduate schools.

The wheel had turned for him, and he is returning to his first love: writing. He has already had some success in freelance publishing, producing feature articles based on his own life experiences or commissioned by magazines. He is currently putting the last touches on his master's thesis. Now that I am a writer as well, and Sam is a teacher, we have a lot to share. Our phone conversations have begun to revolve around correcting papers, conducting classes and getting published, in addition to Miranda, family life and dutiful inquiries about our mutual health.

Adeline did not go back to work after Miranda's birth, taking some courses instead and embarking on a career of writing children's books. She and Sam are very much hands-on parents, and Miranda has become a very sweet little girl, bright and innocent.

Miranda has had her own brush with fame and fortune. When she was four, a Hallmark Hall of Fame show—*Harvest of Fire*—was being filmed locally. Sam applied for a walk-on part in this drama about contemporary Amish people, but did not get it. According to the casting director, putting a beard on him made Sam look more like a rabbi than an Amish elder. But they were also looking for a small girl, and Miranda, dressed in a bonnet and a long dress, did look like a little Amish girl. The job was very exciting for her and she did it well. In the film she comes across as a shy and fearful child—she was really scared of the actor playing the stern, bearded elder, and would not let him pick her up. She got some money out of it (which didn't interest her), her bonnet and a doll-size effigy of herself used in a fire scene in the film. Since the Amish faith forbids creation of graven images, the doll had no facial features but was dressed in Amish clothes.

On the set, Miranda was befriended by the play's star, Patty Duke, who happens to be very fond of children. One day the star was besieged by fans from among the local extras, all asking for her autograph. She evidently felt Miranda was feeling left out, and turned around to ask her for her autograph. The budding actress complied, but since she was still only four, the quality of the document was rather uneven. Nevertheless, it was graciously accepted.

Miranda refers to it as "my movie," and is proud of it, but her parents decided not to repeat the experience by looking for further parts for her. Miranda remembers the glory, but not the stress of the job.

As I am finishing this book, Sam and Adeline had their second child. Jackson Hooper Samuels was born May 29, 1998, making him seven years younger than Miranda. When Jackson was a mere five days old, Miranda was already talking and reading to him and he was reacting to her voice, as well as the voices of his loving parents. Sam recently obtained an editorial position with the University of Iowa publications department. Thus, after some happy upheavals, he and his family can settle down to their new situation.

※　　　※　　　※

When his mother died Bert had only five years of work left. He planned to retire at the customary age of 65, but in 1984 his company downsized and offered retirement incentives aimed at employees in their fifties, but applicable to Bert as well. In the few years prior to that, much of the fun had gone out of Bert's professional life. Designing, building, and starting up new plants had been exciting and satisfying, as seeing concrete evidence of one's efforts always is. But in the 1980s few chemical plants were being built in the United States, partly due to previous over-expansion and partly because of environmental concerns. Bert had to move into metallurgy, still somewhat related to the chemical field, but towards the end of his career he was managing an artificial intelligence project. Instead of being in his glory he had to play catch-up, trying to master a new and very difficult science, not what one would wish for at the end of one's career. Thus, when this opportunity came, he took advantage of it eagerly, effectively retiring at 63—though he was paid fully until he was 65.

People who have an all-encompassing life interest are lucky. After retiring, Bert embarked on what amounted to a second career in art. He attended Parsons School of Design in New York City, and eventually received a certificate in studio art. He proved to be a talented painter, working in pastels, karandash, charcoal, oil and mixed media. He fell in love with the human figure and has concentrated on painting male and female nudes in incongruous, somewhat surrealistic situations. His paintings are very cerebral; anyone can sense it just looking at them, although one often needs a verbal explanation to understand the ideas he is expressing. Over the years he has created about 100 works, many during the earlier years of his retirement, and has had an exhibition in Soho. I don't profess to like all his work, but I like much of it and find almost all of it intellectually stimulating, a remark I could make about much of modern and contemporary art.

By the time Bert turned 70, his energy level began to flag due to the combined effects of age and several fairly serious health problems. I am just getting to that age myself and am beginning to understand the situation. We tease each other about this. Bert always reminds me that he is five and a half years older than I. "Wait until you are my age," he warns me. I kid him about his naps, which have increased to two a day, one in the morning and one in the afternoon (though not every day). The morning nap, he tells me, is not a nap at all. It is merely the continuation of the night's sleep briefly interrupted by breakfast.

Recently, Bert has become interested in collages, combining some elements from earlier work with both "found" and newly executed images, but he is working more slowly than 14 years ago.

After Bert retired I continued working, setting some alternative timelines for myself. First of all, I worried about Bert. Sometimes people have grand plans for retirement, but without the discipline provided by the workplace, they don't follow through. If this happened to Bert, I was going to retire early to provide him with companionship during the day. But it turns out he didn't need me at all! In fact, I was envious of his interest in art; I didn't have any such single driving interest in my life.

Knowing I could work as long as I wanted, I began to think of some possible retirement deadlines. What actually happened was an incredible piece of luck for me. Livingston High School had always employed at least two full-time physics teachers. All through my career these had been men with whom I had good relations but never formed a teaching partnership with. In 1988 the school hired another woman. Barbara came to us because she was excited about our program but also, specifically, because she wanted to work with me. We had met several times at various physics-related functions, and had had an opportunity to share our thoughts about teaching physics. Barbara's previous experience with teaching colleagues was similar to mine. When she came to Livingston, we became a true team, energizing each other and raising our effectiveness and our level of job satisfaction.

We were more than compatible; we had a synergistic effect on each other. Barbara is the most creative physics teacher I ever met and the most dedicated one but, in her own opinion, not overly organized. I am creative as well, though less so. My strength lies in organization, in following through, in thoroughly analyzing ideas both before and after trying them out, and in general pulling the course together for the most effective results possible. We complemented each other, making each of us an even better teacher, and our students responded to the renewed excitement they sensed in us. Computers finally became truly useful and I designed several experiments, some based on computer simulations, others on interaction between lab equipment, measurements and computer use to interpret the data.

Barbara's presence enriched my final years of work. It was a joy to work so closely together with a colleague. Even better, we came to love each other as people and became very close friends. Bert and I were guests in Barbara's home for *seders* (Passover rites and dinner), and for special meals following Yom Kippur. We also celebrated together various rites of passage in our lives.

I agonized over my retirement, anticipating I would miss the school environment unbearably. I did not feel burned-out at all. My energy was sufficient to last through the working day, and the adrenaline carried me through any errands I might have to run after school. But when I got home and relaxed, I could not do anything else. Bert and I even began to go out for dinner during the week whenever I could not face the kitchen. I stopped going to the gym during the week, although I continued walking almost every day on the oval in front of the school, and stopped playing bridge at night. There were so many interesting things to do out there and I had no energy to do them. But would I do them, or would I fall into a rut of shopping and watching TV? And if so, would our finances stand the pressure?

As I grew older, I got more and more interested in money. This is not unusual for my age cohorts in America, whose youth was indelibly marked by the Great Depression. For my own reasons, I too came to see the security in having money "in the bank." I have been brought up on the precept that one does not touch the capital. However, at least according to Bert, money becomes capital five minutes after it has hit my pocket. Mark is always telling us that though Bert and I are very generous to our kids, we live too frugally—even parsimoniously—ourselves. He is exaggerating somewhat, but the habits of financial caution and saving are too deeply ingrained in us to change so late in life.

My retired friends had reported diverse experiences. Lee was teaching part-time in local colleges as an adjunct professor and enjoyed her classes whenever her students were "halfway decent," which was not always the case. But my friend Bernice told me a year after she left, "Klara, I flunked retirement." She has adjusted since, but it took some doing. Ester had retired a long time before. She spent the whole first year traveling and when she got home, developed an anxiety-related hyperventilation problem. Busy, hard-working people often need a more structured situation to provide the transition between work and the life of leisure.

I was determined to learn from my friends' examples. In the spring preceding the event, I planned my impending retirement like a military campaign. And, like in military campaigns, I did not always succeed. Specifically, I planned to follow in Lee's footsteps, and prepared and sent out about 30 resumes to area colleges. I received some responses, but found no teaching position for the fall of 1994. Later in the winter, there were several calls inquiring about my availability, but by that time I had moved on and no longer wanted the responsibility and commitment that came with college instruction.

My retirement activities fall into three categories: volunteering, self-improvement and play. I feel that this country has been very good to me. It allowed me to heal, be productive, raise a family and in general prosper and be happy. While I worked and ran the house, I was too busy to give of my time. I have been given so much; now came the payback time. I am afraid that the above sounds rather self-righteous and self-serving in view of the modest contributions I have made in this field. I greatly admire people who perform true charity.

I do my volunteering though the National Council of Jewish Women, and all of it is based on my teaching experience. I give periodic book reviews at a housing project for senior citizens and for the NCJW itself. I've become well-known at the project and the ladies tell me they always look forward to my presentations. I love public speaking. Like teaching it gives me a pleasurable rush of excitement. One year I taught a physics course at the local community center. I think the average age of my pupils was 80. Of course, there was no homework and almost no math. It was an exercise in presenting pure concepts and relating them to everyday experiences of my class, a method which proved quite successful.

My main assignment, however, was teaching English to a house-bound Russian immigrant. I have been with Olga for close to three years, and by now we have become devoted friends. Olga was a physician in Russia, as were her husband and daughter, but both she and her husband have no hope for a license in the United States. Here, she takes care of her two granddaughters while her daughter studies for the exams required to get her medical license. By her own admission Olga is not a good student; she does not practice English enough when I am not there, and two hours a week is not enough to become fluent in a language, particularly when you are in your sixties. But I have become much more than her teacher. I am her friend, her only regular contact with an adult outside her family, and her window on America. I have taken her and her husband Lev to museums, concerts and ballets, all of which she loves. We discuss public events and life in America, and confide in each other the problems we have. I value Olga. She is the dearest woman and I admire her fortitude, her wisdom, her selflessness, and her unabashed emotionalism and romanticism. The two hours a week we spend together have become as important to me as they are to her.

An important characteristic of my retirement (and I hope of other people's) is to do what I enjoy and nothing I don't enjoy. Nowadays, I love going to school and learning new things. Without any agenda and without the need for credits and degrees, I have taken six college courses at several area colleges, doing all the reading, submitting all the required papers and taking the midterm exams, but not the finals. My choices are eclectic. So far, the courses have included French culture (in French), anthropology, music theory, the intellectual history of Europe and contemporary art. Some of them I have taken alone and some with Bert.

Going together with Bert is particularly gratifying because it gives us both a sounding board for our ideas about the course, the teacher and the other students in the class.

Most of the teachers I've encountered in these courses have been excellent, dedicated and intellectually demanding and stimulating. They share my concern about student apathy and docility. This is particularly obvious when the class consists of college-age and older adults. The older adults, who range from their twenties to late fifties—Bert and I always being the oldest—have a seriousness of purpose. They speak up in class and discuss the material during breaks. Most of the young students do not participate in class discussions or even ask questions. Is it shyness, indifference, or both? Many teachers, though not all, expend much effort to draw out their students. When the young people hear why we are there, they are amazed and unbelieving. To think one could go to school just for fun seems incomprehensible for most. Some, however, express the wish that their grandparents would do the same.

In the last course Bert and I took together at Montclair, a playful rivalry developed between us concerning the grades we were getting. This was a course on contemporary art, and it included trips to New York City museums and galleries. One day the teacher praised a gallery exhibit, extolling the artist's technique in representing glass and metal in her paintings—two very difficult materials to capture on canvas. She specifically mentioned the show catalogue, which she wanted to buy but didn't in the end because of its high price. With some free time on our hands that week, Bert and I went into the city to see a couple of exhibits.

I spoke to the receptionist at the exhibit our teacher had praised, complimenting the curators but expressing regret over the high price of the catalogue. "Only 10 postcard-size pictures for $20? Why so much?" I inquired. The clerk explained it was the high cost of color photographs, particularly when the volume is small. I told her we were visiting the exhibit at the recommendation of a university professor, and debated whether it would be appropriate for me to purchase the catalogue as a gift for her. The clerk, appreciating my quandary, gave me the catalog for free, and of course I passed it on to our teacher. On the very next paper, I got an "A+" and Bert only an "A," whereupon he accused me of currying favor with the teacher and getting an unfairly high grade as the result. It didn't even help that he got a "B+" on the midterm, and I only a "B."

Our assignments in this course involved looking at, describing in detail, and commenting on various pieces of art. Never before have I spent a half hour looking at a single piece of art. This, together with good class preparation, made me see the pieces quite differently. The course dealt only with 20th-Century art, but it gave me the tools and understanding to view any kind of art with more acuity and pleasure. At the last session, while handing in our last assignments, we handed our teacher a note suggesting we get together during the summer for lunch and gallery-hopping, and she handed us a note with the same suggestion, so the course may lead to a new, interesting friendship.

I also attend several series of lectures every year, designed for senior citizens and offered by area colleges and organizations as well as two or three Elder Hostels, all located on the eastern seaboard. Sometimes Bert joins me on these jaunts, other times I go with friends. Elder Hostel is a marvelous invention for the retired if they are eager to learn, as many are, judging from the huge success of the program. A week on location and a chance to get out of the rut, make new friends interested in the same things as I am, is a true boon. It is also gratifying to be exposed to professors who blossom in the atmosphere of love of learning. The locations are often beautiful, accommodations and food adequate if not better, and the prices fair. Encompassing a tremendous variety of topics and activities, for me these sessions are intellectual conversations during which I often learns as much from the other hostelers as from the instructors. One of my favorite Elder Hostel venues is in Hamilton, New York. The programs are run by Le Moyne University and are uniformly excellent, owing to the wonderful professors and local organizers.

All recent research indicates that learning, using one's brain, and concentrating help the elderly to stay mentally alert, but I feel there is even more value in it. Learning new things and diversification of activities stretches the psychological sense of time. There are two ways in which we sense the flow of time: while it is passing and in retrospect. The saying "time flies when you're having fun," is such a truism; it needs no discussion. But time viewed in retrospect is something else again.

We all know that the time of our youth seems to have passed slowly, whereas the middle years have rushed by. There seems to be some biological reason for this but, I am sure, there is also a psychological component. When we were young we learned something new every day, making every day memorable, while in our middle years our lives became routine and repetitious—albeit productive and pleasurable—the days indistinguishable from each other and thus lumped together in memory. Now that I am retired, my activities are varied and I am constantly learning new things, time is stretching again. When I review all I've done, it seems impossible I crammed it all into just four years.

Somewhere between education and play lie my two French-speaking groups, which meet several times a month and include French lessons, lectures, reading a book together, and generally a *causerie* (chat), all conducted in French. I have made several new friends through these gatherings and have improved my ability to speak French, which had been atrophying from disuse.

Play consists of travel, museums, subscriptions to theater, opera, ballet and classical music concerts. Sometimes I go with Bert, sometimes with old school friends, and sometimes with both. It also includes going out to eat, reunions with old friends, visiting the children, and bridge. When I retired, one of my goals was to improve my game and play it more seriously.

When you have lived and worked in one area for a long time, you meet people you know or with whom you have connections wherever you go. My partner in the bridge class was Joanna. I had taught both her children and sat next to her at a concert series in New York. In addition, we both come from Poland. We recognized each other and decided to become permanent partners. We still are, playing twice a week on the average with never an argument or a raised voice. In duplicate bridge, which had caused many a fight and even divorce, this is quite an achievement. In our case we both feel it is only a game, though we always try our best. Our knowledge of Polish is an asset when we want to comment on other players.

The saddest part of getting older is the passing, first of the previous generation, and then of one's own. When parents, aunts and uncles die, we become the heads of the family. We can no longer look to them for support, but are now the sources of support for the next generation. When my father died, I felt truly adult for the first time. But the passing of siblings and friends is a chilly reminder of our own mortality. It is a loss of those parts of our lives that only they had shared. I miss my sister-in-law Roz terribly; she had been like a sister to me. Whenever something exciting happened, or some trouble broke, I would pick up the phone and talk it over with her.

The death of each loved and valued relative or friend diminishes me a little and isolates me from the world. This is an inevitable price of getting older, and the only antidote is to plunge into interesting activities and get involved with new friends while maintaining and cherishing old relationships. I am resolved to attend every wedding, bar or bat mitzvah and even funeral that involves a reunion with friends and relatives.

Yes, the last four years have been busy, productive and fun. I try to arrange my days to allow some rest in between the various obligations and also to hold the number of activities to no more than three per day. It does not always work. Sometimes conflicts oblige me to make a difficult choice between two fun activities, and some days are busier than others. A day with no scheduled activities is like a mini-vacation. Of course, as the years go by, my energy flags more and more, but I started from such a high, intense level, that, at 70, I probably still do more than an average 60-year-old. Bert, who is older and reminds me of it often, has less energy and does less than I, but because of his strong commitment to art, is more focused in his activities.

But the most permanent trace, for me personally, of these recent times has been this memoir. In the next, and last, chapter I will describe the events leading up to the writing of it.

CHAPTER 18

RETURNING
TO POLAND: 1996

I have always enjoyed traveling, and it was in the 1980s that we started the practice of traveling abroad or to the distant reaches of the North American continent every summer. We went to California, the Canadian Rockies, England, Alaska, France (several times), Switzerland, Scandinavia, Spain, Portugal and Italy. But during that time, few tourists went to Eastern Europe. Bert had been to East Berlin on business for his company, and came back to report a dismal, gray and depressing place where it was almost impossible to do business. His company was thinking of selling some technology to the East Germans, but the negotiations fell through.

From time to time, someone who had heard my story would ask if I had any desire to re-visit Poland. I always answered with an emphatic "No!" Indeed, having distanced myself from the tragic past by marrying an American, and by moving away from New York City (a kind of center of refugees from Europe), I was content with my middle-class, family- and work-centered life and reluctant to expose myself to anything that brought the horror back. Having lived through it, I felt that I had earned the right not to have to read books about the Holocaust, or to see films about it. In short, I felt entitled not to have to relive the past. All my friends agreed with this decision.

I did make exceptions. Young people needed to hear about the Holocaust. As time went on, not even their parents were well-informed, not having lived through the war years as adults. In the early 1970s, Livingston High School ran a two-day program called the "Teach In," during which students and teachers gave lessons on a variety of subjects they were experts in. I was approached by David Kramer, one of my Physics students who was interested in the war years, and together we prepared a three-hour presentation in which he talked about the historical background of Hitler's rise to power and I related my personal experiences during the war and answered questions from the audience. Our presentation was wildly popular. We taught in a double classroom to more than capacity crowds. We had to repeat our presentation the next day.

In later years I made several videotapes for Livingston High School relating my personal experiences during the war, and authorized their use by history teachers during the study of the Holocaust. I also spoke several times at our temple, particularly during services commemorating *Kristallnacht* (November 9, 1938 – the Night of Broken Glass).

But still I was reluctant to talk about it. Several years ago I was asked to address a temple Sunday School class. The original time was changed, and I guess I did not properly note it on my calendar. I then proceeded to simply forget this appointment and not show up. The teacher did not contact me, but eventually I realized what had happened and sent her an abject apology. I do not believe, however, that this was an accident. As a rule, I really am a very organized and conscientious person. In my 26 years of teaching I was never late for class. I retired with over 250 unused sick days. At roughly 12 days per year, that must be a record! Why then this sudden attack of forgetfulness? I believe that I accepted this appearance reluctantly, and my subconscious helped me conveniently to forget it. For a while after this occurrence I refused such appearances, but about three or four years ago my attitude began to change.

Several factors contributed to my decision to work through the past. Age, and hopefully some wisdom coming with it, was one. Impending, then actual, retirement reduced some stresses in my daily life. Finally, there was my trip to eastern Europe in 1993. The year before, a group of women teachers from Livingston High School made a trip to Greece during the spring recess. They came back so enthused that they planned to travel abroad in 1993, going to Hungary, Austria and the Czech Republic. I joined the group and spent 10 wonderful days in Budapest, Vienna and Prague.

These countries had not suffered the same ravages of war as Poland did, so we did not see the kind of physical devastation wrought on Poland, other than the result of 50 years of communism in Budapest and Prague. But we did see the consequences of Hitler's deliberate destruction of the Jewish communities. Most of the temples had become museums, and there was little evidence of ongoing Jewish life. All of us were horrified and saddened by what we were seeing, and I received strong support from my friends who understood what kind of memories these sights were bringing back to me. It was a wonderful group with which I could begin to face my past.

This was the first time I had a yearning to go back to Poland. But at the time, I was trying to set the date for my retirement, and was approaching this milestone with great trepidation. On the one hand I continued to love teaching and feared the excess free time upon retirement; on the other hand, I was experiencing a shortage of energy for all the things I wanted to do. Oh, there was enough adrenaline to carry me through the workday without any noticeable loss of energy level, but when I got home, at about 4 p.m., I was drained and could do nothing else. So, it was time to go. I retired at the end of the 1993-94 school year.

The next year was devoted to organizing retirement, which proved as busy (but in a more relaxed way) as work ever was. Toward the end of 1995, I was ready to face Poland, a thought which had been simmering slowly on the back burner for a long time. Bert was not enthusiastic until we read a trip proposal from the Elder Hostel. Here was a chance to stay in only two cities (Krakow and Warsaw) without the turmoil of daily travel, and the sightseeing was to be combined with lectures given by reputable academics on topics explaining Polish history, economy, politics, religion and arts and sciences. So, we decided to go.

In the meantime, a couple of things happened which focused me even more closely on the war years. In late 1995 and early 1996 I gave two lectures at different temples, one on the life in the ghetto, the other focusing on life in the concentration camp.

Steven Spielberg devoted his profits from the film *Schindler's List* to creating video records of Holocaust survivors, and placing them in the archives of five institutions: the Holocaust Museums in Washington D.C., California, New York City, Yad Va Shem, and at Yale University. I was approached about such an interview and gave my consent.

The interview took place in May 1996, just a month prior to our going to Poland. There was a pre-interview with my interviewer, Barbara Johnson. A few days later, the interview proper took me through my childhood, the war years, the adaptation period after the war and a brief summation of my adult life. The tapes are about two and a half hours long. The taping took place in my living room. After taking me through my childhood, the interviewer let me loose to tell the story of my war years. This section took about an hour and a half, which is not long enough to do justice to the topic. All the main facts are there, and a number of anecdotes. Since I always speak extemporaneously, it is more or less random which particular stories get into a given presentation. When I speak as a witness to the Holocaust I feel it important not to use notes in order to maintain for myself and give the listeners a sense of freshness and spontaneity. Incidentally, when my copy of the tapes came in late August, I experienced another period of denial. I could not bring myself to view them for about two months.

Every time I do an appearance, I prepare for it by mentally going over about what I want to say. I am a pretty good public speaker, but I don't speak about my experiences often. So every time I speak, I have to dredge the memories up and, in a sense, relive them while I decide what is appropriate for a given audience. I have addressed teenagers as young as 11 or 12, and groups of senior citizens. I have to decide how much background information the group will need and how many graphic details are appropriate. I have addressed mostly Jewish groups, but during our trip to Poland, I addressed a mostly non-Jewish group, many members of Polish origin. Thus, some tact also comes into play.

❆   ❆   ❆

For weeks before the trip I felt both anticipation and nervousness. How would I feel stepping on the soil which would bring back so many painful memories, but also so many happy ones from my childhood? When we finally got to Kennedy Airport, we met some of the members of our group, and my heart dropped. None of them were Jewish. I had expected a heavy Jewish participation and had counted on emotional support from the group. Would I get it now?

We flew to Warsaw and transferred to a smaller plane to Krakow. At JFK Airport, we had met some of the hostelers; others were already in Krakow. In Warsaw we had a layover, and we tried to utilize it to obtain some Polish zloty as Polish money is not available in the US. This was our first encounter with the usual Eastern-European frustrations: traveler's checks are accepted only in banks, where the procedure takes about two hours because of long lines and the absence of process streamlining.

In Krakow, tired although the trip was uneventful, we were met by a bus and our guide, Dr. Ferenc Szucs, a professor of geochemistry at Slippery Rock University. Ferenc was Hungarian and very experienced in east European travel, but he spoke no Polish, and often called on me for help in communicating with the locals.

After a 15-minute trip through a rather dreary urban landscape, we arrived at the Hotel Visla, our home for the next two weeks. In reality Visla was a sport facility with gyms, soccer and basketball fields, incorporating a hostel in one part of a building. The rooms were a decent size, but primitive to say the least. There was a little armoire for hanging clothes, but no dressers or shelves of any kind. Fortunately there were three beds. We kept open suitcases on the third bed and lived out of them for the next two weeks. Lighting was, needless to say, inadequate. There was a small table in the room which had to serve as a repository for all the odds and ends. The bathroom was a disaster. We knew in advance that Polish water would be undrinkable for us, so the first task was to get some bottled water.

Dinner that night gave us a sign of things to come. We ate in a nearby building at large tables, always waited on by the same two people. The food was monotonous but very tasty – almost always breaded and fried pork, frequently for both lunch and dinner, as well as the ubiquitous mashed potatoes, always accompanied by the same kind of bread. We were served one kind of drink per meal. If there was water, there would be no tea or coffee. At breakfast there was always coffee, but no tea or orange juice. We had brought with us packets of decaf and managed to get some hot water from the waiters who tried to be accommodating, but were clearly overworked.

One of the two servers, a woman, confided in me. She lived with a married daughter and grandchildren, was supposed to be retired, but her pension had not kept pace with inflation so now she had to work to supplement it. Even so she could not afford even the smallest apartment of her own. Pensioners in Poland seem to be worse off than almost anyone else.

When we retired for the night, a new discomfort materialized. In the back of the hotel there was a gas station without access to the street – an inconceivable situation in the U.S., but a common enough occurrence in Poland, where tiny enterprises spring up in all available places. At night this gas station was closed and guarded by dogs. A nearby swimming pool, part of our sport complex, was guarded by dogs as well. So at irregular intervals, but all through the night, something would set off one of the dogs, causing other dogs to respond until the area was filled with a cacophony of barking, starting and stopping and starting again. Sometimes it was impossible to fall asleep no matter how tired you were.

All of us told Ferenc that we would be willing to pay a little more for better accommodations and Elder Hostel took this suggestion to heart. Our hotel was located in a suburb, a 10-minute walk to the tram and about a 20-minute tram ride from the center of town. The trams run in the center of the streets, with the automobiles on the outside next to the sidewalk. Every time a tram stops, all traffic comes to a halt to allows passengers to cross to and from the sidewalk. It must be most frustrating for the drivers, but the trams are numerous, run on time, and many routes are available. Anyway, once you are in the center of town, Krakow is quite walkable.

Across the street was a large university campus with some lab and class buildings, but mostly dorms. Apparently there is no room for them in the center of town, where the Jagiellon University is located. One dorm was 16 stories high and had no elevator. There was also a fairly well-equipped supermarket, and a little restaurant serving hamburgers and hot dogs and charging 10 groszy extra (about 2 cents) for ketchup and mustard. Even in the summer, the place was full of young people, dressed in T-shirts and jeans, and indistinguishable from American college kids.

Creature comforts are, clearly, not easy to come by in Poland. But with initiative, ingenuity and flexibility, one can manage. After their 45 years of communism, the Poles are used to the hardships, shortages and lack of living space. For example, our Krakow guide, a literature teacher named Marta Olbert, lived in a two-room apartment with her mother and her grown son; this was all she could afford. At any rate, everyone looked well-fed and reasonably dressed, although we saw very little elegance.

Krakow is a charming city with a population of about 300,000. It was Poland's capital from the 11th to early 17th Century. The city was never bombed nor fought over in recent history, and since earlier wars were not nearly as hard on the land, Krakow is totally intact. Our first week in Krakow was devoted to sightseeing and lectures. I must say that every professor, regardless of his topic, always mentioned the Holocaust in his or her lecture. They voiced regrets over the Jewish tragedy, but in a mechanical and perfunctory manner, much in the way we murmur condolences over the death of someone we did not know to a bereaved person whom we barely know. For the most part, they were all young people. They expressed a sincere regret, a nostalgia for something they had never experienced, namely the richness that Jews had brought to Polish culture. They mentioned contributions made by Jews to Polish literature, art, commerce and manufacturing. There is a movement among young Polish intellectuals to revive Jewish culture, language and music, but it seems to me so sterile without the Jewish people themselves to flesh it out.

We visited a newly constructed building called the Center for Jewish Culture. This modern building was built with Jewish-American money in 1990 on the site of a prayer house. It houses a Judaica collection, a small concert hall and a tiny museum, showing, at the time, an exhibit by a Jewish Dutch painter, depicting scenes from the Holocaust in a somewhat abstract fashion. Our group heard a concert there performed by Polish musicians for a young, Polish audience. Again, it is not possible to recapture the spirit of Jewishness without any Jews.

We were in Poland during the 50th anniversary of the Kielce pogrom. The president of Poland, Alexsander Kwasniewski, was the first Polish official who apologized for the incident and publicly commemorated it in Kielce where it had occurred, forcing the reluctant residents to participate in this ceremony. Kwasniewski is a former Communist, but this does not mean much in Poland. Under communism, you had to belong to the party in order to get ahead. Thus his membership marks him as an opportunist rather than an ideologue. In fact he is viewed in Poland as a technocrat: young, modern and well-educated. His wife is pretty, has a good figure, dresses well and is a lawyer in her own right. Poles compare her to Hillary Clinton.

On our third day in Krakow, the five Jews in our group, along with a Texas minister and his wife, went to the service in the only functioning synagogue in Krakow, the Remuh Synagogue. It is an old Orthodox synagogue, somewhat dilapidated and quite small. The congregation numbers 150, practically the city's entire Jewish population, but only a few were at the service. The youngest member was about 50. I spoke with her at length. A rather unattractive-looking, heavy and sickly woman, she was single, and although she was born after the war, her mother had been a survivor of several area concentration camps, so she is steeped in camp lore. All the other members are camp survivors.

One of them, when I told him I had been in Bergen-Belsen, said to me, "Ah, you lived in a hotel!" By that he meant that Bergen-Belsen had no gas chambers. I asked them why they had not left Poland. Their answers indicated they had been so beaten down by the Holocaust that they lacked energy and courage to start somewhere else again. They had taken the path of least resistance right after the war. Later it was too difficult to leave Poland. By now, of course, they were all old, sick and retired. They all had pensions and supplemented their income with handouts from tourists.

The service itself was conducted entirely in Hebrew. We, the women, sat behind a curtain and saw none of it. The local women chatted through it all, as women often do when they are banned from participation in the services. After the service, we walked in the Renaissance-era cemetery behind the temple. Some of the gravestones had been secretly buried during the Holocaust and then restored to their old places. The grave of the most famous inhabitant, the great Talmudic scholar Rabbi Moses Isserles, was supposed to have great powers. For centuries people made pilgrimages to visit it. Even the Germans were too superstitious to tamper with it.

But they did break up many gravestones. After the war, the synagogue collected the fragments and built a wall out of them. You can read snatches of the blessings and names – a hodge-podge symbolizing the chaos and destruction of Jewish life in Poland.

The current Krakow Jews do not necessarily live in the area. Kazimierz (so named after Casimir the Great), was originally a separate town, where the king settled the Jews he brought to Krakow. Eventually, as Krakow grew, it engulfed Kazimierz, after which it simply became the Jewish district in Krakow, where Jews lived by preference to be near their own temples, shops and neighbors.

The current Jews of Krakow are free to live where they want, and do so. They tell me they experience little anti-Semitism, but do not fraternize much with the Polish population. Talking to them and attending the service, I felt a great sadness. This tiny remnant, slowly fading away, not persecuted, but isolated, is all that remains of what was once a vital, bustling people. In 20 years there will be no rabbi to conduct a service here, and no one to attend it. No doubt the synagogue will become a museum. I felt a poignancy talking to these survivors. I can't even imagine how sad it must be to live among this small group, with never a bris, a bar mitzvah or a wedding, never the sound of children's voices around you – an eternal punishment for being a Jew.

In all of Poland I never saw a bagel. The bagel, which was invented there, has successfully invaded North America, but never gained even a foothold among the Poles. The same is true of Yiddish words, such as "schlep," "maven" or "nudnik." American English is open to Jewish influences, but Polish is not. All of this confirms the separation between the two peoples, now and before the war. I never had a non-Jewish Polish friend, and neither did my mother. My father had contact with some Poles through his work, but never carried it into his social life. Jews who made it in the Polish world had to do it by total assimilation. Isaac Bashevis Singer was not read by Poles, and neither was Sholom Aleichem.

We returned to Kazimierz with our group and viewed the other three or four synagogues still standing, among them the Old Synagogue, dating to the 15th Century and now housing a Judaic religious museum, but also containing exhibits of the recent history and culture of Jews in Krakow. Except for our group, it was empty. Kazimierz itself is old and shabby; it does not appear that prosperous people had inhabited it even before the war. Aside from the synagogues, it boasts two Jewish restaurants, in one of which our group had lunch. The owners were not Jewish, and neither was the help, but the food was vaguely in the Jewish style. Anyway, there was no pork.

We were entertained by two young men who claimed to be Jewish. Possibly they were. In any case they had a vast repertory of authentic Jewish songs from Poland, including such standards as "Rozhynkes mit Mandlen" and the "Shtelele Belz," as well as of Hebrew songs and such American oldies as "Bei Mir Bistu Shein." All very moving and nostalgic in a pleasant way.

The Germans considered Kazimierz much too grand for the Jews living there, and created the Jewish ghetto further out of town in a much poorer, Polish neighborhood. Today it looks like a partially inhabited slum. In the center of the area there is a drugstore, a shrine to the Polish owner who, for a while, was allowed to keep it open and helped the Jews as much as he could. Eventually, he was denounced and executed. It is here that Spielberg filmed *Schindler's List*. The location is being maintained for tourist viewing, but the main building, the factory, was closed. Nearby, there is a monument to Krakow Jews; it is positioned very discreetly and can only be reached by foot. Most of our group opted not to see it.

I asked the Jewish woman at the synagogue about the Jews who had lived during the war with false papers, pretending to be Poles. I myself know of several such Jews who never came out of the closet. They choose to continue living as Poles. She said that there were a number of them in Krakow. Most are known to the Jewish population, but there is no contact.

She told me one specific story which I found very touching. A Jewish boy was taken in by a Polish woman who brought him up as her own son. In time he became a Catholic priest. When the woman was dying, her action weighed heavy on her soul, so on her deathbed she told him he was a Jew. He took it well and did not reproach her, nor did it shake his faith. He only expressed regret at not knowing it before. "It would not have made me live as a Jew," he said, "but I would have been more sympathetic and understanding towards them."

Members of our group soon found out about my origin and Holocaust history, and they inundated me with questions. Finally, Ferenc and I decided it would make more sense for me to address the whole group together. I did that on the way to the beautiful mountain skiing resort of Zakopane. I spoke for about an hour and a half relating my story, and answered questions. Many of my fellow travelers later approached me privately to express their gratitude. They felt that hearing an authentic war experience enhanced their understanding of, and empathy for, all the suffering and horror that occurred. A personal story always means more than any number of statistics.

Towards the end of our stay in Krakow we made a trip to Auschwitz. I had been dreading it from the beginning. For me, the whole time in Krakow had a schizophrenic element. I was going back and forth between the normal activities of a tourist and the recollections of the long, nightmarish horror in my life. One day I visited a medieval tourist attraction and the next a ghetto where tens of thousands of my people had suffered and which brought back my own memories of like experiences. In fact, the

Auschwitz excursion was followed, incongruously, back in our hotel by a lecture on the current state of Catholicism in Poland.

From the beginning of our trip, Auschwitz loomed as the most wrenching experience of all. Bert told me afterwards he too had been dreading it both on his own account and on mine. While on the bus, I wanted the trip to go on forever, while at the same time I wanted to get there immediately and the whole day to be over. My companions told me later I was a different person that day. The bubbly, smiling woman had been replaced by a taciturn, sad person. I have no pictures from Auschwitz; in Auschwitz, I was not a tourist.

We arrived and saw the railroad siding, silent and abandoned now, with the tracks disappearing into the distance. But I needed only to close my eyes and see the scene as if it were happening right then and there. The train arriving, jammed with exhausted, hungry and thirsty people, each one with terror in his heart. The sudden glaring light after traveling in darkness – the loud, strident voices yelling "Raus!" and "Mach schnell!" accompanied by the barking of police dogs, all done to increase terror and confusion and to extract immediate compliance with the orders, just like my own arrival at Bergen-Belsen. But here this was followed by a selection, a splitting of families, and immediate death for most of the arrivals. For Auschwitz was really two camps: a concentration camp like others in Poland and Germany, and a death factory reserved solely for Poland.

We passed through the now infamous gate with its cruelly misleading "Arbeit Macht Frei" ("work will set you free") motto above, and saw the camp proper. Built originally as military barracks and later enlarged by the Germans, it is the starkest and dreariest place imaginable. About 30 two-story buildings are arranged in three rows, colorless and featureless. There is not a tree, a flower or a blade of grass anywhere to be found. The first thing that struck me is how small it all seemed. Auschwitz housed, if one may call it that, between 15 and 20 thousand people at any time, which meant upward of 600 people per building, and 30-40 people per room. As in Bergen-Belsen, the crowding was incredible – triple-level bunks with narrow spaces in between, and often two people per bed. The sanitary facilities had been designed for hundreds of soldiers, and were primitive at best. They proved to be totally inadequate for the masses forced to use them. Twenty thousand people is the size of a small town. Imagine all those people jammed into a space that could be traversed on foot in less than five minutes.

Today Auschwitz is a museum. Some rooms are maintained as they looked when the camp was in use, showing how the prisoners lived. Some walls show an endless line of photographs of men, all clad in the striped concentration camp garb, with shaved heads, gaunt faces and tortured eyes. Apparently in the beginning, when the camp housed only Poles, the Germans photographed each inmate, but they were soon overwhelmed by the sheer number of the arrivals and the swift turnover (the average life of an inmate was measured in months rather than years) and the practice was discontinued.

Other rooms hold collections of artifacts confiscated from the arrivals who went directly from the train to the gas chambers. One exhibit contains a pile of rusting eyeglasses – twisted, lenses broken, all twined into a giant horrible abstract sculpture – a symbol of what happened to their owners. Another exhibit had a mound of hair. I was surprised to see that all the hair was white. It seems that cut hair continues to age and gray, a bit of information I had not known before. Gruesome articles such as mattresses made of human hair were also on exhibit.

I think the most wrenching exhibit for me was the luggage. Piles and piles of battered suitcases, each one with the name of its owner written across it in big letters – hope springs eternal. And right in front, a brown valise with the name **KLARA** painted in bold, big letters across it. My heart felt squeezed by a powerful hand – my poor namesake – and then: "There but for the grace of God ..." Bert felt the same thing at the sight of this suitcase; he took me in his arms and hugged me.

We inspected several buildings, including the torture cells in the cellar, where once a Polish priest volunteered to die by starvation in place of another man. The Germans were so amazed that they permitted the substitution. Father Kolbe died after great suffering while the man he saved survived the war. On the day of our visit, the Poles were commemorating his death and that of others at the Execution Wall, where prisoners were shot. Flower wreaths had been laid at the wall by returning former inmates. It should be noted that the camp housed many more Poles than Jews during the war, and Poles also consider it a place of national tragedy and horror. In fact they tend to stress that and downplay the Jewish part of the tragedy.

The last place we visited were the gas chambers and the crematorium. These are located outside the main barbed-wire fence, and are rather inconspicuous in appearance. The gas chamber, preceded by the undressing room, was an ordinary-looking, empty area with several square metal columns spaced around the room. Each column had several openings cut into it. On the ceiling there were some shower heads, never connected to any water pipes. After several hundred naked people were jammed into the room, Zyklon B pellets (a hydrogen cyanide compound) were dropped down the hollow columns. Body heat sublimed the pellets and the toxic gases killed the victims in about 10 minutes.

The crematorium next door contained two ovens (the third had been destroyed), looking like ordinary bread ovens in a peasant hut, each capable of receiving two or three bodies. Somehow I was expecting these to be diabolical-looking devices, but this was all so low-tech, so ordinary looking despite the unspeakable evil that went on within these walls. Evil can look so commonplace. A second, much larger gas chamber and crematorium built nearby was destroyed by the Germans before the Soviets entered the area.

From Auschwitz we drove about two miles to Birkenau (also known as Auschwitz II), a much larger and even more inhuman place, housing up to 100,000 inmates, both men and women, and many more Jews than the original Auschwitz. Birkenau was built during the war directly on marshy ground without any foundations. Some barracks were made of brick, but most were wooden. In most of them, there were not even bunks with straw mattresses, but 6'x6' shelves, one above the other, each inhabited by 8-10 human skeletons, crawling into their meager nooks among the sea of humanity. This space was shared with a teeming rat population. There was no heat, indoor plumbing or running water. The four crematoria and two gas chambers built behind the camp were destroyed towards the end of the war.

While our Krakow guide, Marta, was preparing us for Auschwitz, she stressed the secrecy surrounding the death factories in both camps during the Holocaust. Each group visiting Auschwitz is accompanied by an official guide, trained by the museum. While the statistics quoted are undoubtedly accurate, the spin is much less so. Our guide maintained only the German guards directly involved in the mass killings knew about them. They were instructed to speak of it to no one, not even to their families nor their colleagues stationed in the camp proper. Thus the culpability was reduced to a handful of people, and, of course, even they were following orders.

This is an interesting psychological trick. When you downgrade the criminality, you also downgrade the crime. At least this is how it seemed to me, and it made me very angry that countless visitors to Auschwitz get an account trivializing the tragedy by misrepresenting the situation. I was resolved that at least our group would hear a more unvarnished truth.

On our way back from Auschwitz, Ferenc rather tactlessly suggested that I address the group again, but I felt incapable of marshaling my thoughts and, truth be told, I felt totally alienated from them on that day. They were able to shake the horror off in a few minutes and go on to more pleasant topic, whereas it continued to weigh down my spirit for a long time.

But, a few days later, when we left Krakow, I again spoke to the group. They wanted to hear about how I adjusted to normality after the war, and I spoke about that, but mainly I wanted to speak about the implications of what we had seen. This was not an easy task. I was confronting a group of Americans, many of them of Polish descent who were joyfully finding their roots in Poland. Yet I felt I had to speak about the anti-Semitism pervading Poland and contributing to the ease with which the Germans destroyed the Jews. Only in Poland, not even in Germany proper, did the Germans feel free to build death factories, and the knowledge of what was happening to the Jews was very hard to overlook by both Poles and Germans. At Birkenau, the guards and their families lived within sight of the camp and the crematoria. Didn't they ever wonder where the smell of burning flesh, which spread over miles, was coming from? The smell was what first alerted the Polish peasants living near Treblinka to the camp's activities. Railroads pass through towns and villages. Didn't the inhabitants hear the cries of the tortured victims coming out of the sealed cars? Didn't they notice the full trains always going in one direction, and always coming back empty?

I said to the group, "People ask me, 'what could the local population do?'" It was dangerous to help Jews in any way. There is no easy answer to that. But in Denmark, on the day the Jews had to start wearing identifying armbands, the king and the majority of the non-Jewish population wore them as well. When news got out about the impending round-up of Jews, the whole Jewish population disappeared overnight. They were hidden away by their neighbors. Later, at great personal peril, Danish fishermen smuggled over half of the Danish Jews (admittedly a small population) to neutral Sweden. As for the rest of Europe, I said, it mostly stood by passively.

The Germans were quite frank about their hatred of Jews and their general plans for them. After all, Hitler stated his plans in *Mein Kampf*. They were, however, secretive in their implementation of these plans in order to prevent unrest and rebellion by desperate people with nothing to lose. With full knowledge of its fate, the Warsaw Ghetto might have risen against the Germans much earlier and more effectively. Towards the end of the war, individual Germans as well as the German government, seeing their impending defeat, became concerned about the punishment for their atrocities and attempted to cover their tracks. Some people were glad to be deceived. Some still are when they maintain, in the face of massive evidence to the contrary, that the Holocaust never took place.

I recently read an article in the *New York Times Magazine* about Daniel Goldhagen, whose Harvard doctoral thesis, expanded into a 700-page book called *Hitler's Willing Executioners*, created a furor in Germany. The article motivated me to read the book. It is Goldhagen's thesis that the deeply anti-Semitic German population participated willingly, eagerly and in great numbers in the anti-Jewish atrocities. Whatever one thinks of his research and conclusions, he is right in presenting the Holocaust as a moral as well as historical issue. My own experiences, together with common sense, indicate that most Germans *knew* about the ongoing genocide of the Jews, and that many who actively participated in it—enthusiastically or otherwise—attempted to hide their culpability after the war. The Holocaust was a historical event, but we all know that history can be rewritten.

On the last day in Krakow, our Warsaw guide joined us and we said goodbye to Marta, who gave me a picture book titled *The Warsaw Ghetto* – a gruesome pictorial account of that terrible time. She knew that I was speaking publicly about my experiences, and thought the book would get more exposure in my hands. I had learned a great deal from her about the difficult life in Poland, but she and all our lecturers stressed that they were hopeful for the future because of the great enthusiasm of Poles for private enterprise and because, unlike the other Eastern European countries, Poland started its first capitalist years with an emphasis on austerity and capital-building, rather than on instant consumer gratification.

Years ago, we made a trip to Jamaica and noticed that the local population, while needing and exploiting tourism, resented the wealth and comfortable life style of their visitors. Not so in Poland, where people understood the great economic damage done to the country by 45 years of foreign, communist rule, and seemed to understand that it would take time to pull themselves up to Western standard of living. Tourists are welcomed. Local people with whom I talked, such as the beautician who set my hair for about $4, store owners and waiters in our hotel, all questioned me eagerly about how their counterparts fared in the United States. Since we were staying practically on a college campus, I also got to talk to a number of students about their future expectations. It seems to be a wide-open society: people with energy, courage and ideas are doing quite well financially. Plodders are left far behind – wages are low and pensions even lower. It is a very exciting time for some, particularly those with a good, modern education. Of course, those who are not making it resent the successful ones and are apt to talk about "the good old times."

On the way to Warsaw we stopped in Czestochowa, famous for the Black Madonna icon. This picture was supposedly painted by Luke the Evangelist and made its way to Constantinople, then to Russia and, finally, to Poland in 1384. In the 15th Century it was vandalized and slashed by robbers and repainted by Krakow restorers. During the 17th Century, when Poland was invaded by Swedes, the sanctuary of Jasna Gora (Fair Mountain) containing the icon was the only place in Poland still holding out against the Swedes. A battle took place here, during which Polish defenders defeated a much larger Swedish army. The battle was the turning point of the war, and the victory was declared to be a miracle attributable to the Mother of God as represented by the Black Madonna.

This made the painting even more famous than before. Today pilgrims and visitors flock to it by the millions; it is the most sacred object in Poland. The painting is in a large church on top of the hill, and all along you can see pilgrims mounting the hill on their knees. I found it both impressive and very moving. I can see how, to the Poles, it is a symbol of their suffering, of their indomitable survival and of their country in general.

Our guide here was an English-speaking priest who had lived for eight years in New Jersey. Fat and merry, a Friar Tuck type, he told jokes and related easily to our group. He was not too happy when I asked him whether the painting had been carbon dated, and reluctantly admitted that scientists dated the wood to around the 9th Century. He showed us a variety of richly embroidered vestments donated by Polish women and an enormous wall filled with crutches testifying to the many miracles performed by the Madonna. Personally, I cannot believe in miracles, though I do believe in the power of mind over matter. Paralysis sometimes is not of physical, but emotional origin. Such cases can be cured or helped by faith.

The road to Warsaw traveled mostly through fields, rich with the promise of the summer harvest. The land seemed fertile and carefully cultivated, and one could easily see the total flatness which had contributed to Poland's woes. Dotted with small villages, or isolated farms with small stone houses, it is still primarily a rural country, and we passed no other large city on our way to Warsaw, where, early in the evening, we arrived at the Warszawa Hotel. It was an old hotel, but was in a superb location and equipped with a lobby, two elevators, adequate rooms and bathrooms, a beautiful dining room, where at night the orchestra played mostly pre-war dancing music, and even a little store (although it was usually closed).

After dinner we went for a walk on Marszalkowska Street, one of the main thoroughfares in central Warsaw, and right on our corner was a McDonald's (one of three in the city). From the outside it had the fanciest modernistic design I ever saw, but inside the familiar menu – a touch of home. It is a popular meeting place for young people, and was quite full that evening. Whereas normally fast food emporia are anathema to American tourists abroad, it is different in former Communist countries, where they represent modernity and the West to the local population. Stores were full of merchandise, with interesting window displays, and prices seemed reasonable to us, when translated into dollars.

The next day we took the usual city tour, stopping at churches, palaces and war memorials. Naturally everyone was asking me if anything looked familiar, and some things did. But really I had very mixed feelings about this city of my birth.

During World War II, Warsaw went through three convulsions. The first, right at the beginning in September 1939, was the German aerial and cannon bombardment during the siege. That destroyed about 10 percent of the houses, and damaged others. Then in 1943 came the Ghetto Uprising, during which the small section of Warsaw which contained the final, shrunken ghetto was burned completely by flame throwers and incendiary bombs. Then, in the summer of 1944, the Soviets reached the Vistula River and occupied the suburb of Praga, lying on its eastern shore. At this point, the Polish underground ordered a general uprising against the Germans. The underground leadership wanted to do their part in the struggle against Germany. Also they wanted to be the ones liberating

Warsaw, thus making it their own. This was precisely contrary to the Soviet plan. The Soviets viewed the Polish underground, and particularly its intellectual leadership, as their enemy. Content to let the Germans do the job for them, the Red Army halted its advance and watched while the Germans crushed the rebellion in several months of bloody fighting.

By the end of the war 90 percent of the city lay in ruins. Our guide showed us photographs of the area right after the war. It was a vast field of rubble, with not a single wall standing up. The 10 percent of the city still standing was concentrated around the Lazienki Park and the Aleje Ujazdowskie, the wealthiest residential part of the city which, during the war, was closed to Poles and inhabited by Germans and foreign diplomats.

As for the Polish rebels in Warsaw, many were killed. Some managed to escape. The rest were deported to Germany where for the next few months they joined the vast hordes of slave laborers forced to contribute to the German war effort.

Such was the situation in 1945 when, at the end of the war, Poland became a Soviet satellite. The Polish communist government decided to rebuild Warsaw and – defiantly – make it again the capital of Poland. It was one of the few popular decisions the government made. The Polish population was taxed for the rebuilding and submitted to it without grumbling. In 1945 a new Warsaw was designed for a population of half a million. Today there are almost two million inhabitants, leading to severe overcrowding and shortage of residential apartments.

In reconstructing the city, the planners more or less followed the pre-war city map, widening and straightening some streets, and providing more open space and greenery. With some exceptions, the streets have retained their pre-war names, so when you look at the map it all seems familiar. But even knowing the city's history, it was a shock not to see a single familiar sight in the streets. Like all old cities, Warsaw had become a patchwork of the old, the new and the in-between. Most buildings were ornamented with geometric designs, bas-reliefs or stone sculptures, much like the older buildings in New York City. Each building, each block, each district had a character of its own. Now, they were replaced with the featureless boxes customary in communist architecture. The city has lost most of its charm.

Important public buildings were treated quite differently during the reconstruction. They were replicated as faithfully as existing plans and memories permitted. Even old paintings, particularly by Canaletto (brought to Poland by Queen Bona), depicting Warsaw vistas, were used, particularly in rebuilding Stare Miasto (the Old City), a lovely medieval and Renaissance section of Warsaw.

With its narrow, twisted streets and lovely Rynek (market square) enclosed by colorful, narrow buildings, some only two windows wide, metal or wooden sculptures announcing their names or occupations of their owners, and bright colors differentiating them decisively, it used to be my favorite haunt when I was a little girl. Whenever I could talk our current maid into taking me there, I roamed the streets and the stores. I particularly loved a pub located in the cellar of one of the buildings on the square, where one could buy mead – the honey wine so beloved by Poles (as well as Germans and Englishmen). Not that anyone would sell me any alcoholic beverages, but the waiters must have been amused by a little girl wanting to come in and have a lemonade. It made me feel grown-up and I loved to fantasize about living in the bygone times.

Being deep underground, the pub survived and is now a trendy restaurant, one of several on the square, all quite good and reasonable. This area I recognized readily, as I did the Royal Castle and several palaces and government buildings on Plac Teatralny (Theater Square) and Krakowskie Przedmiescie (Cracovian Suburb), but I was after all, recognizing mere phantoms, fake imitations of all that had been.

The Lazienki (Baths) Park had been untouched as well. Here the small summer palace where the last Polish king, Stanislaw Poniatowski, used to live, overlooks a lake, full of swans, and peacocks promenade in front of the main entrance. We circled around for the best view of the palace, from across the lake. It shimmered in the sunlight like a jewel. I remembered that there should be a little amphitheater in the area, with the stage permanently set as a ruin of a Greek temple. Sure enough, there it was just as I had remembered it. It was as if somebody had given me a gift.

Wilanow, on the outskirts of the city, was another place I remembered. Here we visited the palace built by king Jan Sobieski. The palace is rightly called the Polish Versailles, built in Baroque style during the 17th Century, situated in a country setting, with formal gardens, and spacious chambers and galleries, full of paintings and other mementos. It reminds one of its French counterpart, although it is considerably smaller.

What I remembered most clearly is that we all had to put felt slippers over our shoes and glide over the priceless parquet floors, preserving and polishing them at the same time. A source of great amusement when I had visited the palace on a school trip, it was still greeted with laughter and various exaggerated dance routines by the members of our adult group.

Warsaw is full of monuments, old and new, commemorating the war years. There are numerous small plaques all over the city marking places where groups of Poles died in battle or were killed during the 1944 uprising. Of course there is the principal monument to the heroes of the 1944 uprising, realistically depicting several scenes of German oppression and Polish suffering. An even later martyr, Father Popieluszko, murdered by the communists for actively supporting Solidarity, now has his own monument. His grave in the middle of a green lawn is surrounded by heavy stones, connected by iron chains symbolizing the 45 years of communist oppression.

On the edge of what used to be the Warsaw Ghetto is a memorial to its heroes. It is a bas-relief, and looks almost as if the figures were coming out of a doorway. The five figures look vaguely biblical, stern and determined. To one side there is an enormous stone menorah supported by two lions. All very suggestive of the militant, patriotic Maccabeans of Judea. There are also several slabs memorializing the events during the deportation and the uprising. At the Jewish cemetery there is a memorial to Janusz Korczak, showing the doctor leading several small children.

The last day of our stay in Warsaw was left for us to plan. Members of our group went shopping on Nowy Swiat (Warsaw's equivalent of 5th Avenue), to art museums and to visit more churches. One Jewish couple hired a car and went to the birthplace of the husband, 100 miles out of Warsaw, and reported the place utterly changed. Meanwhile, Bert and I went on a pilgrimage to the places I had known as a child.

We started on Sienna Street, where in the courtyard of one ordinary apartment house the only surviving fragment of the Ghetto wall stands, part of the original boundaries. Soon after it was built, the borders were altered and tightened. An attempt was made to have most of the wall run in the center of the streets, reducing the number of smuggling loopholes. The place is not advertised anywhere; doubtless the inhabitants do not welcome visitors.

Sienna Street is an ordinary working-class area where women wear shapeless, flowered cotton dresses and black "old lady" shoes. Bert and I in our sneakers, and I in my slacks stood out clearly as foreigners (mature women in Poland simply do not wear pants), and, on this street, most likely as Jews, since other foreigners would not know or think to come here. We came to a rope cordoning off part of a sidewalk. Seeing that others in front of us were ignoring this little barrier and stepping over the rope, for which we could see no purpose, we followed. Suddenly, an old woman sweeping the street started cursing us at the top of her voice: "*Psia krew! Cholera!*" (Dog's blood and cholera are the two most common Polish curses) and "*przekleci Zydzi*" (damn Jews). She raved on and on.

We continued walking and turned into the gate of 55 Sienna Street. There, maybe 20 or 30 feet of a brick wall stood in the middle of the courtyard in remarkably good condition. A hexagonal plaque attached to the wall announced, "For the dead and the living we must bear witness." The wall was maintained by the United States Holocaust Museum. Two or three bricks have been removed from the middle of the wall. There were several flowers placed in the hollowed out space. The missing bricks have been incorporated into the replica of this wall, on permanent exhibit at the Washington Holocaust Museum to give the latter "authentic power." The wall and its location is once again a powerful symbol of how ordinary the trappings of evil can be.

Moving along, we passed through the large Saski Garden where I used to play as a child and on to Tlomackie Street where the Great Synagogue had been located. The Germans destroyed it on May 16, 1943, marking the end of the Ghetto Uprising and its existence, but its library remains standing and now houses the archives of Jewish history in Warsaw. It looked closed, but I walked up the wide steps to read the notice posted on the massive door while Bert stood waiting in the street. At that instant a young, elegantly dressed woman passed by and, taking the situation in at a glance, solemnly bowed to Bert. Thus, within the space of a half hour, we were exposed to Polish anti-Semitism (characteristically expressed by an older person), and an expression of regret and sympathy harbored (we hope) by the younger generation.

The closer we came to the former ghetto area, the more anti-Semitic graffiti appeared on the walls, with swastikas and "*Jude Raus*" inscriptions. The Poles, of course, claim it is all the work of hooligans, and they may very well be right. I can tell you that walking in the area was not comfortable, and I sensed a hostility I had not felt elsewhere in Poland, but perhaps this was my imagination. Bert told me later he felt the same.

Rymarska Street, where my school used to be, no longer exists. As far as I can tell, right on the spot of my school there is now a Sony skyscraper, one of the few in the city and a landmark visible from quite a distance.

The ghetto area has been rebuilt, right on top of the rubble, into a working-class neighborhood called Muranow. We made our way to Leszno Street (part of which is now renamed Solidarity Avenue) where I had lived the last six or seven years before the war. Since our house was located on corner of Karmelicka Street, the exact location was easy to find. But instead of an imposing Baroque building we found a tenement, with laundry flapping in the breeze on every balcony.

The area is now completely residential, with no stores or restaurants. Where once there was a bustling commercial thoroughfare, now in the middle of a working day there are hardly any pedestrians or cars. We continued walking to Nowolipie, where I was born, but all looked the same: dull and uniform. It was our intention to continue walking to the infamous *Umschlagplatz* and the Jewish cemetery. We already knew that Nalewki Street, where I had lived while in the Ghetto, no longer existed, having seen that edge of the Ghetto during our stop at the memorial to the Heroes of the Warsaw Ghetto.

I had been walking in a fog of memories and regrets, feeling that I was losing my birthplace yet again. Suddenly I experienced a total shift in my priorities: no, you can't go home again! How true that was in my case.

At this point Bert told me he was not feeling well. We could find no place to sit down or get a cold drink. And anyhow, Bert's health was vastly more important than my sad reminiscences. I really think that this was my closure, my epiphany. I knew I would think of these times again, speak of them and maybe even write of them. But I lay them to rest for the time being, to be taken out at will.

It is difficult to summarize my feelings about this trip. I can state unequivocally that it was very tough on both of us. On Bert it was physically tough, and it was tough to see me relive the darkest years of my life. It is a tough trip for every Jew. For me, memories of horror alternated with moments of poignant nostalgia. Doing ordinary tourist things and seeing ordinary life of ordinary people seemed out of place and tactless in the face of such evil and tragedy. It reminded me of what Letty Pogrebin said in *Getting Over Getting Older*: you are only the leading actor in your own life. In other people's lives you play a walk-on part. I felt rather alienated from the people with whom I was interacting so normally. But in the final analysis I was glad I had faced my ghosts and I was very glad that it was over.

AFTERWORD

Since my visit to Poland, I have been speaking about my pilgrimage and my wartime experiences much more often. Most recently, I again addressed the senior class at Livingston High School just after they had viewed *Schindler's List*. Three hundred teenagers sat attentively. Some of the girls and boys cried during my presentation, and one girl was overheard saying that this was her most meaningful school experience. Feedback like that is why I continue to speak on this painful subject.

Shortly after our trip to Poland, Bert showed me a flyer from a local Barnes and Noble bookstore announcing a meeting of a memoir group. Intrigued, we both attended. The meetings consisted of various members reading stories they had written, followed by enthusiastic encouragement by our leader Zella. She made a number of suggestions helping people to get started. All the members present were writing for their children and grandchildren; none were professional writers. Neither was I. I started writing almost perfunctorily, at first, like the others there setting down anecdotes about my childhood. Gradually, I became more and more involved, and the book began to take shape.

It took almost two years to complete, not surprising in view of the many other interests claiming my attention and time. I am a facile writer. I sit in front of my computer and the words flow rather easily. But I can only work a couple of hours in the morning; the concentration required is mentally exhausting. Some parts have been so difficult emotionally that I could not face the computer for weeks at a time. Only the steady encouragement of my husband and the unqualified support of the memoir group could help to focus me again on the task. Bert has heard most of the stories in this book before, but always in bits and pieces. He tells me that it did not come together for him until I wrote it all down in chronological and thematic order. Throughout the writing process, Bert served as my sounding board on thematic and literary issues, as well as my first line editor.

Getting the book published was a totally novel experience for me as well. I learned about query letters, agents, publishers, writer guides and, of course, rejections. I networked as much as I could, getting advice from friends such as John Langdon, an often-published history professor at Le Moyne College, and Rabbi Kasdan from our temple. I followed every lead provided by well-meaning agents and publishers, organizations such as the Holocaust Museums in New York and Washington D.C., and friends involved – however marginally – in the publishing world. Success, when it came, was very sweet. In fact, I framed a copy of my advance royalty check. It is not often that one has a chance to succeed at something so radically new at the age of 70, and I am proud of myself. I truly did not know I had this in me.

Both the trip to Poland and writing this book were cathartic experiences, forcing me to face my past. I know that I can never fully "get over" the evil I lived through, but I have been able to fashion a productive, normal and even happy life. I feel that it is a great accomplishment on my part.

A word on the subject of memoir writing. I have frequently wished that I had asked more questions of my parents about their ancestors and their own stories. My son Mark has become fascinated with our genealogy, and has recently found (in the Mormon genealogy library in Salt Lake City) the wedding certificate of my grandparents Schlomo-Lezar Salamon and Keila Kaczanowska. Although it is written in Russian and hard to translate, the whole family had a sense of triumph and experienced a connection to these long-dead ancestors. Family stories, so eagerly demanded by children, are a glue which helps to define us as a family, and strengthens our feelings of belonging to this basic block of society.

As I get older, thoughts of God and the afterlife intrude more and more into my psyche. I am sure this is normal, since none of us likes to think of going into a void where we will be no more. But whenever I try to find comfort in religion and faith, the specter of the six million slain Jews rises up before me to deny me any solace. On an individual basis I can argue that God gave me a fair share of luck: a good brain, six years of horror balanced by over 50 years of happiness and prosperity, good health and reasonable longevity. But on the vast scale of events I am still bewildered and horrified by the cruel and senseless deaths during our own Holocaust and those of other victimized peoples. The only moral of these stories points to the enormous reservoir of evil in humanity, and this is so frightening that one is tempted simply to say, "Let us close this book and get on with our lives!" On the other hand, maybe the study of the past, not just to know of it, but to learn from it, will lead us to a path of moderation and fairness for all, and will help us to control the evil impulses we are all subject to. May God help us in this work.

A BRIEF HISTORY OF POLAND

Most Jewish people in America know their ancestors came from somewhere in eastern Europe. When they meet me for the first time, and hear that I come from Poland, they tell me about their parents or their great-grandparents, usually with some confusion. Did they come from Poland? From Russia? From Austria? If they refer to themselves as "Litvaks," why is there no mention of Lithuania? What does it mean to be a "Galizianer?"

Indeed, it is confusing because the history of eastern Europe is so turbulent and unique. Thus, I've determined to give you some idea of the history of Poland and to reflect on the causes of the virulent anti-Semitism that arose in this tortured land.

Background

A slogan of recent American politics declares: "It's the economy, stupid." About Polish history, you could say, "It's the geography and demographics, stupid." These two factors have gone far to shape the fate of Poland. When you look at a geographic map of Europe, you notice two chains of mountains running east-west, the Alps and the Carpathians. But east of France, Europe has no mountains running north-south except for the

Urals deep inside Russia, which divide the continent from Asia. Moreover, the central and eastern portions of Europe are flat, with great marshy plains. Except for the marshlands, this was once great primeval forest in the north and grassy steppe in southern Russia. Indeed, the only surviving primeval forest in Europe, Puszcza Bialowieska, once the hunting preserve of kings, is located in eastern Poland.

This vast expanse of flat, indefensible real estate became the natural pathway for east-west migrations, invasions and conquests, particularly after the forests were cleared for cultivation. At times, this area also served as the pathway for Polish conquests or other European adventures in the east (such as Napoleon's campaign in Russia). To the north, the Baltic Sea formed a natural barrier for Poland, as did the Carpathians in the south. But there were no natural borders to the east or west.

The demographics are even more ominous. To the west and south are the German-speaking Prussians, Austrians, Bavarians and other Germanic peoples, all advanced culturally and politically, usually strong militarily, and at times organized into centralized empires (the Holy Roman Empire, the Austro-Hungarian Empire and Bismarck's Germany to name a few). Early Poles recognized the foreignness of these people when they named them *Niemcy*, meaning the mutes or non-speakers. One of the earliest Polish legends tells of a Princess Wanda, who lived in Krakow. Rather than marry a German prince, she threw herself off the top of Wawel Castle into the Vistula River below and died to protect Polish honor as well as her own.

To the east are the Russian and Ukrainian peoples, themselves oppressed by the Mongols long into the Middle Ages and thus not presenting any serious threat to Poland for a long time. It was when the East coalesced into the mighty Russian Empire of Peter the Great that the vise about Poland closed.

But the dangers from these eastern and western neighbors were not only political and military in nature. Poland found herself sandwiched between two implacable enemies, two distinct cultures, and two religions. The Germans were definitely Europeans in their science, arts and religion (though with several serious or even catastrophic lapses). Although Catholicism has been present in Germany for centuries, a strong Protestant movement has influenced its religion since the Reformation.

The Russians made an early commitment to Eastern Orthodox Christianity, but had a political and social system imposed on them by the Asian Mongols. Thus, though Slavs, like the Poles, they were more Oriental than European.

Straddling these two behemoths was Poland, an extremely Catholic country. Poles have always aligned with Rome in religion and with Paris in culture (passing over their perennial enemies in Germany). Despite these ties, Poles cannot escape the inexorable pull to the east. So, when you read this history or ponder the more recent events in Poland, always go back to the fundamentals: in the luck of the draw, Poland got a terrible location and the two worst neighbors in the world. It is against this backdrop that its history unfolds.

Rise of the Piasts

Poles are somewhat unique in that they have lived in the same area since prehistoric times. While some European nations were populated by migrations during the early Middle Ages, recent excavations prove Poles and their ancestors have lived in Poland for thousands of years. There are legends of pagan dukes ruling Poland before 900 CE, but historical records of this era are very sparse.

By the 9th Century, tribes in eastern Europe began to consolidate into relatively stable kingdoms and principalities united by a single language. One of these groups, the *Polanie* (meaning people of forest clearings), gave its name to Poland. The first capital was Gniezno, near present-day Poznan. Here the first Polish king, Mieszko I, accepted the Roman church and was crowned in 960 CE. He was the first historical member of the Piast Dynasty, which more or less retained the Polish crown until 1370.

Although Mieszko I decisively placed Poland in the European camp and extended its borders northeast to the present-day Gdansk area, he failed to establish firm rules of succession. One of his early successors, Duke Boleslaw III Krzywousty (or Wrymouth), came up with the first of several major blunders which throughout history would make Poland the laughingstock of Europe. The oldest male member of the extended Piast family, he decreed, would be first in line to succeed to the Polish throne at all times. I suppose Boleslaw III wanted to avoid the evils of regencies inherent with a traditional succession scheme in which the oldest son of the king becomes crown prince. Regencies were a recognized source of strife in any country and quite common in those days of short life spans.

Confusion and Factionalization

If there ever was a recipe for disaster, it was Boleslaw III's succession scheme. It guaranteed every time a ruler died that leadership would frequently pass to a different branch of the family. At best, a brother would succeed the dead king, but often the crown passed to an uncle or a distant cousin. Moreover, since the central seat of government was in Gniezno (and later to the south in Krakow), it often meant that the new king or prince had to relinquish his own fief to another member of the family (obviously an ally) and, more importantly, dispossess the immediate family of his predecessor, albeit in theory for a nice piece of land in return. Needless to say, the children and widows did not take it lying down, but formed their own alliances and fought back.

In addition, naming the oldest member of the family ruler ensured he would not rule very long (keep in mind again the low life expectancy in those days). In all, after Boleslaw III the Polish crown changed hands over 20 times in less than 200 years, occasionally with rival nobles battling back and forth for the throne. During this period, only five monarchs managed to reign longer than 10 years.

This cycle of shifting alliances soon involved Poland's neighbors, namely the Czechs, Slovaks and Hungarians in the south, the Germans in the west, the Lithuanians in the north and even the Ruthenians (the ancestors of modern-day Ukrainians) in the east. The ever-growing factionalization and forced land swaps led to almost continuous warfare.

By early 12th Century, political disintegration had completely undermined the Polish state, leaving the country with virtually no central government to speak of. Additionally, drawing foreign powers into internal affairs proved to be a dangerous precedent. For the next 100 years, Poland consisted of several virtually autonomous provinces, each with its own king, nobility, administration and agenda. Amazingly, this state of affairs was not a total disaster; it allowed many ethnic groups to settle in the area. In particular, many German burghers migrated to Poland, forming an incipient middle class. Trade flourished and the fertile land continued to be cultivated.

Unfortunately, the multiplicity of kings and courts swelled the ranks of the Polish nobility so that by the early 14th Century the nobles (or *szlachta*) represented 10 percent of the total population. No other European country had so high a proportion. The szlachta ranged from landless, beggared knights to powerful owners of vast estates defended by private armies. In the absence of strong central government, many of the szlach-ta acquired great power and, even worse, assumed a God-given right to that power. While this situation prevented an absolute monarchy, the sheer numbers of these competing noblemen helped to make Poland ungovernable and ripe for invasion.

However, two developments in 1241, unrelated to each other, finally made this situation untenable and prompted the reunification of Poland under a single government. The first was the arrival of the Teutonic Knights. Although international in their original form, this organization came to be dominated by German nobility and, following the failure of the Crusades, began to establish itself more in Europe. Meanwhile, the northern provinces of Poland were being harassed by pagan Lithuanians and Prussians. Duke Konrad I of Mazovie invited the Teutonic Knights to help subdue and Christianize the East Prussians. This proved to be anoth-er major blunder that would greatly alter the course of Polish history. The Knights succeeded at this task only too well; they not only conquered the pagans, they also established themselves in East Prussia and soon became one of the strongest military powers in Europe, bent on south-ward expansion into Poland.

Also that year, Poland suffered a bloody Mongol invasion during which both the Poles and the Teutonic Knights were defeated. Although the Mongols voluntarily withdrew, they continued to antagonize eastern Poland for another 50 years with repeated raids, burning towns to the ground and killing or enslaving their populations. Reunification and a strong central government were imperative to save the country, but con-tinued infighting among the nobility would delay these reforms until early 14th Century.

From Wood to Stone

Salvation finally came from the last two kings of the old Piast Dynasty, father and son. The father, Wladyslaw I the Short, started the reunifica-tion process in 1320 through successful military actions and shrewd political alliances. His much more renowned son, Casimir III the Great (the only strictly Polish monarch so named), ascended to the throne in 1333, further expanding Polish territory through military and diplomatic means. Casimir III also solidified the first coherent Polish central govern-ment in over a century. By his death in 1370, Poland had become one of the dominant countries in Europe.

Casimir III codified laws, rebuilt his capital at Krakow into a magnificent medieval city, appointed loyal governors (called *starostas*) to different districts of the country to circumvent the power of local nobles, built monasteries while expanding religious tolerance, founded many new cities (and encouraged the German burghers to settle in them), and in 1364 founded the University of Krakow, one of the first institutions of higher learning in eastern Europe.

It was also under Casimir III that the first significant Jewish population entered the country. He invited thousands of German Jews to settle in Polish towns and villages and protected them under the 1346 Statute of Wislica, which provided them with legal protection and forbade pogroms and ritual murders at the hands of Christians. It is said of this justly revered sovereign that he found a wooden Poland and left it made of stone. But he did much more than that; by the end of his rule Poland had developed into a cosmopolitan empire in which Poles, Germans, Jews, Ruthenians and even Tartars and Armenians lived reasonably peacefully together. His legacy was to spare Poland the later bloodshed of the Reformation.

Casimir III died without a male heir, ending the Piast Dynasty. He was succeeded by his nephew, Hungary's King Louis, who died in like condition. After Louis died, the Polish aristocracy selected his daughter, the 10-year-old Jadwiga, to become queen. In 1386, she married the Grand Duke of Lithuania, Wladyslaw II Jagiello. This action Christianized Lithuania (which to this day remains solidly Catholic), ended the constant frontier warfare and united the two countries under a much stronger military and political entity, although Lithuania was still considered separate from Poland despite its common leadership. In Wladyslaw II Jagiello, Poland also gained a capable ruler and a great military mind, both very much needed at the time.

The Jagiellonian Era

Jadwiga, who ruled jointly with Wladyslaw II until her death, was a very saintly woman and much loved for her charity, but she died childless in her mid 20s. Wladyslaw then married Sofia Holszanska and founded the Jagiellonian Dynasty, which would prove to be one of the most influential dynasties in eastern Europe.

Meanwhile, Wladyslaw's first task was to deal with the expansionist activities of the Teutonic Knights, who by this time were firmly established in East Prussia. He won a decisive victory at the Battle of Grunwald in 1410, a date which would prove to be a high water mark in Polish history. Polish school children are as familiar with this date as British children are with the Battle of Hastings in 1066, or American children with Columbus' discovery of America in 1492. In addition, the inclusion of Lithuania in the empire added a large territory that served as a shield against the Mongols who still dominated Russia, thus opening the way to more Polish conquests in the east. Wladyslaw took full advantage of this situation, incorporating into his empire Ruthenia (modern Ukraine) and parts of present-day Hungary. Poland was entering its golden age.

The Polish-Lithuanian union lasted for about 400 years, even though the Jagiellonian Dynasty came to an end with the death of Sigismund II Augustus in 1572. The addition of Lithuania, Ruthenia, parts of Hungary and, for a time, even part of Bohemia, made Poland even more multilingual, multinational and multicultural than it had been during Casimir the Great's time. At one point Poland stretched from the Baltic Sea to the Black Sea. Despite its varied population and its comparatively vast territory, almost triple that of the pre-Jagiellonian era, hardly a whisper of the religious strife which was consuming western Europe was evident in Poland. Although a radical Protestant group called the Socinians gained some influence in the Krakow area in the latter part of 16th Century, only to be driven out of the country later by the Jesuits, the effects of the Reformation overall were extremely mild in Poland.

Poland was a model country for its time. International trade was booming, religious tolerance growing, and learning and culture were appreciated by the upper classes. This is the time of Nicholas Copernicus, the Polish monk educated in Krakow who first explained how the Earth revolves around the sun instead of vice versa. It is also the time when the Polish language came into its own. People began to write in Polish as well as speak it (Latin had been the customary written language in the country up to that time).

But, as often happens during a great flowering, the seeds of future destruction were being planted both from without and within. After Sigismund II Augustus died without an heir, the aristocracy and lower nobility stepped in to establish a system of elected kings. Thus their power grew. From 1573 on the Polish throne was determined by the vote of the nobility.

Death by Committee

Eventually the aristocracy formed two legislative bodies, a lower house called the *Sejm* (Diet) and a Senate. By controlling these legislative bodies, the nobility were able to exempt themselves from taxation as well as give themselves other preferential treatments. Although some would call it an oxymoron, the system was moving gradually towards an elective monarchy. While Poland once again was to be spared the excesses of absolute monarchy, they were to be replaced by excessive parliamentarianism. It is hard to say which is the greater evil.

Externally, the greatest danger came from the growing power of Russia. After finally throwing off the Mongol yoke under Ivan III, Russia became an absolute monarchy ruled by the tsars. This system of ruthless dictatorship, rocked by periodic upheavals (both of the palace and popular variety) was the pattern then and in many ways continues to this day. Nevertheless, the sheer size and wealth of Russia, combined with a continuous greed for other countries' possessions, made it a threat to Poland.

The 16th and 17th Centuries saw the election of several renowned monarchs and many ineffective ones. Each election was the result of negotiations among the rival aristocratic houses, who frequently resorted to electing a foreigner being unable to agree on one of their own Polish or Lithuanian members. The foreigner kings took a varying interest in Poland. Some never bothered to learn the language and treated their position as a source of riches, and nothing else. Among the more effective rulers was Stefan Batory, a Hungarian who reigned from 1575 to 1586 and a brilliant general who recovered some lost territory in the east. Two Swedish kings, Sigismund III and his son Wladyslaw IV, also struggled to hold on to the east and north. Sigismund III actually managed to capture Moscow in 1610 and install Wladyslaw IV as tsar. But these campaigns ended with inconclusive results overall.

In 1652 the principle of liberum veto was invoked in the Sejm for the first time. This statute allowed any Sejm member to kill any proposed law simply by calling out "I disapprove" ("*Nie pozwalam*" in Polish). Later, it even allowed a single member to dissolve the Sejm entirely for any reason. In other words, nothing passed the Sejm without unanimous consent. This power came to be used more and more recklessly. In addition to the quarrelsome nature of Polish nobility slowing things down considerably on its own, foreign diplomats and other influential people soon realized the value of bribing a single unscrupulous Sejm member to shout his "Nie pozwalam," thus dissolving an inconvenient session. Talk about lobbying power! Coupled with the election of kings, frequently rendering them mere figureheads, this meant the most powerful governing body in the land was fatally flawed. In my opinion, these twin evils were the main reason for the partitioning of Poland in the 18th Century.

While this was taking place, Poland was suffering under the rule of Jan II Casimir, an irresolute, exceptionally weak monarch whose 20-year reign is remembered as a period of bloodshed and disaster. Under Jan II, Poland experienced the rebellion of the Ukrainian Cossacks, the invasion of Charles X of Sweden, incursions of opportunistic German princes, and the last attempt by Ottoman Turkey to dominate Europe. This onslaught contributed to his abdication in 1668.

Many of these events are ably and feelingly documented in a trilogy of fictional works written in the 19th Century by Henryk Sienkiewicz, known to us in America as the author of *Quo Vadis*. Sienkiewicz not only describes the events of these wars, but also gives us a picture of the touchy, fiercely independent, hard drinking, raucous and battle-loving Polish nobility while contrasting it with the abject poverty and powerlessness of the peasantry.

It is important to note that the feudal state was alive and well in eastern Europe in the 17th Century although it had died out in the western half of the continent years earlier. Feudalism of the worst kind prevailed in Poland, with the welfare of the peasantry totally dependent on the whims of their lords, who were often absent, either playing at court or fighting for the life of the country. The administration of these estates came more and more into the hands of agents, exhorted by the owners to constantly produce more gold. Many of these agents were Jewish, a situation which did not endear Jews to the Polish peasantry.

One last spurt of Polish greatness as a kingdom came with Jan III Sobieski, who ruled from 1674 to 1696, but even this had grave consequences. Jan III won the Battle of Vienna against the Turks, ensuring their dominance in Europe would not spread past the Balkans. As a result, Jan III became immortal in Polish folk history as the savior of the Christian West from the heathens, and deservedly so. But, modern historians point out he spilled a great deal of Polish blood and wealth in the process, weakening Poland while at the same time emaciating the only military power capable of and in a position to check the rise of Russian might.

Partition

After Jan III, the Commonwealth, as the Polish government was now called, declined precipitously. Prussia and Russia both not only indulged in military adventurism in Poland, but also increasingly interfered in Polish internal affairs, forcing upon the country the inept Saxon kings of the Vettin Dynasty, Augustus II and Augustus III, beginning in 1697. If there was any chance for the internal unrest to evolve into an enlightened parliamentary democracy, monarchic or not, foreign interference made sure it did not happen. The Age of Enlightenment which dominated most of Europe throughout the 18th Century never made it to Poland.

Finally, in 1764, Stanislaw II Augustus Poniatowski was elected king. Stanislaw II was to be the last king of Poland. Although a Pole, he came to the throne under dubious circumstances. A former lover of Russia's Catherine the Great, he was decidedly her choice and universally viewed as a Russian puppet. But, almost from the first, he proved his worth by trying to strengthen the monarchy and abolish the liberum veto. However, Catherine thwarted these attempts by promoting unrest in Poland. Of the 11 million inhabitants at the time, one million consisted of Protestants and Eastern Orthodox Christians. Catherine demanded equal religious rights for these groups (they had been curtailed early in the 18th Century). This resulted in a combined rebellion of religious minorities and the nobility against the king, which enfeebled the government and brought chaos to the country.

In 1772, Russia, Prussia and Austria, acting in concert, decided to capitalize on the weakness and use it to justify a land grab. In this bloodless takeover, ostensibly undertaken for the sake of European security, the bandits took one-third of Poland's land.

In the next 20 years efforts to reform Poland's unwieldy government were partly successful. The shock of the partition finally persuaded the Poles to cease their internal squabbling and unite to save their country. The Sejm of 1788 labored for four years to produce the first modern constitution in Europe and the second in the world (after the American Constitution, on which it was clearly modeled). The principle of people's sovereignty was established for the first time, including the middle class along with the gentry. Separation of power between the legislative, executive and judiciary branches was clearly delineated, spelling out in detail the responsibilities of the cabinet and parliament as well as abolishing the regressive liberum veto. Meanwhile, the peasants were emancipated;

education and publishing were on the move, finally spreading the Enlightenment to Poland by the efforts of the growing intelligentsia.

These developments alarmed Catherine the Great, who saw the specter of a strong, independent Poland rising again on her flank. In 1793 Russia and Prussia again partitioned Poland (Austria did not take part in this second partition), this time without an excuse, and chopped off further slices of land in the east and west. This time, however, the Poles reacted. Led by Tadeusz Kosciuszko, a general heavily influenced by the American Revolution and American democratic thought, the Poles attempted to regain the annexed territories. Alas, both the reforms and military actions came too late. Kosciuszko was soundly defeated in 1794 and the reforms never got a chance to take hold. In 1795 the three powers divided the rest of Poland among themselves in a third and final partition. Poland disappeared from the map and—except for a brief period beginning in 1807 when it was a Napoleonic duchy—would not reappear until 1918, 123 years of foreign subjugation later. Stanislaw II was forced to abdicate and go into exile. According to a secret clause in the final agreement, the word "Poland" was to be suppressed forever.

In these partitions, Prussia took most of western Poland, almost to Warsaw. Russia took eastern Poland past the Bug River and close to where the present Russo-Polish border lies. Austria took the balance of the Polish lands in the south, including Krakow and Galicia. So, if you have ancestors who came to the United States during that time, they did not nominally come from Poland, but from Russia, Prussia (which later became part of Germany), and Austria.

A Culture Goes Underground

But, if Poland was defeated, Polishness survived. Poles are always at their best in the most difficult and trying times, and at their worst during times of peace and prosperity. Over a century of foreign domination might have defeated the ethnicity of many cultures. In addition, the Poles now lived under three different regimes, all attempting to eradicate Polish patriotism and culture in varying ways. Polish schools disappeared. Some of the occupying powers forbade all teaching of the Polish language while others permitted it, but only grudgingly. All expression of Polish culture was frowned on and efforts were made to Russify, Germanize or Austrianize the population. In most places, the courts and local governments were also taken over by the occupying powers.

This occupation did not always go smoothly for the victors. There were three major insurrections against the oppressors. These rebellions, in 1830, 1846 and 1863 respectively, all failed and were followed by confiscations, forced exile, further oppression and loss of freedom and, in the Russian areas, deportations to Siberia. Both Russia and Prussia succeeded in turning much of the peasantry against the magnates, exploiting the class divisions in Polish society. Russia allowed a virtually powerless, figurehead Polish state to exist in its zone, but even this was abolished after the 1863 uprising.

But the "organic" rebellion, the work to maintain Polish culture, education and religion (particularly in Protestant German and Orthodox Russian areas), continued throughout the 19th Century. Clandestine schools, often organized in conjunction with and under pretext of religious training, taught about the glorious past, exalted the names of Polish heroes and martyrs and promoted Polish literature. Adam Mickiewicz and Juliusz Slowacki—the two great Polish romantic poets—wrote fiery, patriotic poetry. Mickiewicz and the immortal pianist and composer Frederick Chopin, also a Polish patriot, were among those forced into exile after the 1830 rebellion.

Of course, the three separate parts of Poland participated in the developments of their various occupiers. Industrialization proceeded quickly. In the Russian sector its level exceeded that of Russia proper. Lodz became the textile capital of eastern Europe, and was said to clothe most of Russia (partly with the help of German investment). Coal and iron were mined in Silesia in southwestern Poland and worked in the Warsaw area.

However, profits from these enterprises did nothing to alleviate the poverty of the peasants and the newly risen urban working class. Pressures of a growing population further contributed to the poverty of these groups, resulting in a massive exodus, estimated at 3.5 million people. From Galicia alone, 1 million Poles, Jews and Ukrainians migrated to the United States.

The new political ideas which were spreading throughout Europe also made their way into Poland. Early Polish socialists and communists conspired with their German and Russian counterparts to free humanity from oppression according to their philosophies.

None of these developments were producing any advances in recreating the Polish state. New conspirators appeared on the scene, resurrecting patriotic dreams in the context of new social ideas. Jozef Pilsudski headed a militant socialist party called PPS, while Roman Dmowski fronted the opposing, xenophobic, right-wing National Democratic Party, also known as Endecja (can you find the acronym in that name?). Pilsudski's ideas looked to the past: to the old Polish Commonwealth including Ukraine, Belarus and Lithuania, but with an egalitarian social system and tolerance for all inhabitants. Anti-Semitism was not his style. Dmowski, on the other hand, envisioned a tighter, smaller but purely Polish Poland and opposed all minorities, especially Jews. There was also a small Marxist party dominated by Jewish intellectuals, of whom Rosa Luxemburg was best known. Leaders of all these parties were in and out of jail in Russia and Germany in the late 19th and early 20th Centuries.

Versailles and Resurrection

Much of World War I in the east was fought on Polish territory, and Polish troops participated on both sides. At the end of the war, with American president Woodrow Wilson's help, Poland was re-established. However, the question of its boundaries was troublesome for all parties involved. In the west, the borders were established by a combination of plebiscites, uprisings and Allied intervention. Poland re-acquired much of Silesia, essential for it to become a modern state (to this day most of Poland's heavy industry is in this region).

In the east, matters were decided by a bloody war against Russia. The Soviet Union attacked Poland in 1920, intending to re-capture its pre-1918 boundaries. They advanced almost to Warsaw, but were routed, driven out of the country and pursued as far east as Kiev by Pilsudski's ad hoc Polish military. Although a supremely embarrassing defeat for the Soviets (Joseph Stalin, who was in the Red Army at the time, developed his lifelong hatred of Poland as a result of this humiliation), this would prove to be a mixed blessing for the Poles. Poland got enough of Lithuania (including the capital city of Vilnius), Belarus and Ukraine to infuriate the Russians and Lithuanians, but not enough to form a union of equals. The new Poland included large, disaffected and indigestible minorities. In short, it was a powder keg. In this new nation, there were 22 million Poles, 5 million Ukrainians, 3.5 million Jews, 1.5 million Belorussians, 500,000 Germans, 100,000 Lithuanians and 100,000 Russians. It is widely believed Poland again saved Europe by holding the new Soviet Union in Russia at bay in 1921, but again it was accomplished at a heavy human and political cost.

Polish politics in the so-called Second Republic were dominated by Pilsudski until his death in 1935. There was continuous tension between

PPS and Endecja and by the late 1930s Pilsudski's tolerant stances were beginning to give way to official anti-Semitism. Government suppression of the Jews was considered, but never anything on the Nazi scale.

During the 1930s Poland, like the rest of the industrial world, suffered economic depression. The Jews, involved in trade and manufacturing, suffered even more than the largely rural Slavic population. Pilsudski, who had governed as a sort of Roman-style, intermittent dictator, tended to discount his neighbor, the new German chancellor Adolf Hitler. Poland was fiercely proud of its army, which although large had not modernized much past World War I-level technology. The country's leadership, blind to the military growth of Germany and its own military shortcomings, believed Poland could defeat any German army and acted in an arrogant manner as a result. It did not help that command of the Polish military after Pilsudski's death passed to a rather stupid man: Marshal Edward Smigly-Rydz.

Events were moving quickly. Between 1937 and 1939, Germany annexed Austria and Czechoslovakia, demanded the return of Gdansk (called Danzig by the Germans and set up as a free city in 1918) and the Polish Corridor (a narrow strip of land along Poland's Baltic coast). Finally, on August 23, 1939, Hitler signed a non-aggression pact with the Soviet Union and secretly agreed to partition Poland again. The stage was set for World War II.

A Quick Fall

Eight days after the pact was signed, on September 1, the Germans invaded Poland. On September 17, the Soviet Union followed suit, ostensibly to protect Belorussian and Ukrainian minorities. The Soviets occupied eastern Poland up to the Bug River (as per the secret clause in their agreement with Hitler) while the Germans easily smashed through Smigly-Rydz's largely obsolete army, which was completely unprepared for the blitzkrieg. By the end of the month Poland once again ceased to exist.

Throughout the war Poles were considered an inferior, vermin race (although not as much as the Jews) and were subject to brutal imprisonment, murder and forced resettlement. Both the Germans and Russians were guilty of this. In 1944 the Red Army, now the mortal enemy of the Nazis, stood at the gates of Warsaw while Poles in Warsaw revolted, hoping to aid the Allies and re-establish a Polish presence in the war. Instead of helping the Poles fight the Germans, the Soviets waited across the Vistula River while the Nazis put down the rebellion, deported the survivors and razed the city to the ground. If there was any accord at all between the Nazis and the Soviets, it was to see Polish opposition—and therefore Polish intelligentsia—destroyed.

Rebirth, Communism and Solidarity

The end of World War II in 1945 resurrected the Polish state, but the borders were moved yet again. The Soviets more or less kept the territory they won in the initial 1939 invasion while the defeated Germans were forced to surrender Silesia and some of their own territory to Poland. Vast resettlement projects followed this agreement. Once completed Poland became—for the first time—largely ethnically Polish; Dmowski's dream was finally realized.

But Polish independence was largely an illusion. A puppet Communist government ruled the nation for 45 years despite periodic social upheavals. Today, Poles regard this period as little more than a Soviet occupation. It was not until the rise of Solidarity in the 1980s and the collapse of the Soviet Union that Poland became truly independent. One of the first Soviet satellite countries to make a break from Russian-style communism, Poland has been a relatively stable democracy since 1990 with Solidarity and former Communists forming the main political parties.

The Jewish Experience

Within the history of Poland, there is another story to be told: the story of the Jews and anti-Semitism.

Jews had lived in Poland since the beginning, but, as mentioned earlier, they first came to the country in large numbers at the invitation of Casimir III the Great in the 14th Century. At this time, the Polish authority remained friendly, or at least indifferent, toward the Jews, usually recognizing their worth in the economic life of the country.

The Jewish population increased rapidly after Casimir III. By the 16th Century more than half of the Jews in Europe lived in Poland, about 150,000. Throughout the Middle Ages, Renaissance and after, Poland was the most tolerant country in Europe from a religious standpoint, and continued to attract Jews, who thrived there. The Polish middle class was nearly static, a vaccuum the Jewish influx filled.

By 1939, despite massive migrations to the United States in the decades before, there were 3.5 million Jews in Poland, about 10 percent of the country's total population. Moreover, over half the doctors and lawyers in Poland were Jewish. Large cities like Warsaw and Krakow were about one-third Jewish, and every little *stetl* (small town in Yiddish) had Jews working as artisans or merchants.

Causes of Hate

What then caused the rise of virulent anti-Semitism in Poland in the 20th Century? Most Jews, when asked that question, put the blame squarely on the Roman Catholic Church. There is no doubt the Catholic teaching of Jewish complicity in the death of Christ caused great emotional reaction in this most Catholic of nations, but I don't think this is the whole answer. The Catholics also dominate France and Italy; anti-Semitism in those countries doesn't compare to that in Poland.

In Poland, the church's teachings fell on exceptionally fertile ground. Polish peasants were abysmally ignorant and very superstitious. For example, many believed the Passover holiday could not be celebrated without the blood of a Christian baby. As late as 1940, when my father was in a Soviet prison, he asked a newly imprisoned peasant whether America had entered the war. The reply: "I never heard of this king!"

As mentioned, the feudal state persisted in Poland much longer than in most of the rest of Europe, and while the lords were gone someone had to run their estates. This job fell to the Jews, who squeezed the peasants in order to finance the fighting and other distractions of the distant lords. The peasants came to view the Jews as oppressors; they were the visible presence of tyranny. In addition, peasants could easily convince themselves the lords were not responsible for these excesses. They remained loyal to these lords, with whom they at least shared a common religion and ethnicity.

Another reason for this rising anti-Semitism lay in the comportment of the Jews themselves. Like other ethnic and religious groups they tended to live near each other, forming Jewish districts in cities which, at times, were already called ghettoes (the term was originally coined in Venice, where a smith living in the Jewish district gave the area its name). Rarely were the Jews compelled to live in these districts, however. These ghettoes were always open; the sealed ghetto is a Nazi invention. Moreover, the Jews brought with them their own customs and language. They lived in Poland for centuries but never became an integral part of it.

A Separate, Different People

The Laws of Kashrut were created during the early exiles from Israel, most likely to maintain the Jewish identity in the time of Diaspora. Devotion to the Torah and the Talmud also preserved the Jewish religion and way of life, but at a very high cost. Jews could never break bread with their hosts; the two sides could never get to know and understand one another.

German Jews who came to Poland brought with them a middle German language which evolved into Yiddish, a language heavily influenced by German interspersed with Hebrew, Russian and Polish words. Jews spoke Yiddish for all their internal dealings. Only those who had to deal with the Poles learned a modicum of Polish, and even then they retained their characteristic sing-song accent.

Jewish men dressed in black robes called kapotas and covered their heads with skullcaps while indoors. They also wore long beards and long, curling sideburns called peyes. Most of this was a legacy of the Jews imitating the dress of the medieval burghers, but the fashions of the rest of the world had moved on, so that eventually the fossilized Jewish mode of dress marked them as foreigners.

Jewish food was heavily flavored with onions and garlic. In their synagogues they had no pictures and little ornamentation; men sat apart from women as well. In short, they looked different, smelled different, talked differently, prayed differently and lived differently from the rest of the population, and they did it in ever-increasing numbers. How easy it was to suspect them of evil thoughts and deeds! How easy it was to blame them for the many misfortunes of the Polish people!

The above remarks in no way condone or excuse Polish anti-Semitism. Victims must never be blamed for the crimes perpetrated against them. I am only trying to describe the most likely scenario for the rise of such widespread hatred.

By the 19th Century, while the majority of Jews, particularly in the stetls, remained Orthodox, poor and downtrodden, some young Jews rejected religion and finally assimilated. Some became intellectuals and espoused social ideals such as communism, while others participated in the industrialization of Poland, becoming financiers, manufacturers and capitalists in general. Bright, capable and devoted to education, the Jews soon distinguished themselves in both schools of thought, so that now they could be hated for fostering communism or enriching themselves at the expense of the masses, according to the predilection of the hater. Hitler, of course, managed to hate Jews for both reasons, and in his twisted mind easily reconciled "Jewish dominance of international capitalism and communism" with their "physical and mental inferiority."

A Culture Destroyed

In Poland, grassroots anti-Semitism became particularly strong. During World War II the Polish population either stood by or assisted the Germans in their persecutions of Jews, although there were numerous and notable exceptions. By the end of the war, the 3.5 million Jews in Poland in 1939 were reduced to about 300,000, about 50,000 of whom were survivors of concentration camps or people who lived out the war in hiding or under false Aryan papers. The rest made their way back, mainly from the east, where they had been deported by the Russians in 1941 or had followed the Russian army as it retreated.

But the suffering did not end there. In July 1946 there was a pogrom in Kielce. Forty Jewish men in transit from the Soviet Union to Palestine were killed. Pogroms occurred in other cities; in all, an estimated 2,000 Jews were killed. The official Polish line claims these incidents were provoked by communists, but this does not make much sense. It is much more likely they were a spontaneous expression of brutish anti-Semitism. The participants included policemen, soldiers and workers along with the usual hooligans. Thus it was proven that, in Poland at least, a large presence of Jews is not needed to foster hatred and violence.

The Jews remaining in Poland took due note of the situation and fled. At present there are only between 3,000 to 5,000 Jews in Poland, all elderly, Orthodox and clustered in the large cities. The Jewish-Polish culture is no more.